The Bright Stuff

In an increasingly competitive world, it is quality
of thinking that gives an edge – an idea that opens new
doors, a technique that solves a problem, or an insight
that simply helps make sense of it all.

We work with leading authors in the fields of
management and finance to bring cutting-edge thinking
and best learning practice to a global market.

Under a range of leading imprints, including
Financial Times Prentice Hall, we create world-class
print publications and electronic products giving readers
knowledge and understanding which can then be
applied, whether studying or at work.

To find out more about our business and professional products,
you can visit us at www.business-minds.com

For other Pearson Education publications, visit
www.pearsoned-ema.com

The Bright Stuff
How innovative people and technology can make the old economy new

Arnoud De Meyer, Soumitra Dutta and Sandeep Srivastava

An imprint of **Pearson Education**

London · New York · San Francisco · Toronto · Sydney
Tokyo · Singapore · Hong Kong · Cape Town · Madrid
Paris · Milan · Munich · Amsterdam

PEARSON EDUCATION LIMITED

Head Office:
Edinburgh Gate
Harlow CM20 2JE
Tel: +44 (0)1279 623623
Fax: +44 (0)1279 431059

London Office:
128 Long Acre
London WC2E 9AN
Tel: +44 (0)20 7447 2000
Fax: +44 (0)20 7240 5771
Website: www.business-minds.com

First published in Great Britain in 2002

© Arnoud De Meyer, Soumitra Dutta and Sandeep Srivastava 2002

The right of Arnoud De Meyer, Soumitra Dutta and Sandeep Srivastava to be identified as authors of this work has been asserted by them in accordance with the Copyright, Designs and Patents Act 1988.

ISBN 0 273 65648 1

British Library Cataloguing in Publication Data
A CIP catalogue record for this book can be obtained from the British Library.

All rights reserved; no part of this publication may be reproduced, stored in a retrieval system, or transmitted in any form or by any means, electronic, mechanical, photocopying, recording or otherwise without either the prior written permission of the Publishers or a licence permitting restricted copying in the United Kingdom issued by the Copyright Licensing Agency Ltd, 90 Tottenham Court Road, London W1P 0LP. This book may not be lent, resold, hired out or otherwise disposed of by way of trade in any form of binding or cover other than that in which it is published, without the prior consent of the publishers.

10 9 8 7 6 5 4 3 2 1

Typeset by Pantek Arts Ltd, Maidstone, Kent.
Printed and bound in Great Britain by Biddles Ltd, Guildford & King's Lynn

The publisher's policy is to use paper manufactured from sustainable forests.

About the authors

Arnoud De Meyer is the Akzo Nobel Fellow in Strategic Management and Dean of the Asia Campus at INSEAD. His research interests include international R&D strategy, manufacturing strategy and Internet-enabled innovation. He is the co-author of *Benchmarking for Global Manufacturing* (Business One Irwin, 1992). He can be contacted at: arnoud.de.meyer@insead.edu

Soumitra Dutta is the Roland Berger Chaired Professor of E-Business and Information Technology and Dean of Technology and E-learning at INSEAD. His research interests include electronic commerce, Internet-based learning and process reengineering. His most recent publication is *Embracing the Net: Get.Competitive* (Financial Times Prentice Hall, 2001). He can be contacted at soumitra.dutta@insead.edu

Sandeep Srivastava is the co-founder and CEO of IYCWorld.com, an Application Service Provider in India. He has an MBA from INSEAD. Previously he was an IT entrepreneur and worked for IT companies in India and Saudi Arabia. He is the co-author of *Embracing the Net: Get.Competitive* (Financial Times Prentice Hall, 2001). He can be contacted at sandeep@srivastava.org

To our parents

who first showed us the bright stuff

Emma and Eugeen De Meyer
ADM

Tara Rani and Raj Kumar Dutta
SD

Veena Srivastava and Brij Deo Srivastava
SS

Contents

List of figures ix
List of tables x
Preface xi

PART I
Setting the stage 1

  1 The fateful crash 3
  2 The bright stuff! 25

PART II
Exploring the case studies 43

  3 The genetic power: Charles Schwab, E*TRADE, and Merrill Lynch 45
  4 The simple truth: Wal-Mart, Amazon.com, and Barnes & Noble 65
  5 Goliath and David? GM and Auto-By-Tel 83

PART III
Learning from the past 103

  6 Innovation: lessons from the past reinforced? 105
  7 Innovation as strategy 127

PART IV
Defining the imperatives 139

  8 Co-creation? 141
  9 E-nfrastructure 167
  10 Perpetual metamorphosis 191
  11 Institutionalizing knowledge 211

PART V
Preparing for action 233

12 The backpack 235

Index 245

List of figures

Figure 1.1 The Marketspace model 9
Figure 1.2 Overall degrees of achievement along the Marketspace model dimensions 13
Figure 1.3 Use of the Internet for different aspects of the Customer relationships 14
Figure 1.4 Use of the Internet for different aspects of the Product dimension 15
Figure 1.5 Use of the Internet for different aspects of the Promotion dimension 16
Figure 1.6 Use of the Internet for different aspects of the Place dimension 17
Figure 1.7 Use of the Internet for different aspects of the Price dimension 17
Figure 1.8 Regional comparisons along the dimensions of the Marketspace model 20
Figure 2.1 The chapter plan of this book 37
Figure 5.1 Changes in automobile retailing 89
Figure 5.2 Auto-By-Tel's sales process 91
Figure 6.1 Technological life cycle 108
Figure 6.2 Design of a service operation 116

List of tables

Table 1.1 Major dimensions of transformation in the Marketspace study 10

Table 1.2 Sectors ranked across Marketspace model dimensions 18

Preface

The millennium year indeed turned out to be a watershed year in more ways than one. For instance, the record-breaking "non-inflationary" growth of the US economy took a beating. Similarly, the post-hotmail frenzy around the Internet was definitely doused cold with a matching degree of untouchability for the "dotcoms." To the majority of managers in incumbent companies, the "failure" of the Internet-sponsored onslaught was music to their ears – it was the first sign that the online business "bubble" had burst. Many thought they were right again – the Internet was too esoteric to be applied to their "real" businesses. Most dotcoms have burnt away and even the mighty online leaders such as Yahoo! are on the brink of trouble. What next? Is the Internet a non-starter?

This couldn't be further from the truth. In fact, we think that the hallmark of the first year of the millennium was indeed in making us see the true colours of the Internet. The writing on the wall is written large, bold and clear – the Internet is a far more serious discontinuity than any time in the past. A scramble is on to start all over again. And sooner than we think. "Embracing the Net" is now dawning as an unmitigated imperative and opportunity to all incumbents. All industries that we studied, for example – retail, stock brokerage and automobile – are changing dramatically. Innovation is becoming critical for survival. Further, the nature of innovation is changing. And in all sectors, incumbents are belatedly but surely fighting back to retain their leading positions in the emerging marketplace – sometimes by simply buying up their innovative challengers, the entrepreneurial dotcom startups who are now strapped for cash.

Our research on incumbents around the world shows that most have yet to enhance their competitive advantage using the Internet. A large majority is simply using the Internet as a publishing medium or is satisfied with moving existing business models onto the new channel. Few are creating innovative business models that exploit the true potential of the new technologies. What is going wrong? What else should the incumbents be doing? We begin our exploration of innovation on this theme.

An in-depth analysis of three sets of case studies clearly throws up the new imperative – "Innovation as Strategy." The Internet and innovation seem to be two sides of the same coin. In fact, a small group of successful incumbents have made "innovation as strategy" the centre stage of their corporate strategy. The Internet has made possible a uniquely new strategic anchor for these companies – innovation as an end in itself. The book takes a walk through this bright, innovative stuff.

We ask the following questions: is what we have observed with the dot-coms really unprecedented? Have similar things happened before in business history? By most reckonings, between 1895 and 1905 putting "Motors" in your company's name immediately increased the attractiveness of your company to investors. Though almost all of the "Motor" companies vanished quickly, motorcars redefined distances and time. This it is not the first time that we are confronted with a major disruption in technology. There are some important lessons from the past to be adapted for today and some new imperatives for innovation in the digital era. We base our action agenda upon such lessons.

The new organizational frontier is the "Real Virtual Corporation" – corporations which are able to leverage the innovative power of the Internet and associated technologies to enhance customer relationships to create value, manage integrated supply chains to improve the efficiency of all players and empower their employees to be more productive and innovative. It is about using the power of the virtual to innovate and enhance the real! The Internet is pushing a growing amount of intelligence onto the communication infrastructure and that will have a significant impact on how we produce, deliver and service. This book lays out the framework and action agenda for Internet-enabled innovation in incumbents.

From now on, innovation is going to be imperative for survival, not just growth. Innovation is going to be routine and the quantity of innovation will count no less than quality. The underlying tone of the book is that we are convinced that incumbents can be as nimble footed on innovation as start-ups. We appreciate that this may be a tall order for many incumbents but GE, IBM, GM, Charles Schwab, Merrill Lynch and others prove that it can be done. This is the bright stuff. This is the potential of the Internet waiting to be explored and exploited by you!

We have deliberately kept the book simple, easy to read and as free of jargon as possible. We enjoyed our research into the bright stuff of the Internet and we hope you find the book insightful and useful in order to survive and grow in the midst of the vastly changed competitive dynamics. Good luck on your journey!

Setting the stage

The fateful crash 1

Bookmark

We have been conducting a longitudinal research project over the past five years (1996–2000) to study the extent of business transformation in major global corporations across industry sectors and countries. The study is slowly but steadily becoming a good indicator of the thrust and direction of change in companies and industries on the back of the emerging technologies. The results of the 2000 research are interesting because they demonstrate that most large corporations have been doing little to exploit the unique transformational potential of the Internet. By default, the results also lay down the agenda for innovation in corporations in the coming years.

Our studies show that most firms are doing little beyond the obvious in terms of using the Internet to publish corporate and, in many instances, product information. Few have actively shifted gears and tried to use the Internet to transform their business – to innovate and create new ways of doing business. For instance, less than 20 percent of the surveyed firms allowed for the formation of cyber-communities among customers and very few were innovative in stimulating intra-community interactions.

This chapter initiates an exploration of the reasons why most companies have been poor at harnessing the Internet. The Nasdaq crash of March 2000 has become a turning point in the business adoption of the Internet. No longer is the Internet viewed as a dotcom phenomenon. It is now mainstream. Incumbents such as GE, Boeing, and Citigroup are aggressively innovating by integrating the Internet into their core businesses. A new race has started, this time among incumbent companies. Fasten your belts as we take you off on a new space mission – into marketspace!

A fateful crash

The NASDAQ crash of March 2000 can truly be called a "fateful crash." History may even record it as an event befitting the dawn of a new millennium. The apparent chain of events that followed the crash is all too well known. It started with an innocent-looking deathblow to the dotcoms but most were in fact not amused. The dotcoms were pulling raging eyeballs and page view numbers, but only a few had profitable business models. Apparently, online businesses had limited value propositions on their own. Dotcoms were not the best way to deploy the emerging technologies.

More importantly, however, the March 2000 sentiments reflected a deeper malady – the information technology sector stocks had not recovered by mid-2001 and prospects of a quick recovery weren't bright. The mightiest were reeling under the heat – Lucent, Cisco, Intel – you name them. It was still very difficult to accept that the almost unfailing Cisco had also "erred"; it downsized by 5 percent of its staff strength and announced a gargantuan one-time inventory charge of $2.5 billion in 2001. An exceptional online company like Yahoo! reported a quarterly loss for the first quarter of 2001 (after quite a few quarters of growing earnings) and announced significant job cuts. Expectations from the technology sector were at their lowest ebb in recent history.

But what's so fateful about this situation? The crash may actually have saved us a whole generation of wasted resources – time and money – and given us a greatly enhanced prospect of delivering far better value from the application of Internet-related technologies. Interestingly, it has perhaps also undone a great truth – that history repeats itself. This time history may not really repeat itself and we all stand knocking at the door of unprecedented opportunities. The oft-repeated lesson from history is that whenever a great new technology is discovered/invented, a lot of its early years are lost in trying to impose existing objectives, structures, and processes on it. Subsequently, years of effort, money and dreams are wasted due to a sub-optimal use of the new technology. For instance, the invention of celluloid gave birth to a whole new possibility – the cinema. But in the first two decades after its invention, cinema was simply theatrical performances shown on celluloid; actors behaved as if they were acting on stage. It took nearly two additional decades to understand the new dimensions and opportunities of celluloid and cinema gradually took the shape we know today. Indeed, the crash has short-circuited a lot for us and we can ride the transition much faster and minimize the wasteful route.

But can we actually minimize such a wasteful course? Yes, for sure. For two reasons. First, the Internet is a unique technology, one that is very different from a car, a vacuum tube, or a standalone computing system. It creates a highly malleable and intelligent infrastructure. What happens when there comes a technology that offers "nothing by itself", but enables you to deliver a broad range of new value propositions? When its deployment and use are limited only by our imagination? The fact is that we do not really know how to "best" deploy a technology like the Internet. Your solutions are the ones that now count. The Internet is fast reaching a point where the technology will simply serve to actualize your solutions in letter and spirit. If you get your business objectives right and your execution of operational processes straightened out, your solutions will create a competitive advantage for you.

> **We are still discovering how to best deploy a technology like the Internet.**

Second, and very importantly, many now "extinct" dotcoms have exhibited that they did realize valuable business objectives while conducting their businesses online. In fact, incumbents have been rapidly buying up many of these innovative businesses at low "post-crash" prices. Witness the recent acquisitions of MP3.com by Vivendi, of CDNow by Bertelsmann, and many, many others. Many of these "extinct" dotcoms have found a new lease on life within incumbents and are prospering, albeit in very different environments. Incumbents are also benefiting from the acquisitions – the dotcoms within their bellies are stirring up a whole nest of innovative ideas. The pace of innovation in incumbents is speeding up. This is good news because our research (see following sections) shows that most incumbents have done little so far in harnessing the innovative potential of the Internet.

Wondering why

But then, are you wondering, in spite of what we've already seen on the Internet, what more can happen? Why the innovative power of the Internet has barely touched your life yet? You probably are not wrong to have questions … but do not doubt the revolution!

> Why did we, who love change and typically move quickly to capitalize on it, allow the e-revolution to be led by the small and the new, rather than by large, technology-rich, heavily resourced large companies such as our own? The answer is simple. Big companies like us were often frightened by our unfamiliarity with Internet technology. We thought the creation and operation of Web sites was mysterious, Nobel Prize stuff, the province of the wild-eyed and purple-haired. But as we have gotten more deeply into e-Business, we have come to learn that digitizing all our buying, making and selling processes is the easiest part of the equation.[1]

PART ONE SETTING THE STAGE

Could you guess the subject and author of these words? None other than GE and it comes from the horse's mouth – John F. Welch, Jr., Chairman and CEO of the company.

He educates,[2]

> We have the hard part, hundreds of factories and warehouses, world-leading products and technology. We have a century-old brand identity and a reputation known and admired around the globe, all attributes that new e-Business entrants are desperate to get. And we have one other enormous advantage – Six Sigma Quality[3] – the greatest fulfillment engine ever devised. Six Sigma fits like a glove with e-Business because it allows us to produce and deliver just what customers need when they want it. Six Sigma Quality defines the ultimate in customer fulfillment and satisfaction, just what e-Business requires.

Welch has hit the bull's eye. Indeed, for incumbent firms, the Internet is just the right enabling complement because they already have the hard part – the operational infrastructure, the backend.[4] And among the principal causes for the fall of many once-celebrated dotcoms like Boo.com, Kozmo.com, and Reel.com are backend "missteps." We must emphasize, though, that in many instances these online companies did use the Internet to create new online customer interfaces that offered a welcome new experience for customers. Their backends couldn't sustain that experience. In most cases, the backend was discovered to be inadequate and cost inefficient. But the backend is the real "last mile" which actually touches the lives of customers and thus it's very often the "real face" of the company for customers.

The task is both simple and difficult – match the frontend and backend. But opportunity, immense.

Jack Welch reveals the secrets of GE's success with "e-business":

- Digitizing all buying, making, and selling processes is the easiest part of the e-Business equation.
- The hard part is the hundreds of factories and warehouses, world-leading products and technology as well as the century-old brand identity and a reputation known and admired around the globe.
- Above all, Six Sigma Quality that defines the ultimate in customer fulfillment and satisfaction, just what e-Business requires.

New strategic architecture

Naturally, the effectiveness of companies in re-creating their backends on an Internet backbone will greatly depend on the quality of their existing backend. Of course, all incumbent companies are not alike. Expectedly, the more efficient of them like GE can not welcome the Internet more. Welch adds.[5]

> In the end, all of this going on at GE is about this transformational new technology to better serve customers and to be so good and so fast we become the global supplier of choice. Any company – old or new – that does not see this technology as literally as important as breathing could be on its last breath. I've never been more confident that our most exciting days lie ahead. This "new economy" and "old economy" which we hear about incessantly are just labels invented by pundits. There is, however, something new and something very real that is changing the pace and scope of business as it has never been changed before.

Absolutely, what the Internet is not going to do is to replace the old economy by the new. As we've advocated earlier,[6] the "new economy" is the best thing that has happened to the "old economy." If anything, incumbent companies have a great opportunity – move themselves from the "old" to the "new." We've had many similar situations in the past – radio versus TV, movie theaters versus VCRs – but the old all exist today. The new did not supplant the old; the old took on some of the imperatives from the new. Radio today is not the same as radio some 30 years ago; movie theaters today are not the same as movie theaters 20 years ago. Both changed while moving from the old to the new. And this takes time. But in the case of the Internet, it will take less time.

The more efficient incumbents can not welcome the Internet more.

Consider what is happening in the airline industry. Airlines have historically been very aggressive in their use of advanced information technology. In the late 1970s and 1980s they invested in computer-based reservations systems and invented the application of yield management[7] for managing their inventory of seats and pricing tickets for consumers. The focus in the 70s and 80s was very much on using the computer-based reservation systems to move ticketing away from the airline city offices which then handled 80 per cent of ticketing and reservations, but were very expensive to operate (much like bank branches). This succeeded and by the late 90s travel agents were selling around 80 per cent of all airline tickets.

Enter the Internet. Online ticketing boomed thanks to innovative new entrants such as Travelocity and Expedia. Interestingly, online ticketing remains as one of the most successful business applications of the Internet. Travelocity and Expedia turned profitable in 2001 and rank within the 10 largest travel agencies on or off the Internet in the USA! Airlines, like most incumbents, were slow to realize the transformative potential of the Internet. They hesitated to move online while Travelocity and Expedia built up global franchises within the short span of a few years – on and thanks to the Internet. Only at the start of the new millennium did airlines realize that the Internet gave them the potential to transform their businesses – to recoup the customer relationships that they had abdicated to travel agents in the 80s. While they could not reopen their city offices, they could open virtual offices on the Internet and regain control of their distribution – all at a lower cost and increased revenues (by avoiding the travel agent commissions).

Thus it is not surprising that Orbitz opened its doors to the public on June 4, 2001. Orbitz is the combined online travel agency of five major US airlines – American, United, Delta, Northwest, and Continental. Thirty-two airlines have pledged to sell their cheapest tickets via Orbitz. Orbitz is helping the airlines define their new strategic architectures. Notes Krista Pappas, director of travel advisory services for the Internet consulting firm Gomez, "Orbitz will be a boon to both the consumers and the airlines who are members of it… Orbitz and the delivery of its promised travel services is positioned to revolutionize e-tailing as we know it."[8]

> **Orbitz is positioned to revolutionize the retail travel business.**

We believe that the low sentiments about the Internet in 2001 are only the proverbial lull before the storm. Is the Internet a non-starter? Don't get into nodding in favor. Dotcoms weren't the real face of the Internet. The Internet has not yet really been deployed. From now on, the competition is going to be far more punishing to the less-than-deserving competitors. And this is the real face of the Internet and it's going to be "distressing" for many incumbents. It's time to get going, fast, to avoid being on the wrong lane of the incumbents – on the lane of the trampled incumbents. But before we proceed to circumscribe the Internet-triggered new strategic architecture into a framework, let's have a closer look at a study that we concluded in Fall 2000 to understand the current state of Internet deployment in incumbents around the world.

Research on global business transformation

Empirical evidence from our research supports our assertion that the deployment of the Internet leaves a lot to be desired. One of the authors has been conducting a longitudinal research project over recent years (1996–2000) to study the extent of business transformation, to use the Internet effectively, in major global corporations across sectors. The concept underlying the studies is the Marketspace model, which is depicted in Figure 1.1. The Marketspace model is built on two dimensions: a technological capability dimension and a strategic business dimension.

The technological capability dimension comprises the two aspects that form the very basis of the new capabilities enabled by the Internet:

- **Interactivity**: due to the real-time online nature of the Internet, relationships between organizations and customers are becoming more interactive. This is enhancing the richness of customer relationships and creating new paradigms of product design and customer service; and
- **Connectivity**: the open and global nature of the Internet is fostering the creation of a shared global Marketspace. The radical increase in connectivity enabled by the Internet is giving rise to new communication and coordination mechanisms both across organizations and customers, and also within groups of customers themselves.

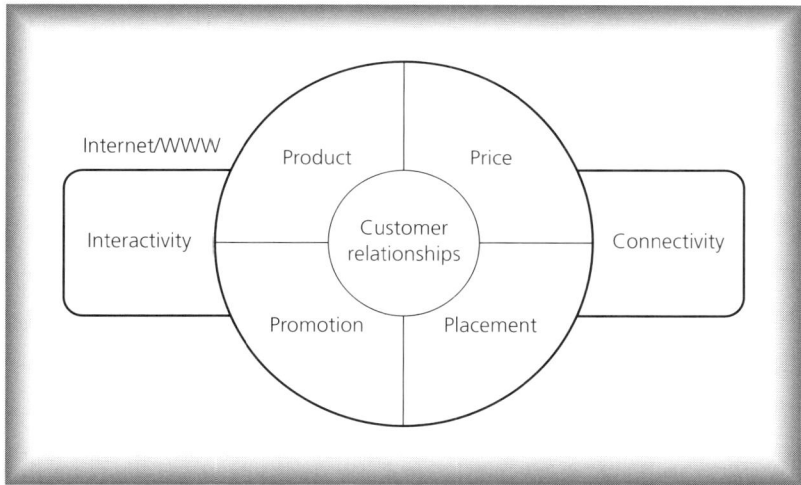

Figure 1.1 The Marketspace model

The dual aspects of interactivity and connectivity are transforming the business models of organizations. We have chosen the classical strategic marketing model of 4Ps – Product,[9] Price, Promotion and Place (or Distribution) as the strategic business dimensions for the research. This model has the dual advantages of simplicity and time-tested acceptance. We have augmented the 4Ps with one C – the additional dimension of Customer relationships, as this aspect is not captured adequately by the 4Ps.

The Marketspace model was used to design a study that probed into the following research question: To what degree are the "4Ps + C" getting transformed due to the real-time interactivity and global connectivity of the Internet? The complete details on the studies are available from publications.[10] In Table 1.1 we have listed the major dimensions along which we evaluated a transformation. Each dimension was mapped out on a set of detailed questions that were tested on a binary scale (yes/no) through a survey with 120 respondents from the Fortune Global 500 list.

Table 1.1 Major dimensions of transformation in the Marketspace study

Technological sophistication

- The ease of navigation of the site;
- The degree of customization possible of the Web interface;
- Speed and ease of access to site features; and
- Advanced technological capabilities

Transformation of products

- The availability of product-related information online;
- The customization of products for individual or groups of customers; and
- The participation of customers in the specification and design of products.

Transformation of promotion

- The use of online advertising;
- The use of online promotions such as sales and discounts;
- The customization of online promotions;
- The participation of customers in online promotions; and
- Links with other organizations in organizing online promotions.

Transformation of pricing

- The availability of pricing information online;
- The dynamic customization of prices;
- The availability of online price negotiation; and;
- The possibility to charge customers for only proportions of products consumed.

Transformation of place

- The availability of online ordering;
- The availability of secured online payment;

- Distribution of products online; and
- The involvement of partner organizations in online distribution.

Transformation of customer relationships

- The provision of online customer service;
- The online identification and tracking of customers to provide customized services;
- The provision of online communications to customers;
- The creation of online communities for customers; and
- The solicitation of online feedback from customers.

The results of this survey are interesting because they demonstrate that much more can be done by incumbent organizations for exploiting the Internet. While media reports of increasing volumes of online commerce are encouraging, our study shows that most large corporations are doing little to exploit the unique transformational potential of the Internet. The results not only indicate the state of e-business transformation in 2000 but also lay down the agenda for innovation for corporations in the following years.

It is worth highlighting here before we enter into details that the results indicate that about two-thirds of the surveyed firms are simply treating the Internet as a publishing medium and most of the remaining one-third appear content with simply transporting their existing business models onto the Internet. Very few firms are actively using the Internet for launching new business models.

About two-thirds of the surveyed incumbents are simply treating the Internet as a publishing medium.

The reasons for the lack of exploitation of the Internet by traditional large firms are multiple and complex. They are more organizational in nature as opposed to being technology related. As outlined by John Welch himself, frequently, "traditional" firms are hostage to the legacies of their own successes. Management in these organizations have risen to the top on the basis of these successes and it is often very difficult for them to detach themselves from historical successes and venture into new territories. For example, France Telecom has been credited with the successful launch of the Minitel videotext service in France more than a decade ago. Trapped by the success of the Minitel, France Telecom had a difficult time, until recently, in embracing the Internet (which threatened to eclipse the Minitel). These and other hurdles to innovation will be discussed in later chapters of the book.

Regardless of what the reasons for the lag may be, lagging incumbent firms from all over the globe risk stagnation and being overtaken by more energetic compatriots or new entrants who are constantly pushing the envelope of innovation. Firms such as Yahoo!, AOL, and Amazon are questioning the rules of entire sectors. In little over half a decade, Amazon has redefined the business of retailing. Traditional leaders such as Wal-Mart are learning a lesson or two from Amazon.

Despite wide publicity about American firms as leaders of the Internet revolution, our results show that large American corporations are not far ahead of their European and Asian counterparts. This is good news for European and Asian managers who often lament the lead of American organizations. There are some indications now that large European firms are catching up with their American counterparts in some sectors. The real issue for all surveyed firms, American or otherwise, is their ability to innovate and move ahead with new business models and novel business practices.

The customer is the right focus as organizations look to exploit the Internet. The study results indicate that such a trend is currently under way among firms. The Internet allows firms to customize their products and services to each individual customer and to deliver a personalized level of service not possible before. However, providing customers with enhanced levels of service and involving them in product/service design requires significant changes within internal business practices. This is not easy and much hard work lies ahead as firms learn how to make life easier for their customers via the Internet. These aspects are dealt with in detail in the later chapters of the book.

Firms from information-intensive sectors such as software, media, and financial services have a natural advantage as they can deliver most of their products and services online. While software and media firms have embraced the Internet for product delivery, some sectors such as financial services have been reluctant. This reluctance may cost them dearly in the future – already, the finance site of Yahoo! is ranked as the number one finance site in many surveys. The physical nature of products need not be a stumbling factor in embracing the Internet, as has been proven by Internet pioneers like Amazon and our research results from sectors such as electronics and computers. Firms in all sectors should actively question how best to exploit the Internet to transform their business practices for competitive advantage.

The results in numbers and graphs

The overall degrees of achievement of the companies surveyed in Fall 2000 along the dimensions of the Marketspace model are shown in Figure 1.2. The overall scores were obtained by aggregating the binary responses for detailed questions comprising each of the six dimensions outlined in the earlier table. A high score (on a scale of 0–100 percent) for a particular dimension indicates an overall high level of business transformation along that dimension. The first observation is that large global corporations have a long way to go to exploit the transformational potential of the Internet. The figures against most of the dimensions are well below 50 percent. Most firms are stuck in the first stage of exploitation of the Internet: publishing corporate and, in many instances, product information. Many have moved to the second stage of using the Internet to facilitate transactions with customers and partners. Fewer have actively tried to shift gears into the third and most interesting stage of Internet exploitation: business transformation. In our survey, less than 20 percent of the surveyed firms allowed for the formation of cyber-communities among customers and very few were innovative in stimulating intra-community interactions.

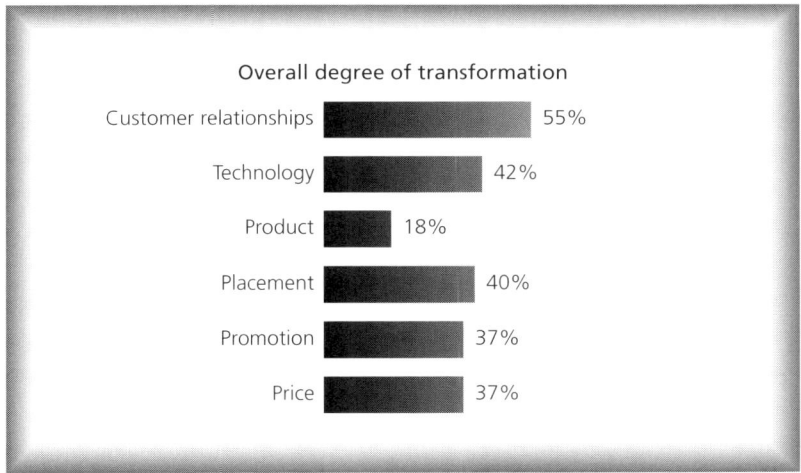

Figure 1.2 Overall degrees of achievement along the Marketspace model dimensions

Despite the low levels of overall achievement, the focus is clear for all corporations: it is on using the power of the Internet to enhance customer relationships. Pharmaceutical firms such as Merck provide customer service online in the form of its product guides which inform consumers about the use of their products. There is a growing realization among corporations that

The customer is the right focus as organizations look to exploit the Internet.

the Internet has forever changed the traditional paradigm of marketing. Gone are the days of mass marketing and remote customer contact. The

Internet has made it possible for companies to focus on building relationships with individual customers and to make direct and personalized contact with each customer.

While a lot has been accomplished with respect to customer relationships, much remains to be done (see Figure 1.3). While a large majority of firms try to identify or track customers, only about half of them offer to keep their customers informed by sending e-mail updates on product releases and other corporate events. Also, a small fraction of all surveyed firms encourage the formation of communities among customers. This is despite evidence that shows that cyber-communities increase loyalty and sales and make customers feel more connected to organizations.

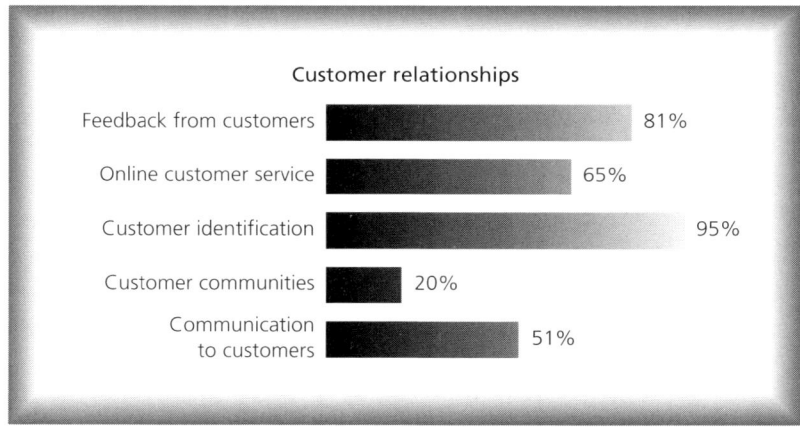

Figure 1.3 Use of the Internet for different aspects of Customer relationships

A high proportion of the surveyed companies featured product catalogs in one form or another (see Figure 1.4), though with varying levels of detail. While most of the catalogs covered the whole product range, only a handful provided information or comparisons with competitor's products. This is interesting because there are many "new" intermediaries on the Web who provide a free comparison of product offerings from competing firms. For example, virtual travel agencies such as Expedia.com provide comparisons of different airline airfares for any particular route.

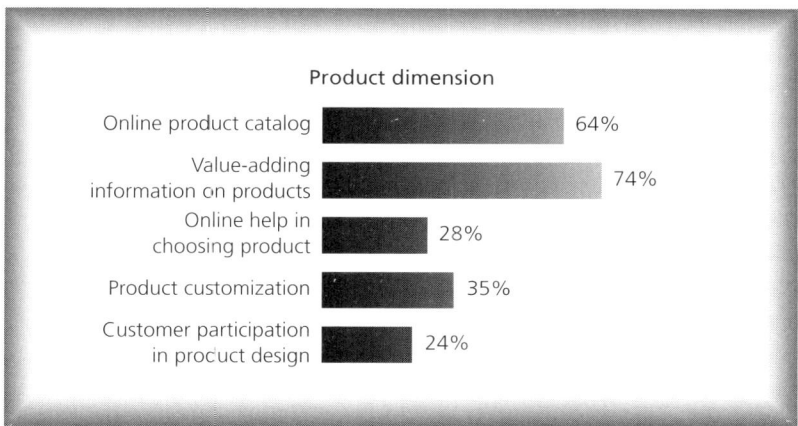

Figure 1.4 Use of the Internet for different aspects of the Product dimension

Many companies make significant effort to provide value-adding information on their products. Volkswagen provides tips for safe driving and helps consumers make the buy versus lease decision by guiding them through the relevant financial details. Most chemical companies provide detailed product specifications and information about the application of their products to aid the purchase decision.

About a quarter of the surveyed firms provide online help to customers in choosing products via expert systems or other automated tools and in some cases via the possibility to interact with human agents. Insurance companies, for example, have the customer answer a set of questions and then suggest the right policy. GM asks potential customers for the features they look for in a car and then recommends a model to suit their tastes.

A smaller proportion of firms allow users either to customize products or to participate in product design online. Disney allows some product customization by allowing buyers to customize commodities like mugs and mouse pads and to design custom greetings (via Design on line). Allyn & Bacon (the Viacom publishing division) allows college faculty to build custom books as course material, by selecting specific parts from available books.

Online advertising is becoming popular with about two-thirds of the surveyed firms utilizing banners and other forms of online advertising (see Figure 1.5). Promotions on the Internet are similar in many respects to promotions in the "traditional" marketplace: price reductions, discounts, and prizes. Thus, many companies have special discounts on Internet orders.

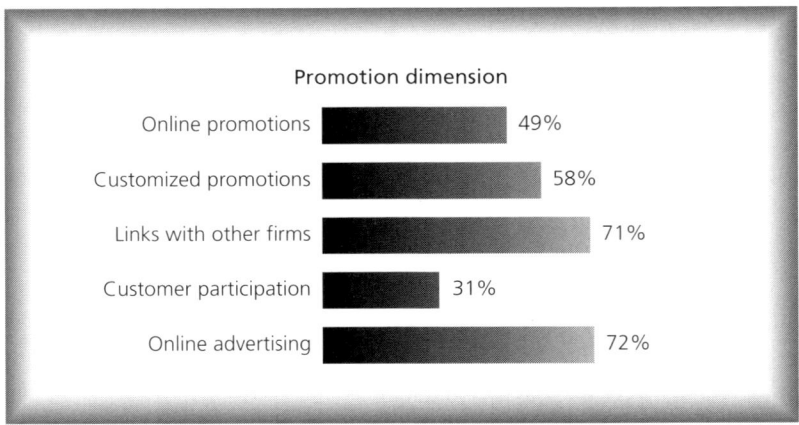

Figure 1.5 Use of the Internet for different aspects of the Promotion dimension

However, the interactive nature of the Web provides firms with a unique ability to get customers to participate in promotions. About a third of all companies use online games and contests to retain the attention of customers. For example, Volkswagen advertises its new car models on its web pages and encourages visitors to enter the contests to win cars. The US Postal Service features contests allowing users to participate in and submit entries for designing new stamps.

Promotions also come by way of links to related sites or sites which might be of interest to customers. For example, the Dutch financial powerhouse, ING Group, provides links to Dutch tourism sites from its homepage.

Less than half of all firms allow online ordering of products (see Figure 1.6). Computers and electronics firms such as IBM not only have self-operated online stores but also provide links to other retailers that sell their products. Given the physical nature of many products, they cannot be distributed online; "soft" products such as software, media, music and financial services can be distributed online. However, only a small proportion of firms are actively using the Internet for delivering "soft" products online. Most firms distribute product-related information, such as dealer or store locations, online.

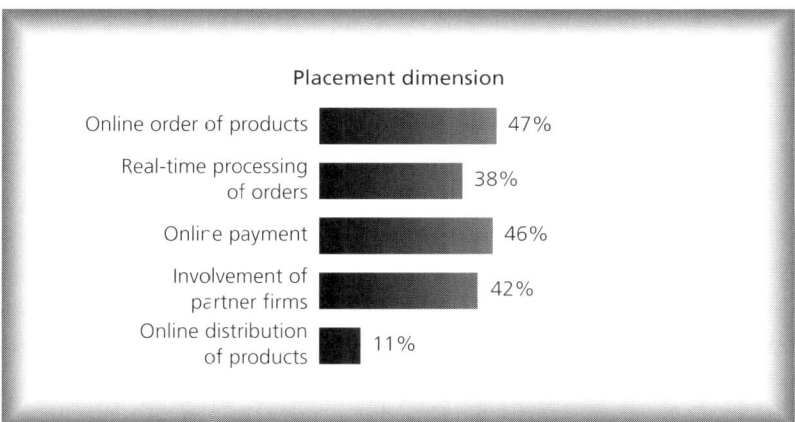

Figure 1.6 Use of the Internet for different aspects of the Place dimension

Most companies that allow online purchases ship goods via UPS or other air/surface mail. Though about half of all firms allow for online payment, only a third of them have the capability to process orders in real time. This highlights the fact that few firms have successfully integrated their frontend web systems with their legacy backend transaction processing and enterprise resource planning systems.

Fewer than 10 percent of the surveyed firms display prices for competing products.

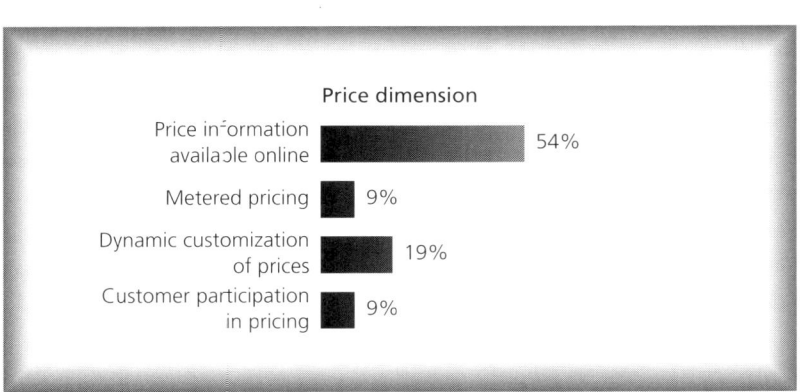

Figure 1.7 Use of the Internet for different aspects of the Price dimension

Table 1.2 Sectors ranked across Marketspace model dimensions

Customer relationships	%	Technology	%	Product	%
Manufacturing	64	Chemical & Pharmaceutical	41	Manufacturing	61
Retail & Wholesale	56	Manufacturing	41	Travel & Transport	54
Travel & Transport	55	Electronic & Computer	40	Telecom & Utility	39
Electronic & Computer	53	Media & Entertainment	38	Electronic & Computer	34
Telecom & Utility	53	Mining, Oil & Refining	38	Media & Entertainment	33
Media & Entertainment	53	Finance & Insurance	33	Retail & Wholesale	31
Mining, Oil & Refining	49	Telecom & Utility	31	Chemical & Pharmaceutical	30
Chemical & Pharmaceutical	48	Travel & Transport	28	Finance & Insurance	29
Finance & Insurance	45	Retail & Wholesale	27	Mining, Oil & Refining	26

Placement	%	Promotion	%	Price	%
Travel & Transport	27	Media & Entertainment	53	Manufacturing	37
Media & Entertainment	23	Manufacturing	50	Travel & Transport	33
Retail & Wholesale	19	Retail & Wholesale	39	Media & Entertainment	26
Manufacturing	18	Travel & Transport	38	Telecom & Utility	20
Telecom & Utility	16	Telecom & Utility	36	Retail & Wholesale	15
Electronic & Computer	15	Mining, Oil & Refining	33	Electronic & Computer	13
Mining, Oil & Refining	11	Electronic & Computer	27	Finance & Insurance	6
Finance & Insurance	9	Finance & Insurance	25	Mining, Oil & Refining	3
Chemical & Pharmaceutical	7	Chemical & Pharmaceutical	24	Chemical & Pharmaceutical	0

Internet commerce and online ordering are hampered by the fact that most firms fare relatively poorly along the Price dimension (see Figure 1.7). About half of all surveyed firms do not display prices for their own products and fewer than 10 percent of the surveyed firms display prices for competing products. A small fraction of all firms offered any form of dynamic price negotiation or customization to customers. The leaders along the Pricing dimension appear to be airline companies, which dynamically vary prices and allow customers to make bids for specific tickets.

Table 1.2 presents a summary of our survey results across the nine surveyed industry sectors. The Manufacturing sector, dominated by the automotive industry, has embraced the Internet as a new medium for growth and customer expansion. Typically, approaching a car dealer to inquire about car features, or worse, to negotiate price is viewed as an unfavorable, often dreaded, experience. By providing consumers with the ability to research, shop, and even finance purchases online, car companies are trying to turn purchasing a car into a fun and interesting experience. A more detailed description of General Motors and Auto-by-Tel is provided in Chapter 5.

Media & Entertainment companies score high in general on the survey results as they are well positioned to conduct business on the Internet. The Internet provides a natural means for them to reach out to larger audiences and to create new products and services by combining their traditional paper-based, radio, or TV content with the newer interactive capabilities of the Internet.

Despite the physical nature of their products, the Electronic & Computer industry continues to be an early adopter of e-business. The innovative use of the Internet by companies such as Cisco and Dell has been much talked about in the media in recent years. We refer to e-business innovation in the Electronic & Computer industry in many of the following chapters.

Many leading firms in the Finance & Insurance sector have been slow to take up on the innovative potential of the Internet.

The Finance & Insurance sector as a whole performs poorly in e-business transformation. Many leading firms in this sector have been slow to take up on the innovative potential of the Internet. It is only recently that incumbents such as Merrill Lynch have started to take the Internet seriously – only when goaded into action by the actions of competitors such as Charles Schwab and new entrants such as E*TRADE (see Chapter 3 for more detail). However, most are still only transporting their existing business models onto the Net; they are yet to creatively harness e-business transformation.

The Retail & Wholesale sector is acting on using the Internet's vast capabilities to increase product sales and to transform the business. While new entrants such as Amazon continue to lead the way in online retailing, incumbents such as Wal-Mart are responding aggressively after a slow start (see Chapter 4 for more details). Firms such as Home Depot and Toys"R"Us have built linkages with online leaders such as Amazon to rapidly build competence in e-business.

The Travel & Transport sector is also a strong performer in the relative sector rankings. This is due to the impressive online initiatives of parcel delivery companies and airlines. This is a sector which has traditionally invested heavily in information technology and thus they are more easily able to move their customer-facing and backend processes online. In some cases, these online moves are transforming the industry – witness the creation of Orbitz as described earlier.

Figure 1.8 depicts the regional variations in the scores of the surveyed firms along the different dimensions of the Marketspace model.

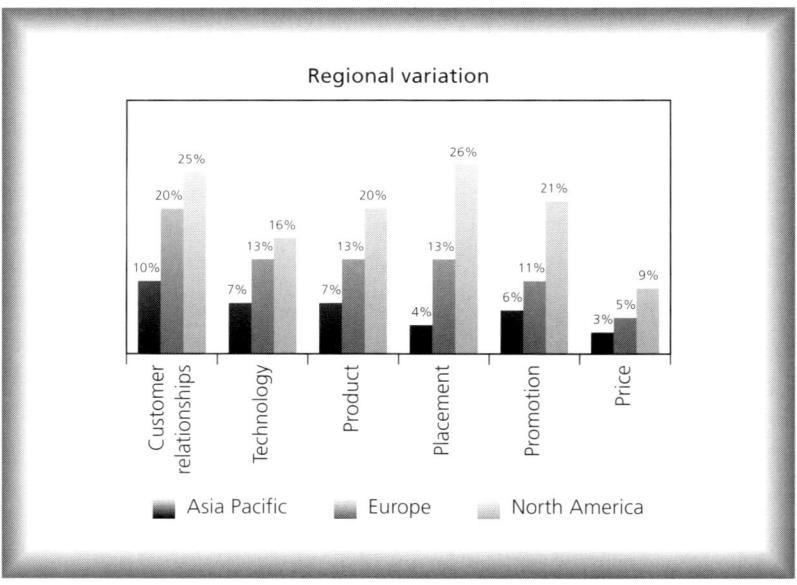

Figure 1.8 Regional comparisons along the dimensions of the Marketspace model

The relative lead of American firms is not surprising because the Internet was born in the USA and even today, a dominant majority of all Internet transactions occur within the USA. American firms also continue to be leaders in investing in information technology. Firms from the Asia Pacific region, primarily Japan, are lagging significantly relative to their counterparts from Europe and North America along all aspects of the Marketspace model. The gap between European and North American firms is less but still significant.

However, it is worthwhile noting that the scores of American firms, along the different dimensions of the Marketspace model, are not significantly higher. This shows that large traditional firms all over the globe are doing little to exploit the unique transformational potential of the Internet. In such a situation, it is possible for European and Asian firms to catch up with their American counterparts in the near future. This appears to be happening in some sectors. For example, Scandinavian companies such as Ericsson and Nokia are rapidly turning northern Europe into a wireless society. A country such as Finland boasts the highest penetration of the Internet in society among all countries in the world and is a showcase for innovative applications of the technology for the rest of the world.

> Our research on global business transformation shows that:
>
> 1 Very few incumbent firms are actively using the Internet to transform their businesses.
> 2 Customer interfaces are the hotbeds of action – firms are focusing on using the Internet to make life easier for their customers.
> 3 E-business transformation varies across sectors – with sectors such as Travel & Transport, Manufacturing, Electronics & Computer, and Media & Entertainment leading others such as Finance & Insurance and Mining, Oil & Refining.
> 4 American firms, while investing more in information technology, have relatively small leads over their global counterparts in e-business transformation.

The agenda

What's apparent from the study? The Internet has failed to touch the core routines of most organizations. But before we get down to exploring exactly why, we need to ask to why we should really be so bothered about the under-utilization of the Internet's possibilities. If it's really useful its usage will automatically pick up beyond the evangelist few. But the point at hand is simple: we think that the potential of the technology

Minimize the loss of resources and opportunities in the innovative application of the Internet.

is immense. We think that it is not simply about the new replacing the old, but rather about the new transforming the old. We think that it is about helping to unleash innovation to create value hidden in businesses. We think that it is about making life better for all. We should thus be bothered. And that's the spirit behind the book, how you can become more innovative and leverage the potential of the Internet faster and more creatively. The book explores how best to use the Internet, today.

And why do we believe that the power of this technology is immense? First, the Internet is hardly "a technology". It's a construct, logical rather than physical. It's the newest infrastructure on which many technologies, devices, and applications will reside. And it's there for good. It's difficult to imagine what it might evolve into. Second, the Internet is inherently a "broadband" infrastructure. A lot of different sets of values can ride over it. A given Internet node could be used for education, commerce, e-governance, advertisement, entertainment, health care, elections, and so many other activities. Once it is there, it is best used for as many purposes as possible. Third, the Internet has a unique associational energy. It grows better as it grows bigger. It has the capability to create the global village. It has very low "spread" costs.

What next? What exactly is the Internet about? The book is devoted to the "bright stuff." To bring out the bright side of the Internet and the resulting competitive dynamics that will unfold soon. In the next chapter we explore the "bright stuff" – the unprecedented promise of innovation that the Internet holds.

Action points

Think about the following questions and issues in the context of your firm:

1. Evaluate how you have used the Internet within your firm over recent years. Have you simply transported your "old" ways of doing business onto the new medium? Or have you transformed the way you do business while moving online? Try to list the different ways in which you have e-transformed your business.

2. Look at competitors in your sector. Do you see any new competitors – companies that perhaps were not there in your competitive horizon just a few years ago? Do they have fundamentally different business models from what you have? List the differences. Are any of these differences due to their unique usage of the potential of the Internet?

3. Look at the Marketspace model again (Figure 1.1) and carefully read through the dimensions of the model outlined in Table 1.1. How does your firm score along the aspects described in Table 1.1? Are you surprised by your score?

4. Do you think that your firm could have done more in recent years to exploit the innovative potential of the Internet? Which organizational strengths have helped you in using the power of the Internet? Which factors have held you back?

Notes

1. www.ge.com. John F. Welch's speech at the General Electric Company 2000 Annual Meeting, Richmond Virginia, April 26, 2000.
2. www.ge.com; speeches of John Welch.
3. Six Sigma is a quality process methodology.
4. We prefer to use the term backend over operational infrastructure to represent the entire operational capabilities – physical assets, processes, and information technology.
5. www.ge.com; speeches of John Welch.
6. Dutta, S. and Srivastava, S (2001) *Embracing the Net*, FT. Com Series, Financial Times Management.
7. Sophisticated mathematical models which vary prices dynamically depending upon availability of seats in different fare categories.
8. O'Donnell, Jayne (2001) "US Airlines team up to sell tickets online," *USA Today*, June 4.
9. We use the term "product" to refer to both products (tangible and intangible) and services.
10. Dutta, S, Amoni, A. and Biren, B. (2001) "Business transformation on the Internet: Results of the 2000 study," forthcoming *European Management Journal*.

The bright stuff! 2

Bookmark

Why do you think some of us remain so excited about the Internet? There is not much truth in the claims in some quarters that it's the greatest invention or discovery ever. But it cannot be denied that it is a discontinuity in the way we handle communications and knowledge. Such a discontinuity is always a period full of opportunities. Now is the Internet's time to show its colors. From previous discontinuities we have learned that many experiments and failures are needed in order to arrive at successful new business models. Let's just approach it without any predisposition.

Is anything "bright" about the current experience with Internet-based business models? First and foremost, it's the best thing that has happened to consumers in many years. Their convenience and value drivers will rule the development of new business models. It has also triggered many incumbents to transform themselves, in some instances beyond recognition. Communicating and collaborating across departments and across organizations has never been easier. Organizations were never as information intensive. And operational processes are increasingly becoming more and more connected with customers. Technology has become a source of continuous innovation. And the best news is that the old and new can reinforce each other: connections between a creative new frontend and an effective existing backend leads to a powerful formula.

Towards the end of this chapter there is a summary of all the subsequent chapters and a roadmap for the book.

A time for experimentation

Add "e" to anything and it should become fundamentally different. For instance, e + business cannot be "business as usual" but something very different. Many incumbents who got on the Net early got it wrong by simply moving their existing business models and processes onto the Net. That was clearly not the way to go. A whole new level of business possibilities are opening up due to the Internet. We are actually living in a defining period. Nothing will remain incrementally changed. We already have reflections of the same in industries like travel, stock broking, music, and book retailing. These have changed beyond recognition. You can "name your own price" for the airline ticket or holiday package you wish to buy; you can conduct stock trading at a fraction of the cost of just a couple of years ago; you can get your favorite music directly from musicians or another music collector.

> **Add "e" to anything and it should enable you to become a fundamentally different value creator.**

Talk to the leaders and you will realize that the Internet is now their backbone. GE, Cisco, GM, HP, Ford, Toyota, and Oracle, all are re-creating themselves on the intelligent infrastructure that is the Internet.

The Internet is a very significant technological development. But it is more than just that. Why do you think some of us are so obsessed with the Internet? Because it offers a revolutionary new infrastructure.

Quite a few revolutions – technological, social, and cultural – have shaped our evolution. There have been other killer applications in the past. The railroad was one of them: it galvanized the first industrial revolution. So were the telephone, electricity, automobiles, airplanes, etc. And earlier we had Galileo's theories about the solar system, Darwin's theory of evolution, and Newton's and Einstein's contributions which changed our understanding of the physical world. At each of these moments in time, people were at first amused and bewildered – airplanes, for example, gave wings to everyone's long-nursed desire to fly like birds! On the other hand, Galileo's theory was considered to be almost sacrilege. But after a while these revolutions or discontinuities helped us to change the world radically.

The Internet is one of these major discontinuities that offer us a unique window for radical change. The others had their time and we learned from them that after an initial period of scepticism and intensive experimentation, a number of new business models emerged, and not always the one that looked like the winner at the beginning. An open mind was needed to spot the potential offered by the discontinuity. Now it is time for the Internet to start showing its real potential. We should welcome it without any predisposition – that's definitely one important lesson from the past.

Looking at institutions, was Ford any less innovative and visionary than the current vanguard of the Internet – AOL, Amazon, Yahoo!, or Cisco? Ford introduced the mass manufacturing that still rules the roost – it's behind the economic growth that the world has enjoyed over the past 90 years. And what about IBM, AT&T, GE, GM? How did these companies conceive, plan, and manage their leadership over the past 100 years? By continuous leadership in technological and management practices and theories. Some old and some new elements were in the melting pot all the time. It was not a case of the new replacing the old. But success came always out of the mutual leveraging of old and new. Naturally, the response of incumbents to the Internet should again be similar – strengthen some of the existing basics, adapt some of the existing practices to the emerging possibilities, and take on some new ways and means.

Do not underestimate the task at hand in adapting some of the existing practices and taking on some new ways and means. For you may not have the luxury of time – it's going to be like the industrial revolution compressed in time by a factor of ten! More importantly, such a source of discontinuity is not likely to appear again in another decade or so. According to Larry Ellison,[1] Oracle's CEO, the transition to Internet computing is the last big architectural change that we will see in computer technology for a long time.

We believe that for the first time in industrial history, technology has accorded the central role to customers. Customers can be themselves again. Individuality is in. Customers will be empowered to design products and services – just the right ones to suit their needs. "Local" or contextual intellectual capital was never more important to living – it's about everything. No longer do customers have to be reduced to nameless numbers in a system designed for mass production. And even more, things only become better as the Internet grows. Stop daydreaming about it. Your daydreams will come true in the near future! Or your competitor may realize these dreams.

Why the bright stuff will happen:

1 The transition to Internet computing is a big architectural change in the business landscape: like any discontinuity we should appreciate its innovative potential and approach it without predisposition.
2 Innovation under conditions of discontinuity does not mean we have to throw everything overboard: success in the past has usually come from melding together the old and the new.
3 The Internet's great potential is to put the customer at the center of the innovation process.

Why do you think all these things became possible? Large-scale Internet-based IT systems are becoming easier for managers to juggle with. There are significant changes in IT management that make it easier to conceptualize, design, build, and manage distributed systems. Again, Ellison puts all this in perspective when he says, "it's because with the Internet, computer and network services will finally begin to look like the electricity utility, the phone utility, or the water utility systems, and economics of scale will really apply." The user interface is also becoming much simpler with the growing adoption of "thin client" (PDAs, mobile phones, network PCs, etc.) user interfaces and decreased "computer literacy" requirements among users.

As a consequence, operational constraints in IT deployment are decreasing significantly. In the past, execution of a plan was challenging because loss of time, effort, and material resources was the norm at functional, hierarchical, divisional, and geographic interfaces. Managing the existing operational infrastructure was difficult due to the high costs of coordination. Change was an expensive proposition. However, all that is changing. The Internet has ushered in global standards that have given rise to the possibility of creating integrated technology infrastructures. Intra- and inter-organizational communication and collaboration are being facilitated on such integrated infrastructures. Connecting to knowledge has become more than a slogan. The power of broadband connections helps us to do more with technology. A well-designed IT "utility" network enables us to connect pools of knowledge together. Organizational processes are becoming more transparent and integrated. An important source of innovation is now being brought into the corporation: customers.

Innovating with customers at the center

Priceline's "The WebHouse Club" was an interesting innovation for customers. It failed but its essence will come alive again with better management of the backend. Prior to the WebHouse Club, major competing retailers, such as grocery chains, had never worked together to allow millions of consumers to save money by naming their own prices. With the WebHouse Club, members named their own price for groceries on the Internet and shopped at those prices at any of over 1,100 participating grocery stores in the New York metro area representing virtually every major chain, including A&P, KeyFood, ShopRite, Grand Union, and Stop & Shop.[2]

WebHouse Club partnered with established local grocery stores and offered consumers a new bargain: save money while shopping at their favorite local grocery store. If any grocer accepted the price offered for groceries through the WebHouse Club, the consumer could go and pick up those groceries at their favorite local supermarkets – savings and delivery convenience at the same time. WebHouse Club would later settle the accounting (or the physical movement of goods) between the grocers that accepted the bid and the grocer from where the groceries were picked up.

> **Incumbents: be open to new ideas. Don't get "Napstered." Or for that matter, "Amazoned"!**

Great revolutions in retail have often been about saving the customer money. For example, Wal-Mart is all about savings. In the past, local grocers offered convenience but Wal-Mart's Warehouse clubs provided lower prices. But in the case of Priceline it offered customers the savings of a Warehouse club with the convenience of their local grocery stores. Potentially this is a "Wal-Martianian" revolution in retail.

A similar scenario is evolving – at a faster pace – in the music industry. You may have closely monitored the Napster saga. Napster has shaken the very foundations of the global music industry! However, Napster or no Napster, history has been made and the music industry's clock can not be turned back. The essence of Napster will thrive – the music that will ultimately sell will be the music that actually pleases your ears. The music industry incumbents appear distressed about all this but the situation could be a win-win for all participants in the industry. Music companies need to listen carefully to their customers. But they didn't listen and allowed Napster to be born. Today they need to capitalize on the significant mutations unleashed in the structure of their industry. If they approach this with an open mind, they can innovate such that they gain together with their customers. In fact, the priority is that they must not let themselves be "Napstered" again!

Let us explore how it can be a win-win situation for all in the music industry. For music companies, the cost of digital reproduction is virtually zero. The cost of digital delivery is also close to nil. The only operational cost is the actual cost of producing the music. There could be a significant increase in the volume of sales if people could buy the specific titles they want and without the disincentive of having to buy the other not-so-interesting titles tagged along with the CD. This conforms to the observation that the sales of singles increased in music stores near universities – the prime locations of Napster users. College students were using Napster to sample the music but then were going out and buying that single – not the entire CD – from a music store. Musicians can get the

> **Cisco and Dell's secret – strengthening customer relationships.**

better part of revenues as royalty. They will also have the benefit of a powerful sales force for free – their fans – to sell their music, and the most powerful of advertisements – word-of-mouth. Music buyers will get more appropriate advice on the entire gamut of music that may potentially interest them! Indeed, the direct vertical and horizontal connections among producers and consumers of music are going to be the two most important levers in the emerging music industry. And that's the interactivity and connectivity that we talked about in the Marketspace model described in the previous chapter.

A less talked about benefit of Cisco and Dell's online business models is that by building online relationships with their customers, it became far easier for them to bring their customers together. Their customers helped to educate each other about making the best use of specific applications and solutions. There is a lot of credibility attached to such communication exchanges. And this has been a major source of customer retention and growth for the two companies. Similarly, for Charles Schwab, using the Internet to strengthen relationships with customers has been like magic to its performance indices – it took Schwab 20 years to get to $100 billion in client assets under its management (1975–95) – but it took less than 5 years to add $500 billion to the same (1996–2000). Essentially, it dramatically increased the leverage of its existing resources. Chapter 3 provides more details on the Schwab story.

Just wait for the spillover. More and more firms will solicit and give heed to their customers' needs and preferences. It's intuitively obvious that such a scenario makes great business sense for all businesses – happier customers lead to better top lines and bottom lines!

> Innovating with customers at the center requires that:
>
> **1** You need to do more than simply listen to customers – you need to make them the core drivers for your innovation.
>
> **2** Customer communities become the new intermediaries – harnessing them effectively will be critical.
>
> **3** Operational processes need to connect the frontends and backends of organizations – seamlessly across multiple channels.

Merging the old and the new

WebHouse Club did not succeed – primarily because the appropriate backend could not be built in time. A large capital commitment was needed to build an effective nationwide grocery store and gas stations network. Key to this was broad participation by packaged goods manufacturers, third-party marketing agents, and a substantial investment in information technology systems. With the stock of Priceline trading at almost a 90 percent discount from its peak, this was no longer possible and WebHouse had to shut its doors on February 19, 2001. However, we do not think that we have seen the last of the concept. WebHouse Club has shown the way for an innovation in the retail groceries market. Customers have valued the experience. It is now a challenge for incumbent grocery chains to make this customer dream come true. To do so, we need to combine the creativity of Webhouse Club with the strength of a traditional provider.

Despite Schwab's obvious strengths in the "online world," it is not ignoring the "physical world." David Puttruck,[3] President and Co-CEO of Schwab, notes that 75 percent of its customers transact online and about 10 percent do the same with touch-tone phone or voice recognition technology. Only 10–15 percent use personal interaction or phone. Yet a whopping 75 percent register for the brokerage service at one of Schwab's offices (retail outlets) – they also want to see for themselves what Schwab does because on an average they put $225,000 with Charles Schwab. Incidentally, Charles Schwab has over 7,000 brokers and 310 retail outlets complementing its online presence. The strength of its relationships with customers is omnipotent. Even as Schwab rolls out its online systems, it is continuing to invest in its existing branch network. Clearly a blend of the offline and the online seems to be necessary for success.

More generally, put the two together – the new customer-centric frontend and the backend – and you have the essence of the new strategic architecture. The marriage of customers and operational processes is possible now. Can you conceive a better scenario? One can be even more radical. Organizations can reduce themselves to being custodians of operational assets and charge rent from customers for using the assets for their gratification. Consumers and organizations are coming in closer sync, just like the two ends of a pendulum. The Internet empowers customers in ways that no other medium has done before. Let customers decide their needs and their fulfillment.

Sir John Bond,[4] Chairman, HSBC Holdings plc, goes further in this direction. He says, "We took the seminal decision that we are at the client end, not the producer end, of the business. The best way to keep clients is by offering the best products available. We say to our internal providers, 'You have to compete for shelf space with [for example] other major insurers in the world.' A major competitive strength is our processing capability, but what we process can come from the best of breed." To him, HSBC uniquely marries customers and operations – seamlessly linking customers to the best deliverables, even outside the operational assets owned by HSBC!

> **Marry customers with operational assets and processes.**

Solemnizing the marriage

Let's look at retailers and see how they may solemnize the marriage between the frontend and the backend. In the current scenario, incumbent retailers and e-tailers seem to be pitted against each other in getting the best fit marriage. David Pottruck,[5] Co-CEO, Schwab, asserts that incumbent retailers are doomed if they remain transaction oriented. If they can change, they take the whole customer experience to a new level and they may indeed thrive let alone survive. And change to what? Matt Maddox,[6] Internet Business Solutions Group, Cisco, offers a significant clue, "The strongest retailers are obsessive about their customers."

Are the strongest retailers the most obsessive about their customers? So it seems. Others, the vast majority of retailers, display a lack of empathy in their interactions with customers; the vast majority do not put their heart next to their head while reaching out to customers. On either side of the buyer–seller dyad the interactions are not cherished. The buyers do not always make repeat visits to retailers by design. They usually do not have much to distinguish one from the other. For these retailers, the cost–benefit trade-offs underlying increasing involvement with customers have largely been virtual. While the benefits could be articulated, the costs of changing legacy processes and systems were prohibitive for most of them.

However, the Internet removes a lot of these constraints. Now retailers can more easily develop the memory to catalog exchanges with customers and reach to the bottom of their value anchors in buying decisions. And that supports a growing relationship that touches both the head and the heart of individual customers. New entrants such as Amazon have demonstrated a lead in exploiting the Internet to this end (see Chapter 4 for more details). But involvement requires something else too – looking into each other's eyes, literally! And on this count incumbent retailers should feel more assured; they at least have ample opportunities to do that – in their stores! It's quite evenly poised between the new entrants and them.

Witness the success of Wal-Mart in blending store-based and online retail. Despite a late start, Wal-Mart has moved aggressively in online retail in recent months. It is, however, not trying to copy Amazon! It is using its online presence to complement its physical stores. Some of the best-selling items in its online stores, such as Rolex watches, are not even found in its stores. Why stock items that are not in the typical purchase basket for most of the suburban and rural customers visiting its stores? At the same time, try ordering plastic cups online. You will not be able to do so. Why stock an item that costs less than a dollar but incurs more than five times that amount in logistics costs? It is not just a case of selective stocking of products. The synergies are real. Wal-Mart utilizes data from its online store to optimize its shelf-space utilization!

Amazon is also no longer a pure e-tailer. It has opened physical warehouses to better connect its frontend with its backend processes. It wants to control critical aspects of the backend processes to ensure the highest levels of customer satisfaction. It is not yet opening physical stores, but is partnering with other physical retailers, such as Toys"R"Us, to exploit in-store customer relationships. Barnes & Noble is finally realizing the value of its physical book store. Initially it managed Barnes & Noble.com as a dotcom at an arm's-length relationship with the parent bookstore company. Eventually, it realized that tremendous possibilities for synergy lay between the physical and online book presence. Customers in bookstores can research online from kiosks in stores. Online customers can return books at any bookstore. The synergies are many (see Chapter 4 for more details).

More out of less: Bisecting the back-end

Interestingly, even the flip side of being closer to customers' hearts is no less bright! There your apparently good cost savings in reaching to the bottom of the heart. Have the cake and eat it too! Explains[7] Jacques A. Nasser, CEO, Ford, "[online presence] is only the tip of the iceberg. The more significant thing is how it would be changing us from designing and buying components for different number of models available, to production and distribution. When you design for 100,000 customers, the complexities that you go through are very high – you have to guess what they may want." He adds that online you understand customers quickly and save a lot of complexity, and change design and engineering according to the explicit needs and demands of customers – no more guessing. And the online experiences cannot be denied because the cost of distribution of cars may be as high as 30 percent of the price that customers finally pay. (Chapter 5 outlines some of these transformations in the automobile manufacturing and retailing sector.)

To be sure, the Internet could make your backend much more valuable if you could bring about a closer connection between your backend and customers. You could get more from your backend. No, we're not talking about simply sweating out the assets. It's possible to get more out of less. Indeed, the real value creation opportunity is about increasing the productivity of physical assets by leveraging them to the hilt. What's the new strategic imperative then?

Effectively bisect the information and physical parts of the backend and take the information part online. Untangle the two. On the ground, the two are hardly distinguishable and the bisection will boil down to giving birth to a knowledge asset; create it out of the minds of the people and desk research of documents.

How do you get more out of less?

Consider what Cisco has done with its call centers. As little as seven years ago, Cisco was a relatively small company – with about 6,000 employees worldwide – but was facing torrid growth rates. Traditionally, customer queries were answered by technical engineers. However, given the rapid worldwide growth facing Cisco, answering queries by simply hiring more technical engineers was not a valid option. Cisco decided to extract the knowledge required for answering 80 percent of simple customer queries and package it in a series of interconnected expert systems which it launched online. The knowledge component of a critical customer service process was put online. Today about 80 percent of all customer queries are answered online via the automated system. Technical engineers are able to add higher value by answering complex customer queries. Cost savings are tremendous – in fiscal year 2000, Cisco's revenues almost doubled, but its call center staff size did not budge!

There are other advantages of bisecting the information and physical backends. For example, interactions with customers can reduce the experimentation necessary to create a satisfying product. This is a great advantage because it leads to better capacity utilization of the physical backend. The physical backend will always have limited capacity – it's a scare resource; the physical backend is capital intensive and technologically circumscribed.

Also, a network of alliances can be established to use the capabilities of other partners under your "supervision." That will ensure the availability of production capacity without having to waste financial resources to develop a diverse production capacity to address a wider spread of customer demands.

> The bright stuff is for real:
> 1 There are real savings to be earned from closer connections between your backend and customers.
> 2 Valuable knowledge assets can be created by bisecting the information and physical parts of the backend and taking the information part online.
> 3 A network of online alliances can be established to get more out of less for your customers.

The result: a key change in manufacturing economics – custom manufacturing can become as efficient as mass production. At Cisco, suppliers not only make all the components and perform 90 percent of the subassembly work but also even do 55 percent of the final assembly. So suppliers regularly ship finished Cisco computers to Cisco's customers without a Cisco employee ever touching the gear. This results in savings of between $500 million and $800 million. "We can go from quote to cash without ever touching a physical asset or a piece of paper," boasted the then executive vice-president Donald J. Listwin. "You've heard of just-in-time manufacturing. Well, this is not-at-all manufacturing."[8]

And if you're getting worried about losing touch with manufacturing competence, you're misplaced. "We develop the entire process, and we know what every supplier is doing every moment," said Carl Redfield, senior vice-president for manufacturing. Cisco designs the production methods and uses the Internet to monitor operations at its contract producers around the clock. But it's qualitatively different from the EDI put in place by the likes of Wal-mart and Sears, where the 80:20 principle applies and only the 20 percent of the suppliers giving 80 percent of the value were linked to the costly EDI system. And it's dissimilar from the traditional outsourcing in another way. Cisco invests time, money, and resources into developing systems that are integrated with the technology infrastructures of its partners. In fact, Cisco has a group of about two dozen individuals who are dedicated to helping their partners become part of the virtual manufacturing process.

The bright stuff

As the book goes to print, it is fashionable to print obituaries about ex-dot-coms and berate their founders for greed and business immaturity. However, we believe that many (not all, for sure!) dotcoms had very good ideas – in fact, in many instances ideas that will remain and change entire industries (as is the case with Napster). Most of the failures of dotcoms did not arise from a dearth of ideas, but from an inability to execute flawlessly and from the lack of appropriate backends and processes. Consequently, many customers were dissatisfied and turned away from them. It is great to have the lowest price on Buy.com, but it is of no use if the gift you ordered for Christmas arrived after New Year! They were unable to connect their customers with their backends.

The Internet in fact holds a bright future for incumbents.

This is where we believe that the Internet in fact holds a bright future for incumbents. The window of opportunity that is now offered to incumbents is really the bright stuff we talk about. As articulated by John Welch in the previous chapter, incumbents have tremendous assets that they can leverage in this Internet era. In a recent study published by the Boston Consulting Group,[9] the same argument was made. We quote from them:

> As the leaders build these capabilities [to expand the possibilities of B2B e-commerce in Europe] they will change the balance of power in many fields of competition. Most of the winners will be successful *offline* businesses that have understood the potential of e-commerce and worked persistently to realize its benefits… . Incumbents that embrace the opportunities and master them will gain sufficient advantage over those that delay.

But as our research (Chapter 1) demonstrates, even among the leading incumbents, only a handful of them have been able to confidently start building that ability. Obviously, the key question is why so? Because it requires a major transformation in strategy and organization. People, policies, and processes, all need to change radically. Customer interfaces need to undergo a major restructuring to fuse the online and offline channels in a seamless unity. The operational infrastructure and supply chain need to be overhauled.

This seems to be a tall order? Yes and no. Yes, because there is a lot of hard work required. No, because one can act smart. One can be innovative. And fortunately, the Internet and innovation are two sides of the same coin. The Internet provides a unique infrastructure for innovation. You remain focused on innovation, you thrive. Innovation should be a strategic end in itself. Let innovation permeate every decision, activity, process, and function.

How to reconfigure your organization for innovation? Simply, as the dominant generic strategy, innovation should be the key result area for all employees in your organization. We have chosen to use three case studies in three different sectors – financial services, retail, and automotive – to illustrate how leading incumbents and new entrants have each tried to craft innovation as their dominant strategy. These three case studies are used to arrive at four important elements of a change agenda for incumbents – each of which forms the subject of a separate chapter.

A brief introduction of each chapter in the book is detailed in the following paragraphs. A graphical representation of the chapters and a roadmap for the book is presented in Figure 2.1.

The genetic power: The next chapter is anchored around a study of Charles Schwab, the pioneering discount broker and the leading online broker. One of the more celebrated instances of an incumbent organization quickly reasserting its leadership in the exploitation of the Internet in its business, Charles Schwab always had that edge for innovation in its genes. It's a vivid example of how the right combination of technology and leadership can lead to innovative breakthroughs, and how innovation as strategy is strongly correlated with the quality of the organizational infrastructure. The chapter also details the increasing commitment of the leading brokerage incumbent Merrill Lynch to the Internet and the rapid growth of the new entrant E*TRADE. Together they provide a glimpse into the innovations triggered by the Internet and associated technologies in the financial services sector.

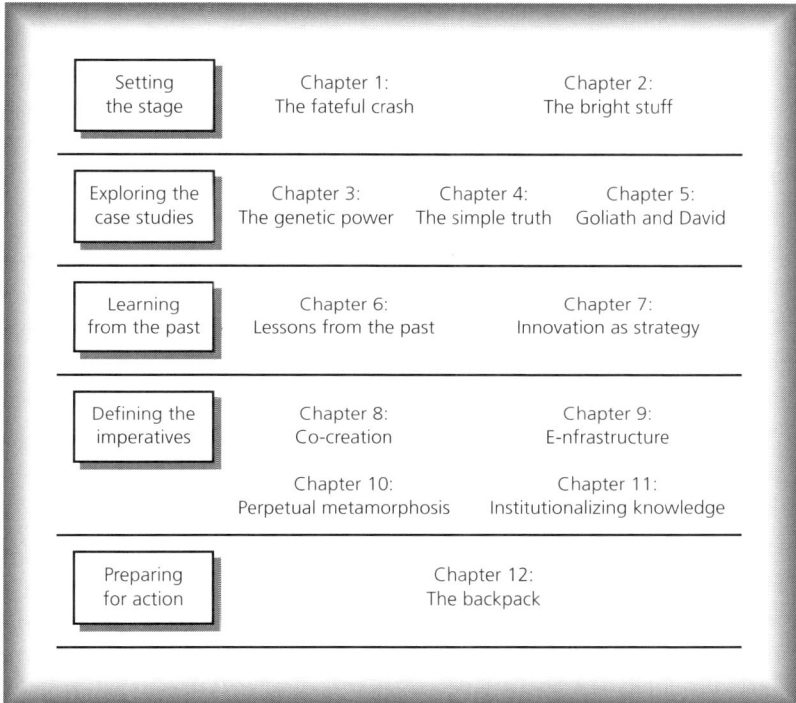

Figure 2.1 The chapter plan of this book

The simple truth: Expanding on the theme of the previous chapter, Chapter 4 explores how the world of one of the biggest corporations – Wal-Mart – doesn't seem to have changed. It continues to do the same old thing – customer care at its best. There is a lot new about doing old truths better. Wal-Mart.com's CEO Jeanne Jackson asserts, "… we're not going out there to do leading-edge technology. We're doing things that make the shopping experience easy." Once again the message is unambiguous – the new economy is the best thing to have happened to the old. And appropriately, the Amazon case strongly co-relates the impact of visionary leadership and strong vision on innovation. Barnes & Nobles.com provides a complementary perspective on the need for innovation to become a way of life. All three companies share a strong focus on customers – customers as the source of innovation.

Goliath and David: Chapter 5 rounds up the case studies with a focus on how General Motors has taken to the Internet after being prodded into action by new entrants such as Auto-By-Tel. The chapter establishes why incumbents must play the game with new entrants and illustrates why doing that is not easy. In the automobile industry the Internet has changed the economics of the industry and leading players in the industry are busy reconfiguring their mutual relationships. It becomes evident that the Internet is a uniquely innovative infrastructure reflected in the wide spectrum of innovative responses of the incumbents. Similar to the role played by E*TRADE in the brokerage industry, Auto-By-Tel exemplifies how the Internet can unleash a rapid stream of innovation in a relatively stagnant and complacent industry.

Lessons from the past: After having explored innovative changes in different sectors in the preceding three chapters, we need to ask ourselves whether what we observe is really unprecedented. Have similar things happened before in business history? Is there really a difference between what we see happening today and what happened at the beginning of the twentieth century in the automotive industry, or in the 1950s with the introduction of the transistors? Indeed, it is not the first time that we are confronted with a major disruption in technological trajectories. The lessons learned by nineteenth-century entrepreneurs may actually be a treasure chest for the entrepreneurial imperatives of the digital era. Can we learn something from these past experiences with other innovations? At the same time, we should be open-minded and ask ourselves the question: what is really different today? Answers to these questions form the core of this chapter.

Innovation as strategy: We observe some designs in the actions of firms E*TRADE and Schwab, Auto-by-Tel and GM, or Amazon and Barnes & Noble that are fundamentally different from having a great "innovation strategy." We have chosen to call those new designs "innovation as strategy." It is epitomized by innovation as a way of life, as the common thread running longitudinally, as well as latitudinally, in an organization. The actions of GM, Barnes & Noble, Amazon, Charles Schwab, and others prove that the world has changed. The previous cases emphatically indicate that the significant assumptions behind successful business models are being questioned. This chapter identifies similarities across the cases to outline four imperatives for innovation that are outlined in more detail in the following four chapters.

Co-creation: Innovation as strategy is rooted in customers. Ironically, one of the more effective vehicles for innovation is to stop thinking! Stop anticipating what your customers may want. Ask them. Involve them. Does this excite you? There cannot be a better recipe for innovation (and growth) in business. Co-creation demands destination-bound operational capabilities – the ability to cater to the individuality of your customers. But such an ability requires a comprehensive reengineering of customer interfaces. And the Internet has a major role to play there. Besides, the Internet has created a new opportunity – the ability to comprehensively service each customer. As you would expect, co-creation is not without serious pitfalls – pricing strategies will become the biggest area of managerial misjudgments. Read this chapter to put these issues in perspective.

E-nfrastructure: What do you need to implement co-creation? First and foremost, middle-of-the-road organizational attributes cannot support the demands of the emerging opportunities. Organizational infrastructure is becoming ever more important in the quest for excellence and innovation. Three elements of the infrastructure – organization, partners, and information technology – provide a highly fertile substrate for growth through innovation. A naturally innovative organization is critical – people, structure, and culture should be leveraged for innovation. A lot of competence and knowledge about better serving your customers lies with your suppliers and resellers. How do you partner effectively with them to innovate continuously? Moreover, the person versus machine dichotomy is meaningless now. The imperative is to integrate the two seamlessly to create new value. This chapter contains the blueprint for the emerging organizational architecture.

Perpetual metamorphosis: Successful companies are not just innovative once or twice, but continue to reinvent themselves many times during their existence. They are neither easy on themselves nor complacent about their successes. They have little fear of going through drastic strategic restructuring and reorganization of their competence bases. And their leaders are willing to adhere to bold long-term decisions. Perpetual metamorphosis is becoming a way of life. It's finally survival of the adept. The biological truth is descending upon economic life (and death). The Internet is redefining innovation cycles and creating a new urgency for perpetual metamorphosis within incumbents. How to engage in perpetual metamorphosis without losing your sanity? This is the focus of this chapter.

Institutionalizing knowledge: A new economy is emerging built on knowledge and innovation in which knowledge will not be just another asset to be managed besides people, property, and capital. Knowledge will be the asset to be managed and the other assets will be the means for the competitive management of knowledge. Organizations will have to learn to master the knowledge–innovation (K-I) cycle, to master knowledge institutionalization. Fortunately, the Internet provides a unique infrastructure for this. But knowledge institutionalization has to be worked upon at two levels – one with internal knowledge (organizational and operational) and the other with external knowledge (customer related). The two must fuse to be strategically meaningful to organizations. The challenges of institutionalizing knowledge are described in the chapter with the help of two detailed examples – Xerox and Arthur Andersen.

The backpack: The message in this book is simple – innovation is going to be routine. From now on, innovation is going to be an imperative for survival, let alone growth. The quantity of innovation will count no less than the quality. And there will be no simple shortcuts or organizational islands for innovation – you're an innovator or you aren't. You'll innovate both how you do business and what your business is all about. And innovation will not be a "cost center." The Internet is creating a unique infrastructure – customizable, intelligent, and scalable – and it's the new Edison's laboratory. Take as much of your assets and processes online as possible.

Let's take off with the first case study – the genetic power.

Action points

Answer the following questions for your organization:

1. Try to imagine a few scenarios. What if you got "Napstered"? What would that look like in your sector (if your customers could suddenly and easily exchange your products and services amongst themselves)? What if you got "Amazoned"? How feasible are these scenarios? What are their implications for your organization's strategy?

2. Have you merged the "old" with the "new" in your organization? Can you list a few examples of these "mergers" from the recent past? How have the older legacy aspects of your business been affected by the Internet? How easy were the changes? Does any of this surprise you?

3. How connected is your organization to your customers? Can you name a few recent innovations that arose directly as a consequence of more intense connections with customers? What are some common features of these innovations? Can you recognize some patterns among them?

4. What is the "bright stuff" for you? Identify some specific examples where you have already created value using the Internet. What can you learn from these examples? Can you identify ways in which the Internet can create additional value in your business?

Notes

1. Based on Ellison's quote on p. 58, *Fortune*, May 24, 1999.
2. www.priceline.com
3. http://www.ge.com/news/podium_speech.html
4. Based on Richard C. Morais' 'Bull-terrier banking', *Forbes Global*, July 24, 2000.
5. www.ge.com; speeches section.

6. Alison Gardy and Mard Naman, "The do's of online retailing," www.cisco.com
7. www.ge.com; speeches section.
8. Port, Otis (1999) "Customers move into the driver's seat," *Business Week*, October 4.
9. The Boston Consulting Group, May 2001, "Incumbents take the initiative, harnessing the power of business-to-business E-commerce in Europe," available through www.bcg.com

Exploring the case studies 11

The genetic power: Charles Schwab, E*TRADE, and Merrill Lynch

Bookmark

In this first set of cases we'll study how some companies in the financial sector have been using the Internet to redefine their industry and consolidate their leadership. These cases bring out how entrepreneurship at the top has always been the way of business in winning companies. In particular, all three companies, Charles Schwab, E*TRADE, and Merrill Lynch, have used innovation to create undisputed leadership in their chosen markets. As you read, focus on Schwab more for understanding the organizational face of a winner, E*TRADE for innovative dimensions of online scalability, and Merrill Lynch for the typical response of an industry leader.

Change in the brokerage industry

Deep in the bowels of Charles Schwab's San Francisco headquarters, in the offices of its electronic brokerage division, there is a glass cabinet containing the relics of the company's past forays into cutting-edge technology. The Pocketerm, a clunky hand-held device that downloaded stock quotes through an FM receiver, dates back to 1982. Schwabline, a terminal that gathered market data over a phone line and printed it out on a roll of adding-machine paper, was state of the art in 1986. There are also souvenirs of online-trading experiments, including boxes of software with names like the Equalizer and StreetSmart. What you won't see in this technological curiosity cabinet, however, is the latest product in Schwab's long line of technology gambles: its investing Website, www.schwab.com. The Web venture has turned out to be most conspicuously not a dead end for Schwab. It represents arguably the most successful embrace of e-commerce by any major corporation outside the technology industry.[1]

While the Internet is increasingly transforming our life on multiple fronts, it has already transformed the rules of the brokerage industry. With a few mouse clicks, an experienced Net navigator can today tap into Wall Street research reports on publicly traded companies, view up-to-the-minute stock quotes, gather reams of performance data on thousands of mutual funds, check out the latest rates on bank loans and save up to 80 percent on traditional brokerage commissions by trading securities on the Web. Pioneered by E*TRADE, Internet stock trading service providers have mushroomed since early 1996. The user-friendliness, accessibility, speed, and low fees of online trading have challenged established full-service and discount brokers and changed the way people invest. Even Charles Schwab, a firm which practically invented the concept of a discount broker, has not gone unchallenged. Leading incumbents such as Merrill Lynch have been forced to recognize the potential of the Internet to unleash disruptive innovations.

The brokerage industry

The brokerage industry facilitates investors' purchases and sales of securities by providing investment advice, processing and execution of buy/sell orders, record keeping, and market making (maintaining inventories of securities to sell on order). It's a lucrative and high profile sector of the larger investment industry but it's highly cyclical too. Although it's possible[2] for two investors to trade with each other directly, a usual transaction will tend to employ a brokerage firm to get the assistance required in the legal aspects of buying/selling securities. In theory, the choice of a broker should be simple – there are a whole lot of them – but in practice it's not easy. The sheer variation in the quality of services each provides can make the choice very difficult.

The service provided by brokers can be classified into three categories depending upon the portfolio of services provided. The first category of brokers is called "full-service" brokerage firms; Merrill Lynch and Morgan Stanley are the leading full-service brokerage firms. These firms have a large number of retail offices connected to their headquarters and, through the headquarters, to major (stock) markets. Institutional investors, such as pension funds, also deal with such retail brokerage firms but they normally deal through separate divisions within the firms.

The two other types of brokerage firms are regional brokerage firms and discount brokers. The former concentrate on full-service broking within a limited geographic area. The discount brokers offer "bare-bones" services at low cost; fewer services than "full-service" brokerage firms at substantially reduced commissions. Investors who simply want to have their trade orders executed without any investment advice avail of their services. However, over the years the level of information and services provided "free" by the discount brokers have increased to include perks such as telephone hotlines, live share prices, financial planning tools, and newsletters containing investment advice. More interestingly, discount brokers have had a very critical role in shaping the competitive pressure in the entire brokerage industry.

The winners – once the pioneer and always a pioneer.

Mayday 1975 holds an important place in the US brokerage industry. That day, fixed brokerage commission rates ceased to exist in the US and that was presumed to herald the dawn of a new age on Wall Street. Mayday's purpose was to expose commission rates to competition, on the assumption that previously the NYSE had fixed commissions at a rate higher than competitive levels, and that with competition, rates would drop.[3] While Mayday changes did directly affect commission rates, both for institutional and individual investors, in retrospect it produced broader consequences – leading up to what we see today. Interestingly, many brokerages took the opportunity to raise commissions! But Schwab will always have a special mention here – Schwab defined discount brokerage – it slashed commission rates. It ushered in "do-it-yourself" low-cost trading and custody services.

And another turning point in that history is Internet-based stock trading. Pioneered by E*TRADE, Internet stock trading services have mushroomed since early 1996. The user-friendliness, accessibility, speed, and low fees of online trading have challenged established full-service and discount brokers and changed the way people invest. Within this fast-growing segment, which holds over 15 million of the approximately 80 million accounts managed by full-service brokers and traditional discounters, the market-share war is on with some early winners: Schwab leads with 35 percent market share; next comes E*TRADE with a 15 percent market share; and traditional giant Fidelity commands 13 percent of the market.

In this following case study, we focus on Schwab, the leader and the "click and mortar" broker, and E*TRADE the pioneering online discount broker. And the reaction of the biggest of all – Merrill Lynch – is included to understand the rapidly changing dynamics of the brokerage industry itself.

The roots run deep

The leaders have always been pioneers. It runs deep in the organizational psyche. Post 1975, more than 25 years later in 2001, Schwab still has a special place in the brokerage industry. It's as if innovation is its only strategy: it lives to innovate! Innovate to serve customers better. Its single-minded focus on customers is the force behind its pioneering role all these years. All other organizational goals seem almost automatically to follow innovation as strategy. It has created a new model of financial services that melds technology and people to provide an integrated "high-tech" and "high-touch" service for investors.[4] As early as 1979, in a "bet-the-company" move, it invested in a mainframe computer system. The successful implementation of this automated transaction and record-keeping system only added to the conviction of the management that technology can be a key growth driver. Dawn Lepore, CIO, said, "At that stage, Schwab was a private company with an entire net worth of $500,000. Well, the contract for the software was also $500,000. In essence, Chuck (Charles Schwab) bet the company on technology. When he talks about that decision, he often recalls that he was so nervous that when he reached for the pen to sign the contract, his hand was shaking." In fact, Schwab has always been like that – ready to experiment to innovate.

Schwab bet the company on IT technology. In 1979!

Schwab was incorporated in California in 1971; it adopted the name Charles Schwab & Co., Inc. after Charles R. Schwab became its owner and President in 1986. Initially established as a full-service broker, it competed with traditional brokerage firms such as Merrill Lynch. It began with a very simple idea: "to provide investors with the most useful and ethical brokerage services in America."[5] And evidently, it has lived up to it in letter and spirit all these 30 years. Post 1975, Schwab grew significantly through investment in technology, continuous product and service development, and innovative customer service delivery systems.

E*TRADE, the pioneer in e-trading, also has a similar pioneering legacy. On July 11, 1983, a doctor in Michigan placed the first online trade using E*TRADE technology. What began with a single click over 17 years ago has now taken the world by storm. Today, E*TRADE customers can be found in all 50 states in the US and 119 countries from Aruba to Zambia. Created as a service bureau in 1982 by Bill Porter, a physicist and inventor with more than a dozen patents to his credit, the early E*TRADE provided online quote and trading services to other brokerage firms like Fidelity, Charles Schwab, and Quick & Reilly. Over time, it led Bill to wonder why, as an individual investor, he had to pay a broker hundreds of dollars for stock transactions. With incredible foresight, he saw the solution at hand: someday, everyone would own computers and invest through them with unprecedented efficiency and control. In 1992, E*TRADE Securities, Inc., one of the original all-electronic brokerages, was born and began to offer online investing services through America Online and CompuServe. Then, with the launch of www.etrade.com in 1996 (a few months ahead of Schwab's online initiative), demand for E*TRADE's services exploded. A revolution was born.

In 1996, Bill handed over the reins to Christos Cotsakos, a decorated Vietnam War veteran and a well-known management "revolutionary". "We've continued to build a global brand that resonates with consumers because it has soul and passion, and credibility," noted Cotsakos in his early years at E*TRADE. "The E*TRADE brand is on fire, and we're just getting started in building the world's leading electronic personal financial services company," he added.

For the quarter ending March 31, 2001, E*TRADE recorded a net revenue of $330 million, down from $417 million for the same period last year. Net income from ongoing operations stood at $868,000 compared to a net loss from ongoing operations of $672,000 in the same quarter last year. Customer accounts grew to over 3.7 million (approximately double that of 1.8 million accounts a year ago). Early 2001, it also opened a "real world store" – in New York City. The E*TRADE center's 30,000 square feet of retail space brings knowledge to investors and savers in a high-tech and high-touch experience.

On the other hand, at the end of March 2001, Schwab served 8 million active online accounts with over $870 billion in customer assets through 342 domestic branch offices, four regional customer telephone service centers, and automated telephonic and online channels. For the quarter ending March 31, 2001, the Company's operating income was $120 million on revenues of $1.2 billion. The respective figures for 2000 were $323 million and $1.73 billion. In both cases, however, the revenues declined following the general downturn in the economy in the following quarters.

The design behind

Not surprisingly, Schwab's Internet success was no accident. It happened because the co-CEOs Schwab and Pottruck had build an organization that thrived on excellence – an excellence based on innovation. The first chapter in Schwab's journey into e-commerce opened in late 1995 with a series of messages to chief information officer Dawn Lepore from one of her research groups.

> The group, she remembers, wanted to show her some experimental software that would allow Schwab's different computer systems to talk to one another. It was the sort of project that software designers love: challenging, technically complicated, and intended to solve such an obscure problem that it was difficult to explain its merits to anyone but other techies. So, prior to inviting Lepore to see it, they cobbled together a separate piece of front-end software that would show one possible application out of many. Lepore scheduled a demonstration and brought along one of the company's biggest technology nuts, (Charles) Schwab himself.[6]

As it turned out, the application the engineers chose was a very simple Web-based stock trade. Their program allowed a Schwab server to take an order from a Web browser on a PC, route it through all of Schwab's sophisticated backend systems and mainframes, execute it, and send a confirmation back to the PC. At the time, most existing Web trading systems required that orders be printed out and entered by hand into another system, sort of defeating the point of automated trading. Lepore's computer researchers were less interested in online brokerage than in winning Lepore's approval to continue work on their obscure middleware project. But Lepore and Schwab instantly recognized the implications of the patched-together demo. Says Schwab: "I fell off my chair." Comments Dawn, "At Schwab, we're sometimes accused of being 'change junkies.' And despite our focus on innovation, we're constantly worried that we aren't doing enough."

Schwab's Internet success is no accident. Innovation has been designed into the genes of the company.

Within a matter of weeks a project team started working on the Web trading application development. To bring adequate focus and resources to the team, the team leader, Gideon Sasson, was specifically recruited for the project. The team operated under an ambiguous title (perhaps that was the reality) at the beginning and reported directly to Pottruck. The team had a very clear mandate but enjoyed all the freedom and flexibility to short-circuit the usual bureaucracy for all financial, intellectual, and strategic resources. And e.Schwab was born.

A similar story was being played out at E*TRADE. Costakos joined the company just a few weeks after the launch of Web-based brokerage services. He was quick to see the potential of Etrade.com and made it the anchor for the future strategy of E*TRADE. E*TRADE was reinventing the world of online investing by making "empowering the customer" its central theme. The company's online documentation described it as follows:

> E*TRADE is changing the entire value proposition of the financial services industry by applying the power of technology and the power of the Internet to the business of investing. Technology enables E*TRADE to offer more value to the self-directed investor. E*TRADE has shifted the balance of power – from the temples of finance to consumers...

Cotsakos, CEO, added, "By listening to our customers and continuing to innovate, we strive to give them what they want when they want it. We are focused on creating a business that's built to last, as we build our destination brand for the long term. Because of our all-electronic model, E*TRADE is able to continually innovate and increase personalization of our offerings for our customers." He added, "It's a leadership strategy of vision, culture, technology, brand, and innovation. [Simply put], delivering by continuously creating a new kind of company. We're still in the vanguard of a lifestyle revolution. We're still giving the power of the few to the many. We're still creating the future of financial services."

According to Media Metrix[7] reports, E*TRADE has been the world's most visited online investing site for the most part of 1999 and 2000. E*TRADE believes that its customers chose it because its products and its brand resonate with their changing lifestyle. It's also among the more profitable of the online businesses. Its annual revenue per customer is $547 and its gross margin of 62 percent is also among the industry's finest. And in early 2000, it returned to profitability 12 months ahead of schedule. Back in the summer of 1998, Cotsakos had, like Charles Schwab, also bet the company – on the Internet. He had proposed a plan to quadruple E*TRADE's advertising budget – effectively turning one of the few profitable Internet companies into an unprofitable company overnight. The board balked initially but Cotsakos did not give in. He persisted over hours of discussion in his arguments to attract customers and build brand quickly and eventually won the board over.

Cotsakos' unique leadership style has been central to the success of E*TRADE. An article in *Business Week* (February 7, 2000) described it thus: "He's spending gobs of time crafting a culture for the Internet Age that at times seems downright bizarre, and at other times brilliant. But it's always pure Cotsakos: edgy, out there, theatrical, and bursting at the seams with enthu-

> "At E*TRADE, we're an attacker, we're predatory. We believe we have a God-given right to market share."

siasm. Cotsakos sums it up in five words: 'A lust for being different.' That's shorthand for his attempt to build a company that's jammed with people who are wildly creative, arch competitive, yet so closely knit that they're almost family." Costakos comments in the same article: "At E*Trade, we're an attacker, we're predatory. We believe we have a God-given right to market share."

Courage for success

Technology leadership has always played an important role in Schwab's ability to outperform all. The company was one of the first firms to introduce 24-hour touch-tone trading service. In 1984, it first offered online trading with PC-based trading through the proprietary Equalizer software – which had a small, dedicated user group of about six people who met in a Silicon Valley garage. StreetSmart was introduced in October 1993 to give online access to brokerage and investment information services and it was a big success with about 200,000 to 300,000 customers. By 1994, TeleBroker (a touch-tone telephone trading facility introduced in 1989) and other online brokerage services were handling over half of Schwab's customer calls! And by 1996 e.Schwab was established as a separate, standalone division of Charles Schwab to provide customers with "web-based" online trading capability and significant discounts from Schwab's standard commission rates.

By 1997, Schwab had two different offerings – e.Schwab (only online) and Charles Schwab (the traditional retail operation as well as the online service of its own). e.Schwab customers paid $29.95 for reduced services, while the Charles Schwab customers got a 20 percent discount on the regular rates (which left them at about a $65 price point) but they also received the full gamut of services. Some customers used to visiting retail offices to meet representatives and speaking to representatives over the phone were suddenly cut off from them when they opted for e.Schwab services. They could only get to the representatives via e-mail and only one phone contact was allowed free in a month to get advice from the representatives. If you could not do with e-mails alone, you had to retain the regular Schwab account. This commission structure did not augur well with most of the customers – e.Schwab was rocking the whole boat and something had to be done. It was writ large that customers did not want two disparate delivery channels! The regular ones felt that they were paying more and the e.schwab ones felt they were getting less service.

Worse, Charles Schwab and David Pottruck soon realized that there was no going back to the usual services without e.Schwab.[8] It was developing into an unpleasant either-or situation: e.Schwab or no Schwab. They both realized the great opportunity that e.Schwab was, but there was a cost. While it was cheaper and highly scalable, switching to the low online commission could cost Schwab nearly half the company's revenues (then). The dilemma was particularly a new economy phenomenon – over 30 percent of Schwab's stock was owned by employees besides the major stockholding by Schwab and other top managers. A major cut in revenue was risky. The entire company had to see the same new numbers and the vision around the horizon to work cooperatively towards the new online Schwab. But finally, Charles Schwab and Pottruck took the plunge: $29.95 Web trading for all – Schwab chose to be wholly online though all branches stayed and its customers could get their advice too. But there was only one trading mode and all the other services were optional. The estimated pre-tax profit implication of this move was between $125 million and $150 million. To a company that earned, in 1997, $250 million dollars, this was no small decision. Its stock price went from $41 to $28.

CIO Dawn Lepore adds: "If you wait until a technology is widely adopted before you try it, you've lost your market advantage. That is why we were early entrants on the Web and we have such a big share of that market."[9]

But that sounds too simplistic? How do you merge the two entities organizationally? Pottruck started realizing that taking the $150 million hit was perhaps the easier part of the decision and bringing back e.Schwab into the Charles Schwab fold was a tough call. E.Schwab had developed to be culturally dominated by the spirit of its creation – independent and fast. It was also dominated by technologists because the product was highly technical.

The key strengths of Charles Schwab:

- Visionary leadership – the courage to "bet the company."
- Customer centricity – a deep belief that what's good for customers is good for the company.
- A culture of innovation – continuous experimentation is the philosophy.

Finally, in January 1998, Schwab took the plunge – there was only one Schwab after that. And in yet another commitment to people, Gideon Sasson, the initial project leader for e.Schwab, was made the head of the electronic-brokerage unit. It was perhaps the first time in Schwab's history that anyone from a technical project had moved to a senior general-management position. The transition was difficult and involved taking all

Schwab employees into the company's confidence. Among other things, Lepore gave Web access to Schwab's 4,000 branch and phone reps so that they too could see the technology's benefits.

Schwab wanted its employees to realize that the core values of the corporation had not changed in its move to the online world. Great service and customer focus had been the underpinnings of Schwab's success over the years. They would continue to be so in the future. And employees were key to this vision of the future. Pottruck noted, "We really are a full-service brokerage firm – but a different kind of full-service brokerage firm. In our model, the customer is in control, as opposed to the broker. In our model, we are demystifying investing, rather than trying to keep it 'mysterious' as a means of tying our customers to us. We educate and empower our customers so they can manage their own money – with some help and assistance from us if they want." He emphasized, "The old image of Wall Street is dead. And while the Internet has empowered and freed investors, the new definition is not just about technology. It's all about finding the right combination of people and technology."

At Schwab, it's all about finding the right combination of people and technology.

Changing landscape

Schwab has appropriately earned its place in Internet history. *Fortune* magazine cites it as one the best companies to work for in America and one of the most admired firms in the securities industry. And it remains focused on "creating a world of smarter investors." It's continuously getting closer to its customers and trying to make their investing lives easier. For example, in November 2000 it launched a toll-free Service Hotline to offer investing services in Vietnamese and it expects to offer a dedicated website in Vietnamese in the future. It already provides such services in Korean, Chinese, and Spanish.

Its commitment to investors is also borne not by the fact that in October 2000 it launched a new multifaceted multi-channel program called Women Investing (www.schwab.com/women) to inspire women to increase their own financial knowledge and share that knowledge with family and friends. The site followed a study that underlined that women tend to have learning styles different from men's and that many women have a strong preference for learning from other women in a collaborative and interactive environment. The website is organized into several key sections. "Talk/Share/Learn" provides links to a message board for women investors, a series of interactive workshops, weekly forums, and the ability to pose questions to an investment adviser. The "Life Event Series" provides easy-to-use tools and tips on topics that have a particularly big financial impact: making a job transition, raising money-wise children, getting a divorce, and planning for retirement. "Our goal is to inspire women who are already experienced investors to share their knowledge as role models and money mentors, and we want to make it easy for them to do that," notes a company manager.

This new resource underscores Schwab's ongoing online and offline efforts to empower investors with the knowledge and confidence they need to make the best possible investment decisions. Earlier in February 2000, it had launched Schwab Learning Center featuring interactive courseware. Noted Gideon Sasson, "These courses enable people to learn at their own pace, on topics that interest them, to help them become more informed and better investors." The Learning Center complements Schwab's other consumer education initiatives like Webshops, a series of workshops hosted by Schwab's 335 branches with the goal of educating 240,000 people about the tools and benefits of investing online, by the end of 2000.

Success by empowerment

E*TRADE's route to success has been built on a simple theme: "empowering people." It's about finding new ways to help people manage their money. E*TRADE was the first firm to give its customers direct control over their investment activities, offering them an integrated and customized access not only to their portfolios, but also to data, research, and analysis as well as information on their holdings and the markets. In order to better service the diverse financial needs of its customers, it started offering a wide range of services in a seamless package to its clients. For example, through its Business Solutions Group (BSG) it provided an electronic stock plan solution for over 3,500 leading corporations. E*TRADE Business Solutions™ pioneered a full spectrum of stock plan management services, including plan administration, compliance, employee communication, and online transaction capabilities.

> **E*TRADE's route to success has been built on a simple theme: "empowering people."**

In April 2000, E*TRADE launched E*TRADE BANK after acquiring Telebanc, US's largest pure-play Internet bank, and the initiative has been a fair success. The bank is booking new accounts at double the rate it was before the re-branding and it's the nineteenth-largest federally chartered savings bank in the US. More importantly, the cross-selling between banking and brokerage is accelerating and the cost to bring an existing brokerage customer to the bank is a fraction of the cost to acquire a bank account from the marketplace. It added $500 million additional deposits in the bank in the first quarter of 2001.

> The key strengths of E*TRADE:
>
> - The first-mover advantage of a pioneer.
> - An innovative positioning of value delivery – "empowering people."
> - A focus on continuously evolving the business model.

It has extended the relationship with some BSG clients to provide an E*TRADE "Virtual Credit Union" solution for their employees. These companies are able to offer their employees packaged E*TRADE services, including banking and brokerage, through the company intranet. It also plans to install E*TRADE branded ATMs in the companies' corporate headquarters and major facilities, to connect people to their finances in the simplest and most convenient way possible.

E*TRADE's success has been noticed by the markets. On March 1, 1999, E*TRADE became the first online investing service to be added to the Standard & Poor's (S&P) MidCap 400 Index, a group of 400 domestic stocks chosen for market size, liquidity, and industry group representation. The S&P MidCap 400 Index is used by more than 95 percent of US managers and pension plan sponsors to measure the performance of the mid-size company segment of the US market. E*TRADE was the first securities and financial services company to be awarded the CPA WebTrust seal of assurance by the American Institute of Certified Public Accountants (AICPA). E*TRADE also was ranked the number one overall online brokerage service in several quarterly reviews conducted by Gomez Advisors, a leading independent authority devoted to online financial services.

A continuous evolution

Despite having pioneered online trading, E*TRADE soon realized that multiple touch points were necessary for satisfying customers. In 2000, E*TRADE started aggressively enhancing and expanding its customer service operations with multiple offline touch points. Suzi White, Vice President, customer service at E*TRADE described it thus:

> It is often customer service that separates a company from its competition, whether it be electronically or via the human touch. Our goal is to provide the highest level of electronic assistance for maximum customer convenience. We also empower our customer

service representatives to ensure that each and every investor has an exceptional customer experience. With continued dedication and focus, E*TRADE is looking to set a new standard for customer service in electronic commerce.

In May 2000, it completed the acquisition of Card Capture Services, now called E*TRADE Access, and that gave it control over 9,600 ATMs and its first step towards building its "high-touch, high-tech" presence. It will add 1,000 ATMs in Target stores nationwide over 2001–2003. In August 2000, it acquired Versus Technologies which is helping it create an electronic trading platform for institutional customers. It already has over 650 institutional customers worldwide and the platform connects investors, institutions, investment dealers, exchanges, and alternative liquidity pools to one another worldwide.

In September 2000, it opened the first E*TRADE Zone in the Roswell, Georgia SuperTarget Store. It will take the number to 20 by the end of 2001. These high-traffic locations will eventually feature ATMs and full-service E*TRADE financial kiosks, offering brokerage and banking capabilities, electronic transfer of funds, streaming media, and much more. The concept has the potential of exposing the brand and products to 50 million consumers nationwide per week, and at just one-tenth the cost of what it takes to maintain a free-standing branch. It also completed the acquisition of LoansDirect in first quarter 2001 to offer consumers access to mortgage and home equity loans. New products. New ways to reach new customers.

And on April 4, 2001, it opened the E*TRADE Center, a financial services superstore with over 30,000 feet in downtown Manhattan to give consumers value-added financial services and educational content in a high-tech, high-touch experience! E*TRADE Center has four levels of interactive technology. The bottom floor of E*TRADE Center features a professional trading services area for E*TRADE's active investors where they have the ability to place trading orders and conduct business. E*TRADE Center's mezzanine level offers a forum for high net worth customers to conduct financial transactions and receive personalized attention from financial service associates. Educational seminars are offered to consumers on the top level, adjacent to the E*TRADE gift shop, bookstore, and Mangia Café. Also accessible within E*TRADE Center are three deposit-taking E*TRADE Bank ATMs available to customers 24 hours a day. In addition, the Center has partnered with Aether to provide wireless demonstration stations for investors interested in learning about wireless financial services.[10]

The original online pioneer has taken the plunge into a blended "bricks and clicks" model. CEO Cotsakos noted in a press release statement, "E*TRADE Center is a milestone in our blended approach to financial services, which combines an emphasis on electronic delivery with a physical presence to provide customers with a high level of personalized service. In the changing market environment, it's important for investors to know they have both electronic and physical access to information, products and services to meet their individual investment needs."

E*TRADE has been intensely focused on building its brand. To further strengthen the E*TRADE brand experience, it uses state-of-the-art customer relationship management (CRM) technology to first identify those who would most benefit from certain financial products and services, then alert them to that availability. Through this expanded CRM initiative, E*TRADE is able to integrate all available data and market research to form a single view of customers. It's heavily focused on scalability – "when we get bigger, we just get better." From E*TRADE Bank to ATM machines, from Target Stores to BSG, it's effectively bridging the "last mile."

The inevitable

Merrill Lynch, the preeminent brokerage firm, didn't think of the Internet as a strategic opportunity, until 1999. It suffered from the classical lapses of leading incumbents who are at times slow to realize the implications of a disruptive technology. In the case of Merrill Lynch, it saw a rapidly changing world in which $30 (and lower) trades were competing with its usual full-service commission of $200 a trade and its margins were facing a decrease of 80 percent or more. Customers were being empowered to buy and sell at almost the same price as brokers and their traditional bonds to full-service brokers were getting weaker by the day.

However, the day of reckoning was December 28, 1998, when Schwab's $25.5 billion market capitalization increased for the first time over Merrill's capitalization of $25.4 billion. The impossible had happened. A one-time newcomer, Schwab, had upstaged the leader. Merrill was much bigger than Schwab on almost every measure ($11.4 billion vs. $1.9 billion in equity, $1.5 trillion vs. $600 billion in assets under management, and 66,000 vs 17,400 employees), but the market had given a higher score to Schwab. "It judged that Schwab got the Internet and Merrill didn't," noted a Merrill manager. "That was about our manhood."[11]

Merrill soon realized that inaction was not a course of action in the face of innovations launched by Schwab and E*TRADE.

Merrill soon realized that inaction was not a course of action. Something had to be done to counter the innovations unleashed by Schwab, E*TRADE and others. As a lead article in *Business Week* noted, "The stakes in this conflict are staggering. At risk is everything from the legacies and careers of Merrill's executives to the firm's ability to stay out of the arms of suitors such as Chase Manhattan Bank. At the heart of the battle is Merrill's fight to remain king of the financial hill."[12]

> Lessons from the experiences of Merrill Lynch:
>
> - Being big does not make you safe – new players will eventually catch up with you.
> - Inaction is not a viable course of action in the face of innovation – a leader has to be ready to lead the pack.
> - Incumbents have tremendous assets which can help to make the transition online.

Merrill started with a process to rethink every aspect of its business – from retail customer contact to corporate customer needs, from research to brokerage to asset management. Jerome P. Kenney, Merrill's chief strategist, noted, "We concluded that the firm had to be converted to an Internet-based firm." Departing from its usual practices, Merrill reached out to hire a leader from outside the brokerage sector, John McKinley from GE Capital, as its first Chief Technology Officer.

The year 1999 was a year of new beginnings for Merrill Lynch. It decided to play an aggressive game of catch-up with the rollout of two innovations.[13] The first was Unlimited Advantage^{SM}, a relationship offering a full spectrum of financial services, including ongoing professional advice from a financial consultant and virtually unlimited transactions for most investors "by mouse, by phone or by human being," for a single, asset-based fee. And in its first six months, Unlimited Advantage^{SM} attracted client assets at a rate more than 20 times faster than previous fee-based accounts. Assets in client accounts with online access soon exceeded $300 billion for Merrill Lynch. The leader started taking new interest in reshaping the emerging competitive landscape.

The second was Merrill Lynch Direct^{SM} (ML Direct) for self-directed investors, offering low-cost online trades along with a robust suite of information, research, and financial modeling tools. "We're tremendously excited to be launching ML Direct," said David H. Komansky, Chairman and CEO. "Backed by the full global resources of Merrill Lynch, Merrill Lynch Direct^{SM} combines content, intelligence and innovation to create the smartest place for the self-directed client to invest online. No matter how you may wish to approach the market – whether by working with a professional Financial Consultant or self-directing a financial portfolio online – you can do it at Merrill Lynch."

John L. Steffens, Vice Chairman and head of the US Private Client Group, added that "Merrill Lynch Direct offers far more than just online trading execution. With features such as real-time account positions, tax-management information, the Global Investor Network for research, banking services and online shopping with an exceptional Visa® Signature Rewards program, self-directed investors will be able to use this site to help manage all aspects of their financial lives." In addition to investing, Merrill Lynch Direct offered individuals and small businesses access to a host of vendors, from Toys"R"Us to Barnes & Noble Inc. Merrill's CEO David Komansky emphasized, "We are trying to build different mechanisms to be able to attract people to our portal – our clients predominantly – and to strengthen the overall relationship."[14]

Acting on the Internet was initially very difficult for Merrill. Like most leading incumbents, it had got complacent by success and isolated from customers who were screaming for online access. Then there were the 17,000 commissioned brokers who threatened to revolt if Merrill embraced the Internet. The existing business of its brokers that ML Direct threatened to cannibalize by offering trades for just $29.95, the same rate Schwab charged, was a major cause of friction at Merrill Lynch. Merrill's management worried that its successful brokers could easily move to competing Wall Street firms and take plum client accounts with them.

The culture of the firm also did not help. Merrill had an image as "a Luddite firm" and it had to change "from a high-cost bureaucracy to a tech-savvy, change-friendly, flat organization that operates on razor-thin margins".[15] Further, it long held that individual investors should adopt a disciplined investment strategy and that online trading increased the propensity of being caught unaware in market machinations. But once it became a market reality that the investors were taking the online plunge, as evident from the success of E*TRADE and Schwab, the choices for Merrill Lynch were rather limited.

However, more than anything else, Merrill Lynch's attempt to switch to fee-based accounts heralded a transformation in the relationships between its brokers and their clients. For years, it had been pushing its brokers to shift more customers from paying commissions for every transaction to paying an annual fee based on a small percentage of total assets. Many brokers balked because they felt they had more control of their own earnings in a commission-based system. At the end of 2000, only about 7–10 percent of Merrill clients' assets are in fee-based accounts.

Is Merrill becoming an e-commerce company? Or is it a financial services conglomerate with primary focus on brokerage?

Merrill Lynch has been increasing its online commitment by the day. In April 2000, Merrill Lynch and HSBC Holdings plc announced plans to create the first global online banking and investment services company through a groundbreaking 50:50 partnership. The new company has been created to serve individual customers across the world except in the United

States, providing the industry a very comprehensive and innovative range of online banking and brokerage services for consumers who prefer to make informed investment decisions for themselves.

Similarly, in July 2000, Merrill Lynch announced the launch of www.holdrs.com, which provides helpful online tools and information for investors who wish to take advantage of Merrill Lynch's HOLDRS. The website, which enables investors to evaluate their holdings through a combination of interactive tools, was created in response to the significant interest from a wide range of investors seeking a single, integrated source of information about HOLDRS. Merrill Lynch's adoption of the Internet is increasingly getting "Net-set-go."

Reactions from unexpected corners

Till now we have looked at companies from within the brokerage industry. Merrill Lynch, a long-time player, put up an effective counterstrategy against an early technology leader such as Charles Schwab, and a newcomer such as E-TRADE. The Internet has made it possible to allow companies from outside the core brokerage industry, but who have an infrastructure to reach out to customers, to get interested in offering financial services.

Innovative new players will force "legacy companies" such as Merrill Lynch, Charles Schwab, and even E*TRADE to (again) reevaluate their business models.

A look at Yahoo! can provide some indications of this. Yahoo! operates one of the most popular financial destination sites on the Internet: Yahoo! Finance (quote.yahoo.com). At this site, customers can access, free of charge, a wealth of financial information and tools. Yahoo! Finance allows customers to create customized portfolios and track their holdings, obtain information about stock price movements, observe earnings surprises, and collate buy/sell recommendations from a number of industry analysts. A number of chat-forums allow investors to participate in online discussions about different sectors and/or firms. Yahoo!'s Finance area is one of the most popular sources for up-to-the-minute financial information on the Web. Its tax center (www.taxes.yahoo.com) provides a complete and comprehensive resource to help users complete their tax returns on the Internet!

More importantly, new players can skip online broking and jump to the "next stage" if the following trends are any real indications:

- **Customer gatekeepers**: Companies such as Yahoo! are rapidly positioning themselves as gatekeepers to cyber-customers. Today, these gatekeepers provide customers with free access to a wealth of value-adding information on a variety of topics. If these organizations emerge as the cyber-destination of choice for a large segment of cyber-customers, then their roles *vis-à-vis* customers and content providers will change significantly.

- **Direct Public Offerings (DPOs)**: Unlike traditional Initial Public Offerings (IPOs), a DPO is a "best-efforts" offering made directly by the issuer itself without the help of any underwriter as an intermediary. Several sites for DPOs have been established over recent years to form databanks of potential investors for DPOs. It is certain that the influence of DPOs will increase as the penetration of the Internet increases in society. Even though the number of firms offering DPOs (via the Net) is increasing, the market remains restricted to small and medium-sized companies in the US.

- **Bulletin boards for secondary trading**: Large institutional investors have used closed electronic networks (such as the Island System and the "POSIT" system – Portfolio System for Institutional Trading) to trade shares amongst themselves since the early 1980s. As security and reliability concerns on the Net are addressed, such closed trading will enlarge to include small investors via the Internet. Already bulletin boards are emerging where investors can trade stocks amongst themselves. Examples include Real Goods (www.realgoods.com), PerfectData Corporation (www.perfectdata.com), and Internet Capital Exchange (www.inetcapital.com/).

By actions like these, the cyber-gatekeepers can actually start redefining the boundaries of the brokerage industry. Innovation emanating from these upstarts will force "legacy companies" such as Merrill Lynch, Charles Schwab, and perhaps even E*TRADE to (again) reevaluate their business models.

Issues

The long-term impact of the Internet on the brokerage industry is still unclear and evolving. As this book goes to press, the dotcom carnage does not seem to have an end in sight. The market capitalizations of most online players, including Charles Schwab and E*TRADE, have decreased significantly. E*TRADE's shares have descended 90 percent to the $6 range – from a high of $60. Analysts have dropped earnings estimates for these firms by 30–50 percent for 2001. Most players are being forced to react with draconian measures. Charles Schwab stunned everyone on March 22, 2001 by laying off about 13 percent of its employees – 3,400 in total. E*TRADE is embracing the "bricks and clicks" model, having realized that it cannot mistake the "promise of the Internet for a guarantee" for success.[16] Most industry observers expect a wave of consolidations in the sector before firms move up towards increased margins and stable profitability trajectories.

> "One should not mistake the promise of the Internet for a guarantee."

Undeniably, the second half of the 1990s was an incredible period for innovation in the brokerage sector. Regardless of how many players eventually survive, retail brokerage has been transformed forever. Customers are empowered now and they are not going to go back to the "old dependence" on brokers. Brokers are being forced to question the value they add to the process. They can no longer thrive simply as over-paid order-takers. Thanks to the Internet, stock-broking has changed in fundamental ways. However, the end scenario is far from clear. The idea of fully automated agents running people's portfolios in linked electronic financial markets is no longer far-fetched; it is merely far off.[17] Internet-based bulletin boards for secondary trading are rapidly emerging and challenging the role of the broker-dealer, both traditional and Internet-based. Advances in security and reliability on the Internet are lowering the barrier to using the Net for direct trading among investors. Banking on the global access provided by the Internet, many firms are launching Direct Public Offerings (DPOs) to sell equities directly to interested investors without the traditional intermediary of an underwriter or a syndicate of underwriters.

The above cases have illustrated that innovation is a continuous process of change. There is no time to rest. Experimentation is mandatory. One has to be always on the offensive. It is also about more than simply technology. Organization and leadership are critical for success. At times, management has to take significant risks. It takes guts to bet the business. The essence of the transition lies in the cultural setup and encompasses issues like speed and empowerment and the way the structure and formal decision-making aids (policies and procedures) support these traits in the organization. Clarity and communication of the imperatives, the implications of the changes across all ranks, an appetite for continuous learning and unlearning supported by the structure and the reward systems in the organization, the ability and experience of living with the anxiety so inevitably attached to a process of learning and transition – all have an important bearing on this change process.

Perhaps it is apt to end this chapter with what Charles Schwab has to say about the Internet's impact on his business: "We are just beginning to grasp what it is."[18]

Notes

1. Schonfeld, Erick (1998) "Schwab puts it all online," *Fortune*, December 7.
2. Sharpe, William E., Alexander, Gordon J. and Bailey, Jeffery V. (1999) *Investments*, PHI Inc., pp. 22–3.
3. Blume, M.E., Siegel J.J., and Rottenberg, Dan (1993) *Revolution on Wall Street*, WW Norton & Company, pp. 161–3.
4. www.schwab.com. The case draws on material from Schwab's website. The quotes are taken from speeches available on the site.
5. Schwab Annual Report 1995: http://www.schwab.com/SchwabNOW/SNLibrary/SNLib030/1995/viscomm3.html
6. Schonfeld, Erick (1998) "Schwab puts it all online," *Fortune* special, December 7.
7. http://www.etrade.com/cgi-bin/gx.cgi/AppLogic+About . . . Media Matrix (8/00).
8. Schonfeld, Erick (1998) "Schwab puts it all online," *Fortune* special, December 7.
9. "Betting the bank," *Information Strategy*, September 1997.
10. E*TRADE press release, April 4, 2001.
11. "Merrill's E-Battle," *Business Week*, November 15, 1999.
12. "Merrill's E-Battle," *Business Week*, November 15, 1999.
13. Quotes available on site www.ml.com
14. "Merrill's E-Battle," *Business Week*, November 15, 1999.
15. "Merrill's E-Battle," *Business Week*, November 15, 1999.
16. Business Week Online Extra, Q&A with E*TRADE's Christopher Cotsakos, March 26, 2001.
17. "A survey of technology in finance: Turning digits into dollars – fixing what is broking (part 5 of 8)," *The Economist*, October 26, 1996.
18. www.schwab.com

The simple truth: Wal-Mart, Amazon.com, and Barnes & Noble

4

Bookmark

With a market capitalization of $219 billion,[1] Wal-Mart dwarfs Amazon.com.[2] Wal-mart has succeeded by paying diligent attention to some good old-fashioned business values – create value for the customer and provide the highest levels of customer service. Wal-Mart re-created the retail industry some decades ago with its unique model of mass-market retailing. However, it stumbled when faced with the Internet revolution. In little more than half a decade, Amazon.com has built a formidable global brand from scratch and established the benchmark for online retail excellence. While it struggles to become profitable, Amazon.com has taken the mantle of leadership in online retail, at least for the last few years. Barnes & Noble is another interesting player in the ongoing retail revolution. Owner of one of the largest physical bookstore chains, Barnes & Noble struggled to catch up with Amazon.com and was left in the dust as Amazon.com kept moving rapidly from books to music to electronics to garden equipment and on to other product categories. Read this chapter to see how these players are innovating and redefining the retail experience, but at the same time applying some old and simple truths about how to put the customer at the center.

Wal-Mart[3] – holding ground

While Charles Schwab and the brokerage industry is a great story of putting technology to work for customers, there is another industry that has seen major innovative changes. In fact, the real Internet game has just started in this industry. The retail industry is home to one of the most innovative online start-ups – Amazon.com. Amazon.com's trail of continuous and seemingly unstoppable online innovations is in no small part responsible for ongoing dramatic changes in retailing. However, the industry leader – Wal-Mart – is not giving up. Wal-Mart knows its context – successful retailing is all about customers – and is appropriately applying the Internet to that end.

"Although our office is located in California's Silicon Valley, our heart and spirit are still in Bentonville, Arkansas, the corporate home of Wal-Mart Stores, Inc.," notes Walmart.com about itself.[4] Founded in January 2000, Walmart.com is jointly owned by Wal-Mart Stores, Inc., the employees of Walmart.com, and Accel Partners, one of Silicon Valley's most respected venture-capital firms. Although Wal-Mart is the majority owner, Walmart.com is an independent company with its own board of directors and management team. The location of its headquarters in the San Francisco Bay area gives it access to the world's deepest pool of Internet and technical talent but it firmly positions itself as a retailer. It's headed by Jeanne Jackson, former CEO of Gap's Banana Republic unit and head of Gap's Internet division.

The heart and spirit of Walmart.com is not in Silicon Valley but Arkansas.

Wal-Mart took its time to launch its online foray, sometimes astonishing observers with some of its actions. For example, in late September 2000, Walmart.com decided to close its online store for several weeks to remodel the site and to make the site more friendly and easier to use. Analysts were shocked! While other e-tailers could revamp their site while keeping their stores running, why did Wal-Mart have to close down its store? A lead story in *Business Week* (November 6, 2000) asked: "After more than 4 years of false starts, is Wal-Mart losing its zeal for the Web?" However, CEO Jackson was emphatic that the decision to close the site was done with the best interests of customers at heart. It would be much easier to do a complete overhaul of its front- and backend systems and manage the transfer of giga-bytes of data with the system entirely shut down. And she noted, "This is a marathon. It's not a sprint."

It is true that online sales make a small fraction of Wal-Mart's total sales and thus Wal-Mart had the luxury of being able to close its online store for a few weeks; but this is also indicative of Wal-Mart's unique approach to online business. A very deliberate and complementary role is developing for Walmart.com and it's expected to strengthen the many things that have made Wal-Mart a universally known brand – things like excellent vendor relationships, highly efficient back-office systems, an unswerving commitment to Sam Walton's "Always low prices" philosophy, and an unrivalled group of experienced retailers who strive each day to make the customer number one. A lot of things have changed since the first Wal-Mart opened in 1962, but some of these things never did. Wal-Mart has the goal of ensuring that you'll continue to get the highest value at the lowest prices. And you'll always be greeted with a warm welcome, whether you walk through the door of your local Wal-Mart store or turn on your computer to visit Walmart.com. In fact, Wal-Mart believes that the Internet is only going to make these differentiators sharper.

Its online strategy is evolving with the aim to make the best of both the worlds. For example, a store item that only sells about one a month – like a milkshake maker – might be moved to the online site so the store can use that shelf space for a faster-moving item.[5] In addition, customers may research products online and come to the stores to buy them. Or, a store that doesn't carry something a customer wants, could locate it for him or her on the website and arrange to make it available. The Web offers a whole new opportunity – more effective shelf-space utilization – a critical success factor in retailing. And unlike any other online store, it had the advantage of carefully picking up the online merchandise so as to minimize cost of service. "We had [before] silly stuff on our site," Jackson noted. "What were we doing spending $9 to ship a 19-cent lip pencil?"[6]

Describing the factors that had led to Wal-Mart's phenomenal success in the brick-and-mortar world, a Morgan Stanley analyst wrote:[7]

> One of Wal-Mart's key store opening strategies was related to real estate – the company would find inexpensive land with large amounts of space, but with good traffic flow, and would then rely on word of mouth and low prices to drive lots of traffic. And then Wal-Mart would offer consumers its nearly unparalleled shopping convenience, huge product selection, and low prices.

To date, a key factor of Wal-Mart's popularity with consumers is its hometown identity. Shoppers are personally welcomed at the entrance by People Greeters. Each store honors a graduating high school senior with a college scholarship. Locally made merchandise is frequently and proudly displayed. Associates (employees) determine where charitable funds are donated. At its core, Wal-Mart is a place where prices are low and value and customer service are high – every day. Wal-Mart carefully controls expenses to maintain its low price structure. Customers do not have to wait for a sale

The industry's most efficient and sophisticated distribution system is at Wal-Mart.

to realize savings. Backing the hometown flavor of a Wal-Mart store is the industry's most efficient and sophisticated distribution system at work at Wal-Mart. The system allows each store to customize the merchandise assortment to match its buying community's needs.

Commented Sam Walton (1918–92) as he accepted the Medal of Freedom from President George Bush in March 1992: "We're all working together; that's the secret. And we'll lower the cost of living for everyone, not just in America, but we'll give the world an opportunity to see what it's like to save and have a better lifestyle, a better life for all. We're proud of what we've accomplished; we've just begun." His legacy is writ large at Wal-Mart in its three unqualified principles:

> Key strengths of Wal-Mart:
> - A uniquely coherent and strong organizational culture.
> - A customer-centric organization.
> - An efficient and IT-intensive logistics operation.
> - Increasingly seamless integration between Wal-Mart.com and the physical stores.

- *The "10-foot attitude"*: One of Wal-Mart's secrets to customer service is its "10-foot attitude," handed down to it by Wal-Mart founder Sam Walton. During his many store visits, he encouraged associates to take a pledge with him: "... I want you to promise that whenever you come within 10 feet of a customer, you will look him in the eye, greet him and ask him if you can help him." Now, how will you translate the "10-foot attitude" on to a website? It starts with striving to build a site that is easy for customers to use – working every day to bring a better shopping experience. The online store will always be a work in progress, but one thing won't change: the commitment to keep customers" needs at the top of the priority list.[8]
- *Lower prices*: Sam's adherence to his pricing philosophy was unshakable, as one of Wal-Mart's first store managers recalls: "Sam wouldn't let us hedge on a price at all. Say the list price was $1.98, but we had paid only 50 cents. Initially, I would say, "Well, it's originally $1.98, so why don't we sell it for $1.25?" And, he'd say, "No. We paid 50 cents for it. Mark it up 30 percent, and that's it. No matter what you pay for it, if we get a great deal, pass it on to the customer." And of course that's what we did." The pricing philosophy at Walmart.com is

the same as it is in Wal-Mart stores. When the former gets a price break from a supplier, it passes it along to the customers, often in the form of a "Rollback." You'll see lots of Rollback signs on the site, just as you would in any Wal-Mart store.

- *The Sundown rule*: It's a rule that is taken seriously at Wal-Mart. It's standard to get things done "today" – before the sun goes down. Whether it's a request from a store across the country or a call from down the hall, every request gets same-day service. This is the easiest to adapt online.

Amazon.com – the spirited way

> We have one strategy at amazon.com – provide the customer with the best shopping experience. Amazon.com's heart and soul is all about making shopping better for customers.
>
> Jeff Bezos, Founder and CEO of Amazon.com.[9]

Sounds similar to Wal-Mart's mission? It seems to be more than a coincidence – Amazon seeks to be the world's most customer-centric company. And it was born with this mission in July 1995. Not surprisingly, the spirit and evolutionary chart of Amazon is unique. Sam Walton's dream, realized in 1962 with the opening of the first Wal-Mart store, is the only comparable mission. In 1995, redoing Sam Walton through the Internet was indeed very innovative – it hadn't become any easier in all these 32 years. To that extent the very concept of Amazon was innovative.

The company creatively applied technology to deliver personalized services and flexible merchandising. According to CEO Bezos, "We'll be redecorating the store for every customer."[10] By the current reckoning that means 25 million stores for its 25 million customers. It innovated a virtual store that provided some simple but effective changes in the experiences associated with a traditional store. The store greets customers by name. Customers can read reviews on any product from fellow customers. The store offers almost universal selection – you name it and you get it – it carries every book, for example. Customers can get increasingly pertinent suggestions on purchases of gifts.

Amazon seeks to be the world's most customer-centric company.

Amazon.com opened its virtual doors in July 1995, selling books and it has maintained its leadership position in online book sales to date. It launched its music store in June 1998, and by the end of October 1998, it became the number one online music seller. In November 1998, it launched its video store and repeated the feat in one quarter. It seems well poised to repeat the performance in electronics goods in 2001. CEO Bezos reaffirms, "We're not a book company. We're not a music company. We're not a video company. We're not an auctions company. We're a customer company."[11] "Clearly, Jeff has an 'I'm going to own the world' mentality," notes venture capitalist Timothy M. Haley of Institutional Venture Partners. "Indeed, potential rivals fret about how to avoid getting 'Amazoned'." [12] And customers seem to reciprocate the sentiments with liberal praise.

> Your site is dangerous. I could easily spend half my salary here. I love bookstores and libraries, but frankly, I find more of the titles I want on your site, and they're so easy to order, and the interface is so friendly that I think this new vice is going to corrupt me permanently.
>
> *Comment from an Amazon.com customer,*
> *Anne Tourney of Mountain View, California*[13]

Amazon is indeed very meticulous in creating the customer experience. While offering a host of features, it keeps the graphic content in its website minimal in order to enable users to download pages quickly. Also, the company invested heavily in developing proprietary software and systems that provided robust backend support. It's always looking for new and innovative ways to take the drudgery out of shopping and create a better customer experience. For example, 1-Click and Gift-Click make shopping easy and hassle-free, and Wish List takes the uncertainty out of gift giving. 1-Click securely stores billing and shipping information so that each customer needs only one click of the mouse to buy a selected item, rather than entering the same information over and over again for each purchase.

Amazon is always looking for new and innovative ways to take the drudgery out of shopping and create a better customer experience.

Its book-return policy thoughtfully complements and builds confidence in the quality of its editors' recommendations by allowing customers to return any book recommended by them, even after it has been read. "It doesn't matter how dog-eared or worn it is," CEO Bezos notes, "Even if you ripped out the pages because you thought the book was so bad, you can still return the pieces to us for a full refund."[14] Previously, the company's returns policy required books to be in unread and new condition. All these initiatives result in a satisfied and committed customer.

Amazon's commitment to service customers better takes many innovative forms. It ran a contest in 2000, Toy Quest, inviting kids to design and create their dream toys. Each child aged 12 and under could send his or her toy-invention ideas to the Amazon Toy Quest for a chance to become a famous toy inventor – because Amazon was to manufacture and sell the winning toy. "Innovation is incredibly important," said Jeff Bezos. "We want to see what kids will come up with when they are given the chance to create the world's coolest toy – we want to know what it will look like and what it will do. Toy Quest will bring kids' toy inventions to life, capturing the creativity and magic that lives in their imaginations."[15] The winning inventors saw their dream toys brought to life. Amazon also awarded each grand-prize winner a $10,000 college savings bond, as well as 7 percent of his or her toy's sales royalties in the form of a college savings fund.

Early forays

In the context of Amazon's spirited run in the pursuit of online opportunities, Wal-Mart's early forays into the Internet world may seem not as high profile but yet it's interesting and educating. Wal-Mart had always aggressively harnessed alternate channels of distribution, such as warehouse clubs and super centers. To address the potential of e-commerce, Wal-Mart went online in July 1996 with websites for Wal-Mart and SAM'S CLUB. At that time it did seek to build an impressive assortment of products and services to be available on the Internet while offering Wal-Mart's Every Day Low Prices. It wanted to be the absolute value leader on the Internet.

> Key strengths of Amazon.com
> - Visionary leadership.
> - The pioneer's lead.
> - Best-in-class online customer service.
> - A unique leverage of technology,

To realize the ambition, it worked in cooperation with Microsoft to develop standard Web-retailing procedures. It offered customers a simple site layout and shopping system that would be the same each time they visited the online retailer. The site featured "greeters," which met customers at the "doors," "shopping carts," guaranteed secure transactions, "customer favorites," and new products for Internet users. By September 1996, Wal-Mart's site ranked in the Top 25 shopping sites.[16]

Wal-Mart introduced innovations in its online channel from time to time. Its site offered more items online than it did in its giant stores. In fact, the site's best-selling products in 1998 were Rolex watches and Nike T-shirts – items not even found in Wal-Mart stores.[17] In 1997, the company introduced a new category of fresh seafood to the website. Customers could order from a selection of five different seafood offerings and have the items delivered to their doorstep within 24 hours, freshness guaranteed.[18] The company endorsed a new payment card security mechanism, jointly developed and endorsed by all of the major payment card companies, called Secure Electronic Transaction (SET), in 1997.

Wal-Mart expanded the music category of its online site by more than 100,000 selections in 1997. Overall, by 1997, the product selection expanded to more than 140,000 items. It offered products in 27 main categories ranging from sporting goods to fresh flowers. Wal-Mart also aggressively attacked any attempt by the upcoming online retailers to steal its competitive advantage in terms of superior store management know-how. It filed a lawsuit in 1998 against Amazon to protect its former associates from giving out the knowledge of its proprietary and highly confidential information systems. The lawsuit was settled out of court in 1999 with Amazon agreeing to reassign some former Wal-Mart Information systems associates and vendors to tasks different than their assignments at Wal-Mart.[19]

By 1999, Wal-Mart had become openly receptive of the challenge and stated:[20]

> Wal-Mart is in retail business and for that reason we look at any form of retailing as a competitor. The Internet has some very interesting aspects and will definitely serve as a growing market as we move into the 21st century.

However, the skepticism that had held Wal-Mart back from a full-fledged response against online channels was evident at times:[21]

> Very few, if any, Internet retailers have made a profit, and issues like cost of delivery, merchandise returns and data security all have to be resolved before this business model is validated... when and if the business proves viable, we will be there with the technology, distribution, assortment and the lowest price.

In the meantime, business continued as usual – the Wal-Mart division opened 41 new discount stores and 167 new Super centers in 2000, and SAM'S CLUB division opened 13 new domestic clubs. Wal-Mart International opened 77 units in 2000. It also opened 4 regional, 6 food distribution centers and 12 Neighborhood markets in 2000.

Barnes & Noble.com – little time to think?

Barnes & Noble was perhaps most directly affected by the advent of Amazon.com. However, its online entry was reactionary to start with. Even Wal-Mart was comparatively far more aggressive on the Internet. Born to the USA's largest bookseller, Barnes & Nobles Inc., a Fortune 500 company, Barnes & Noble.com clearly had a great legacy. Founded in 1917, it had grown by innovatively redefining a bookshop. Book stores as community centers, for example. Everything from the design of its stores to the selection of its titles to the training of booksellers reflects that philosophy. It hosts community events, author readings and signings, and performances within its stores. The company was the first to discount books and advertise on television in 1975. In 1985 it launched its own publishing division that specialized in rescuing out-of-print books by reissuing them in quality, affordable editions. In 1991 it pioneered the "superstore" concept. These huge locations combined a wide selection of titles with experienced bookselling staff and a warm atmosphere that included cafés, magazines, community events, and well-stocked children's sections. And in May 1997, its online subsidiary Barnes & Noble.com opened on the World Wide Web. In May 1999, Barnes & Noble.com (www.bn.com) undertook the historic public offering on NASDAQ raising $468 million, an unprecedented sum for an Internet IPO at that time.

The young one has come a long way since May 1997 – it's the second largest, and one of the fastest growing, online distributors of books. Its revenue for 2000 reached $320 million, 65 percent growth over the last year. Its losses, without capital charges, stood at $155 million. It invested $175 million in 2000 in various acquisitions. It now ranks among the top five Web properties in the world[22] and is one of the biggest online destinations among brick-and-mortar companies. The cumulative number of users increased to 7.3 million, up 80 percent over the last year. Looks impressive? Not really when you look at the comparable figures of Amazon. The first quarter 2000[23] sales for Amazon stood at $695 million with a net loss of $255 million. But it expects pro forma operating profits by the end of 2001. It also increased its inventory turnover from 9 in the first quarter of 2000 to 12 in the same period in 2001. Its books are sold in over 160 countries and have 29 million users. More importantly, in first quarter 2000 Amazon's US Books, Music, and DVD/Video segments reported a fully allocated pro forma operating profit in those segments. Why has bn.com lagged behind in spite of its illustrious history?

The torch of innovation did not move on to bn.com from its parent.

Apparently, the torch of innovation did not move easily to bn.com from its parent. To be fair, however, the umbilical cord between the two was cut away from day one. The online business was kept at arm's length and there was limited integration between the two. In fact, even investors gave a lukewarm greeting to its IPO and its shares were trading at 36 percent of the offer price on the issue date. "For a brand name franchise a typical first day performance is upward of 200 to 300 per cent… Investors were concerned about the relationship of the online unit with its parent company", commented an analyst in the *Financial Times*.[24]

When compared with Amazon.com, bn.com was offering nothing new essentially – customers could search and choose from thousands of new and out-of-print titles, read reviews and excerpts. To top it, it did not really exploit some major possibilities of leveraging the existing assets of Barnes & Noble stores for creating superior values for customers. Some of the "real world" assets that could have been very useful include the following:[25]

- *Experienced booksellers.* Its culture of outgoing, helpful, and knowledgeable booksellers consisted of over 30,000 full- and part-time employees.
- *Marketing and community relations.* Each store has its own community-based calendar of events, including author appearances, children's storytelling hours, poetry readings, and discussion groups.
- *Mail-order business.* Its mail-order business that shipped more than 1 million packages to more than 50 different countries provided the infrastructure for special order processing that was required to fulfill orders on the Internet.
- *Relationships with publishers.* It had established relationships with more than 20,000 publishers. It meant that costly and time-consuming backend processes like order entry systems, replenishment systems, etc. were already in place.
- *Relationships with authors.* This was a very powerful differentiator. Long-standing relationships with authors meant better support from the authors in initiating and conducting author–reader interactions.

However, of late things seem to be getting focused. In September 2000, bn.com and Barnes & Noble, Inc. announced major integration initiatives. Internet Service Counters powered by bn.com were being installed in all 551 Barnes & Noble superstores. The new counters will enable customers to order any book or other product through bn.com at any Barnes & Noble store. Bn.com customers may return books and music CDs purchased to any Barnes & Noble store and receive merchandise store credits.

Bn.com is extending its business model to leverage the offline world.

Bn.com is extending itself to the B2B arena, where its Business Solutions program provides Fortune 1000 companies with a turnkey Intranet bookstore, enabling them to streamline and control their book purchasing process. In September 2000, bn.com also announced plans to acquire Fatbrain.com, Inc. (www.fatbrain.com), the third-largest online bookseller specializing in professional and technical titles for the corporate marketplace. Fatbrain.com's Web-based services reach more than 3.5 million employee desktops at almost 350 Fortune 1000 companies worldwide. Fatbrain.com helps organizations capitalize on business information and professionally published materials by streamlining its management and distribution, enabling delivery in digital and/or hardcopy format directly into the hands of employees, partners, and customers.

Barnes & Noble University, an online distance-learning forum offering free classes, got under way in August 2000. The broad-based curriculum covered a range of subjects, from gardening and classical music to Shakespeare and organizing stock portfolios. In May 2000, bn.com pioneered Same-Day Delivery service to its Manhattan, New York customers. This rapid delivery service enables the huge residential and working population of Manhattan to get delivery within hours of virtually any book in print from today's bestsellers to the most hard-to-find titles from small publishers. The service also includes delivery of more than 100,000 music CDs.

More significantly, bn.com is now clearly focused on its vision – to be a leading provider of digital content. It seems to have come out of the shadows of Amazon and dedicated itself to strengthening its position as an e-knowledge company. Besides the initiatives already discussed, bn.com has made strategic investments in some additional companies whose products and services are compatible with its core business. For example, the company has invested in enews.com, the Internet's leading site for discount magazine subscriptions; BuyEnlarge, which uses state-of-the-art technology to produce prints and posters on demand; notHarvard.com, the pioneer in developing online branded universities; and MightyWords, a digital content provider.

Internet success – the Wal-Mart way

Wal-Mart launched a new Wal-Mart.com store on January 1, 2000, featuring numerous personal shopping aids, a travel service, and a photo center to meet the growing variety of needs of more than 90 million customers that shop at Wal-Mart stores weekly. Quite like bn.com, the year 2000 saw a renewed commitment of Wal-Mart to its online strategy. The number of online book, music, video game, and home video titles alone increased tenfold. The number of items presented online was over 500,000. "This is a journey for us, not a race," said Glenn Habern,[26] senior vice-president of new business development at Wal-Mart. "There have been many that have speculated and placed expectations on our progress; however, we have remained focused on our customers and their expectations of us. Wal-Mart.com's new store is being designed with them in mind." And in a wide-ranging strategic alliance with AOL, it is now providing the vast majority of Wal-Mart communities with convenient, low-cost access to the Internet. This is especially important for those who live in smaller Wal-Mart communities that have been affected by the "digital divide."

Not unexpectedly, Wal-Mart again revamped its site in September 2000. Jackson[27] introduced the revamped Walmart.com site as, "Our home page in one glance shows everything available in the 'store,' in categories. Very clean, very simple. Customers can sort things by price, brand or most popular items. And the checkout is very clean. But we won't do one-click checkout. To be customer-friendly, we must give them an option to bail." Jackson asserts that although industry pundits may not find Walmart.com's site particularly fashionable, it is the product of some very conscious choices. "But we're not going out there to do leading-edge technology. We're doing things that make the shopping experience easy. My mom isn't going to make a transaction on the Net until it's easy for her to do."

Jackson[28] considers the existing measures of website success such as eyeballs, page views, and traffic to be of lesser importance. "You will not see any of those measures in a report from Walmart.com. Every single metric we're putting in place is about building a strong foundation with our customer base, so that long term we can build the right kind of a house." The emphasis on customer relationships will also affect Walmart.com's choice of business partners: Jackson said her company will seek "value-added alliances."

> **"You will not see any of those measures (e.g. eyeballs, page views and traffic) in a report from Walmart.com."**

For example, rather than trying to attract more visitor traffic by linking with a site like Travelocity, Jackson and her colleagues decided that Southwest Airlines offered good value for their customers. The Walmart.com site will provide a link to Southwest so customers can order airline tickets online.

And the million-dollar question? Which company would profit when an order was made online and picked up at the store? Jackson noted, "Whether there's a commission – because we created the site that enabled the sale – or whether we get the sale and pay rent to the store, one way or another we'll make money. The entire boat will float by both ends rising."[29] Obviously, Wal-Mart seems to be in clear knowledge of what it's heading towards.

Continuous innovation

How has Amazon been holding out its position? Apparently, the secret is continuous innovation. Not all of these innovations will survive, but the constant drive for perpetual metamorphosis is a recipe for success. Just have a brief look at some of its simple but innovative services.

Amazon was among the first to offer its customers the ability to send personalized voice messages, free, with every electronic greeting card (www.amazon.com/cards). With this voice-greeting option, card senders can sing a song, recite a poem, or add whatever best expresses their thoughts to a friend or loved one. And it is indeed easy. To attach a private voice message, visitors can simply select a card, click "Add a voice greeting" on the card's personalization page, and call a toll-free number to record the message privately. Each card is sent immediately after the voice message is recorded. Card recipients will hear the greeting over their computer immediately upon opening the card – there is no download required. Those without sound capabilities on their computers can call a toll-free number and listen to their special greetings over the phone.

Amazon and author M.J. Rose made publishing history when her book *Lip Service* hit the street to become the first self-published novel discovered online. Rose was a participant in Amazon Advantage, a free program that solves two of independent authors' biggest problems: visibility and widespread distribution.

Amazon.com's constant drive for innovation is a recipe for success.

Three years ago, when Rose was turned downed by traditional publishers, she decided to establish her own imprint, Lady Chatterley's Library, and publish her novel herself. After enrolling in the Advantage program, *Lip Service* generated such a buzz from the large volume of positive reader reviews that the publishing industry was forced to take notice. As a result, *Lip Service* became the Literary Guild's first selection drawn directly from online sources, and it is the first self-published novel the book club has ever acquired. Subsequently, Pocket Books bought the North American rights to republish *Lip Service*.

"My dreams of driving cross-country selling books from the trunk of my car became a nightmare when every independent bookstore I approached refused to stock a self-published book," noted Rose. "Through Amazon.com and the Advantage program, my dreams became a reality. Amazon.com Advantage gave *Lip Service* the same prominence, immediate availability, and level of exposure as a best-selling novel from a larger publisher."

In April 2001 Amazon announced an interesting alliance – an agreement to re-launch Borders.com as a co-branded website powered by Amazon.com's e-commerce platform. The co-branded site, expected to debut in Fall 2001, will feature the vast selection of books, music, video, and DVDs available at Amazon.com as well as continue to offer content unique to Borders.com, including store location information and in-store event calendars. Amazon will be the seller of record, providing inventory, fulfillment, site content, and customer service for the co-branded site. Following the success of its much-lauded deal with Toys"R"Us, this alliance aims to exploit the unique online strengths of Amazon.com with those of best-in-class "offline" retailers in a "win-win" situation. Amazon.com is actively exploring other similar partnerships. These alliances are also proof of a subtle evolution of Amazon.com's strategy. It is demonstrating the flexibility of its e-commerce platform and transforming itself into a Web-enabler.

This is in alignment with Amazon.com's focus on building a core competence in technology excellence. Here is what Stewart Alsop, a critical observer of trends in the Internet sector, had to say about Amazon.com (*Fortune*, April 30, 2001):

> Most people think of Amazon.com as an e-tailer, and value it for how it sells products and distributes them. Those people make the fundamental mistake of comparing Amazon.com with other retailers and direct-marketing companies.
>
> I think of Amazon.com as a technology company. It may be the only company to have mastered the use of technology in serving individual customers. No other outfit comes close to tracking what its customers do and using that information to make its customers happy. The result: As time goes by, I find myself buying more and more stuff from Amazon.com and feeling good about it. I actually look forward to getting e-mail messages from Amazon.com promoting stuff that I buy. They are the only commercial e-mails that don't irritate me – the only ones.

"I think of Amazon.com as a technology company."

Amazon has a custom-designed multi-terabyte data warehouse built by Oracle. It has employed some of the most sophisticated data analysis tools from SAS Institute and e-marketing software from Epiphany to help personalize its business approach to each individual customer. An example of how it may work is as follows:[30] "Amazon.com decides to offer a 20 percent discount to 20,000 people in an effort to sell excess inventory on a particular kind of camera. Database marketers at the company use the Epiphany application to identify people who have purchased camera equipment or supplies in the past, while statisticians use SAS Institute tools to rank other customers on their likelihood of buying. The results are combined, and the email offer is sent out." The result is extremely effective!

Amazon.com also continually invests in new technologies. For example, it was among the first to add m-commerce – mobile commerce services – in late 1999 in response to market research predictions about the potentially rapid take-up of m-commerce by mobile telephony customers. To build the best-in-class m-commerce service, Amazon.com assembled an impressive set of partners, including Sprint Corp.'s Sprint PCS, Verizon Communications Inc., and Nextel Communications Inc. It adapted its patented "one-click" system to the mobile platform, enabling customers to buy merchandise with a single tap on the phone keypad. Software was also created to post recommendations for purchases to customers over mobile phones, much like what it does online. Though Amazon.com has decreased its resource commitment to the mobile platform in the first part of 2001 (due to increased profit pressures), it has built a formidable set of assets in its (mobile) "Amazon Anywhere" initiative – something which can be spun off as a provider of m-commerce technologies (to other firms) in the near future. Another source of revenue in the offing.

Amazon had also been very different in its backend management from the very start. It did not follow the "pure-play" route. It built its own warehouses, for example. But its own inventory is a very small fraction of the number of titles it offers. It relies on rapid fulfillment from major distributors and wholesalers who carry a broad selection of titles. This sourcing model enables it to turn very high inventory rates and reduce inventory-holding periods to less than five days. The "collaborative filtering"[31] technique used for recommending books keeps the rate of returns at only 1 to 2 percent, which provides a huge potential of favorable deals with publishers who have the largest stake in reducing returns.[32] It deploys automated interfaces for sorting and organizing its orders to enable it to achieve rapid and economic purchase and delivery terms. For orders that cannot be filled from its inventory, its proprietary software selects the orders that can be filled via electronic interfaces with vendors and forwards the remaining orders to its special orders group. It has developed customized information systems and trained dedicated ordering personnel in sourcing out-of-print books and other hard-to-find products.

While other e-tailers have been able to copy one or a few of Amazon.com's innovations, none of them have been able to match the pace and scope of Amazon.com's amazing history of innovations – both big and small.

Issues

In this chapter we had three interesting examples of how companies are innovating with the new technological possibilities to redefine retailing. Amazon redefined the online landscape, Wal-Mart is bringing its store-based success formula to the Net, and Barnes & Noble had difficulties in transferring its innovative approaches to a different medium.

> **No other retailer has been able to match the pace and scope of Amazon.com's amazing history of online innovations – both big and small.**

In March 2001, there was an interesting buzz in the media about a possible deal between Wal-Mart and Amazon.com. It made a lot of sense to many. After all, Wal-Mart remains the undisputed leader in physical store-based retailing and Amazon.com is the king of online retail. Bricks and clicks seem to be way forward in retail. With Amazon.com's stock getting mauled in the dotcom carnage, why not combine the "best retail bricks" with the "best retail clicks"?

The buzz finally turned out to be only that – only a buzz and not a reality. However, the excitement around the idea shows that innovation is alive and well in retailing. The new model of retail – effectively combining store-based and online retail – is being defined. Leaders such as Wal-Mart and Amazon.com are constantly experimenting – while keeping their anchors fixed on customer value creation and excellence in service. They are perpetually metamorphosing their business model. And they have a technological and organizational infrastructure that enables them to succeed with innovation as a strategy. In the end both Wal-Mart and Amazon.com may well be successful. If so, success will be based on the speed and effectiveness with which these companies can continuously reinvent themselves, the degree to which they can transfer their know-how from one medium to another (and eventually institutionalize that knowledge), and create an organizational culture that is in line with the requirements of doing retail through the Net.

Notes

1. As of June 19, 2001.
2. Market capitalization of $4.5 billion on June 26, 2001.
3. Taken from company documents found on its website, www.walmart.com, and from the 10-K SEC Filings at www.sec.gov
4. www.walmart.com

5. Based on the report "Wal-Mart.com CEO Jeanne Jackson does some remodelling," from Knowledge@Wharton, Special to CNET News.com, November 11, 2000.
6. Based on the report "Wal-Mart.com CEO Jeanne Jackson does some remodelling," from *Knowledge@Wharton*, Special to CNET News.com, November 11 2000.
7. Based on "The Wal-Marting of the Web?", Morgan Stanley Internet retailing report 1997.
8. www.walmart.com
9. Amazon.com's press release, January 26, 1999.
10. Littman, Jonathan (1997) "The book on Amazon.com," *Los Angeles Times* magazine, July 20.
11. "Q&A with Amazon's Jeff Bezos," *Business Week*, May 31, 1999.
12. "eBay vs. Amazon.com," *Business Week*, May 31, 1999.
13. "Customer comments," www.amazon.com
14. www.amazon.com
15. www.amazon.com
16. Wal-Mart, 1997 Harvard Business School Case 9-797-099.
17. Steinhaufer, Jennifer (1998) "Old-line retailers resist online life," *The New York Times*, April 20.
18. "Seashore to your door within 24 hours," Press release, July 30, 1997.
19. Press releases October 16, 1998 and April 5, 1999.
20. "Interview with the chairman," 1999 Annual Report.
21. "Interview with the chairman," 1999 Annual Report.
22. www.bn.com
23. www.amazon.com
24. "Slow start for IPO of internet bookseller," *Financial Times*, May 26, 1999.
25. From 10-K, Barnes & Noble, Inc., 1999.
26. www.walmart.com
27. Based on the report "Wal-Mart.com CEO Jeanne Jackson does some remodelling," From *Knowledge@Wharton*, Special to CNET News.com, November 11, 2000.
28. Based on the report "Wal-Mart.com CEO Jeanne Jackson does some remodelling," From *Knowledge@Wharton*, Special to CNET News.com, November 11, 2000.

29. Based on the report "Wal-Mart.com CEO Jeanne Jackson does some remodelling," From *Knowledge@Wharton*, Special to CNET News.com, November 11, 2000.

30. Foley, John, Konicki, Steve and Hulme, George (2000) "Amazon's IT Agenda," *Information Week*, November 6.

31. Collaborative filtering is a technique used by Amazon to make recommendations to a particular customer based upon analyses of the purchasing habits of other similar customers.

32. "Leadership Online: Barnes & Noble vs. Amazon.com (A)," HBS Case 9-798-063, 1998.

Goliath and David?
GM and Auto-By-Tel

5

Bookmark

This chapter takes our exploration further by describing how incumbents, even if late entrants, can succeed. We see how General Motors (GM), quite an icon of a huge stable organization, slowly but confidently seized the opportunity thrown open by the Internet. It not only matched the new entrant start-ups but also stole a march over its traditional rivals. Auto-By-Tel (ABT), the pioneer, exemplifies how online opportunities can change the economics of an industry; it has reworked the fundamental dynamics of the industry. Explore the ABT case to see how innovative possibilities exist in every industry – even in the mature sector of automobile manufacturing and distribution. GM's response to ABT demonstrates that innovation cannot be matched by increased efficiency alone; innovation against innovation is the only way. Focus on how incumbents can play the game, if they act confidently. GM was among the first incumbents in the automobile sector to react, in 1997, with "GM BuyPower"!

The starting point

We may be so overwhelmed by Wal-Mart and Schwab that we might almost miss out an equally interesting business coup. One of the "mightiest" of corporations on earth, General Motors, has played a key role in the application of the Internet in its industry. Contrary to its traditional reputation as a huge bureaucratic organization, it has actually led the more nimbler siblings, including Toyota and Ford, in seeking the Internet as its new fulcrum for change. The following paragraphs provide a telling story of how Internet-enabled innovations have changed the face of the biggest industry of our time – automobile production and distribution. A fundamental change has begun in the way vehicles are designed, manufactured, distributed, and sold. Some automakers are going beyond that too. Ford's CEO Jacques Nasser, for example, is talking about redefining his business boundary to cover the entire life cycle of the vehicle – from sourcing to assembly to scrap. Ford already has acquired businesses, on both sides of the Atlantic, which are "outside" its existing portfolio of activities. For instance, it has acquired Kwik-Fit, a quick-repair business in the UK, and a vehicle recycling business in Florida.

In the case of the automobile industry, the trigger for change came from an online entrant. Auto-By-Tel (ABT) initiated simple customer-oriented changes in the way the industry operated. The changes turned out to be so powerful and the technology so enabling that within five years the face of the industry has changed significantly. ABT must be credited with having shown the power of the new technology to incumbents like GM.

There has been a fairly consistent reduction in manufacturers' suggested retail prices, totaling around 10 percent, throughout the 1990s. Tough luck for the manufacturers: their costs had to follow this trend. To top it, dealer incentives in absolute terms have remained mostly stable in that period and customer incentives have increased. While car manufacturers have done a good job of cost reduction at their ends, a good part of their savings have been appropriated away by distributors and customers. At times, the cost-focus of automobile manufacturers has been almost absurd. A report by the *Economist*[1] noted how Ford was redesigning ashtrays, yielding a paltry saving of *25 cents a vehicle.*

Even worse, new cars that used to account for a bulk of the profits in yesteryears now account for less than 10 percent of the profits for retailers.[2] The focus of the retail business is now shifting to selling used cars (used car sales

> **The changes turned out to be so powerful and the technology so enabling that within five years the face of the industry has changed significantly.**

exceed new car sales by over a factor of 3), servicing, and financing. The new car business has become more of a "must do" to sustain other profitable businesses. As a consequence dealers need continued and further incentives to pay sufficient attention to new car sales. This further precipitates the squeeze for automakers. There are many other causes for discord too – from the sharp competition between dealers to the high costs of financing inventory, supporting commissioned salespeople, and paying for advertising.

Auto dealerships are changing

Car sales in the United States as well as in the rest of the world take place through retail dealers and distributors. All of GM's automotive-related products, for example, are marketed through retail dealers and distributors. The United States alone has more than 22,000 dealers. GM has approximately 8,000 vehicle dealers in the United States, 900 in Canada and Mexico, and 5,000 outlets in the rest of the world.

Almost all over the world, dealerships are generally local businesses and usually lack sufficient expertise and technical training to handle the technological sophistication of modern cars. They also have not historically attached sufficient importance to customer satisfaction with respect to the services they render. But this is not entirely their fault and the entire industry operates along similar lines. Very often automakers try to sell what they can produce instead of producing what they can sell. And over time, in order to protect their businesses, dealers have used local political influence to create legal barriers: for example, laws inhibiting manufacturers from setting up competing outlets and preventing them from selling direct to customers. There are significant legal barriers – even today – against automobile manufacturers approaching or selling directly to customers. These laws have become a blocking factor in the transformation of the auto retailing industry. Competition among dealers of the same company over exclusivity of territory, antagonism between auto manufacturers and dealerships over profit sharing, etc. have created conditions of tension.

In the US over 30 states have enacted laws that prevent automakers from selling vehicles online, and the dealers' considerable lobbying strength seems to be growing. A US District Court judge ruled in July 2000 that Ford, which tried to sell used cars online through its FordPreowned.com site, could not sell vehicles over the Internet in Texas – one of the nation's top automotive markets. And most of these states also require new owners to pick up their cars at a dealership. Yet, over 40 percent of buyers used the Internet before taking a decision on the car they bought and over 5 percent of all automobile sales in the US were finalized online in 2000.

Several structural changes were visible in the past few years in the auto retailing business:

- *Consolidators*: Financial consortiums from outside the auto industry (and in some cases, groups of local dealers) have tried to accrue economies of scale by integrating dealerships and getting them to operate together. For example, United Auto Group controls over US$4 billion sales per year and Auto Nation records over US$16 billion in sales per year.

- *Car superstores*: Used-car mega-stores like Huizenga's AutoNation and Circuit City's CarMax have made a big impact on car retailing. Price tags are equitable and customers have a vast choice of vehicles without the overhead of haggling with the salesman. These superstores typically pay salaries proportional to customers' satisfaction with their service, instead of commissions.[3]

- *Manufacturer initiatives*: Automobile manufacturers are also selectively consolidating their dealerships. However, they fear that these consolidated superstores could become more powerful and demand price cuts and other concessions and perhaps even begin selling cars from other manufacturers. For example, Ford in partnership with local dealers is consolidating (in some states in the US) existing showrooms into a smaller number of superstores, with separate local service centers close to where people work or live. The dealers keep majority ownership, and licensed salespeople continue to sell cars. Volkswagen is going through a similar exercise in Europe.

> **"Simple" innovations have changed the face of the biggest industry.**

For dealers it has also become more difficult to make money and they are losing market share to a new type of a competitor: online sales. The eventual sale still happens at dealer premises and used car-selling giants like AutoNation and CarMax. But the online availability of comprehensive listings of dealer costs and Manufacturers' Suggested Retail Price are increasingly shielding customers from dealers' tactics. Of course, an educated consumer does "help" the dealer to shorten the negotiation process but at the cost of reduced margins. While 75 percent of car dealers have their own websites, a good part of the online retailing business has been captured by new intermediaries such as Auto-By-Tel (ABT). The fact that we have a new type of intermediary is to an extent paradoxical, since many believed that the Internet with its freely available information would foster direct contact between sellers and buyers. However, the new intermediaries have discovered new ways to add value to customers. One ABT customer, Brad Saviello, of Atlanta, Georgia noted:

> I had been bargaining for a car with a local dealer for two days and was within US$800 of the invoice price listed in the "net". Before I committed to the deal, I decided to try ABT after reading an article in Inc. or Success. To my surprise, I was contacted within two hours of submitting my request and was offered the same car I had been negotiating for US$100 over invoice by another local dealer. In addition, the financing rate was 0.4 percent better than either of the banks I normally use. The whole process took all of one day. Amazing! The total savings between the sale price reduction and the interest savings over the life of the car are almost US$1260. Thanks![4]

Is the retail side of the automobile industry the new business opportunity? Reported to be of the order of $600 billion a year in the US, it is clearly an area with great opportunities for improvements and new value propositions. Perhaps there's an opportunity for manufacturers in reengineering their sales and distribution to get a greater reward for increasing efficiencies in their operations. Let's spend some time in the next pages analyzing the innovations that Auto-By-Tel has implemented and how those innovations have influenced the whole industry.

Yours innovatively – Auto-By-Tel!

> We're going to give the customer a proficient purchase process that will deliver the lowest price and the least amount of stress they've ever had purchasing an automobile.
>
> Auto-By-Tel (ABT) Co-founder and then CEO Peter Ellis[5]

Ellis launched ABT on the Web in 1995, with only four employees, from a small office. To consumers it offered much wider choice and peace of mind with its comprehensive solution for all points on the automotive life cycle. At the same time it created a network of accredited dealers and automotive services partners to reach online car buyers and owners in the most efficient way. Through this network, consumers could find a haggle-free, competitive offer. For its direct-to-consumer service for buying new vehicles, it offered a real-time online inventory of thousands of vehicles, instant up-front pricing, multiple trade-in options, competitive financing and insurance, and at-home or office delivery. It's online auction services allowed consumers, dealers, and consignors to transact new and pre-owned vehicle purchases in a live "bid" environment.

ABT removed the stress out of the process of buying a vehicle.

A purchase request would be routed to the nearest participating dealer and a return e-mail was sent to the consumer with the dealer's name and phone number and the name of the dedicated manager at the dealer. Buyers could get a graphic depiction of the exterior, interior, and mechanical components of the vehicle, allowing buyers to identify items that are scratched, broken, or in need of mechanical attention. Buyer and seller profiles, escrow and transportation services were also available.

Before establishing ABT, Ellis himself owned and operated 16 dealerships and other automotive businesses, credentials that he had in common with many of ABT's top executives. This gave the company's leadership a unique understanding of both the dealers' and the customers' requirements. ABT had done its homework well. Given the fragmented market with 49,000 dealers (of all kinds) it could put down the problems clearly as:[6]

- a perceived overabundance of dealers;
- increasing advertising and marketing costs;
- high-pressure sales tactics with consumers;
- large investments by dealers in real estate, construction and other expenses and;
- highly negotiated sales process with relatively little information regarding manufacturer's costs, leasing costs, financing costs, etc.

Thus, the values it hit upon for the consumers were: information on specifications, selective dealers involvement, insurance and financing options, resources such as Kelley Blue Book, Edmund's, IntelliChoice, etc. – in all, a different vehicle purchasing experience. It also sought to close the loop within ten days of the submission of a customer's purchase request by contacting the customer again by e-mail to check the quality of his or her experience.

Dealers benefited from this system by saving costs, getting more leads, better customer relationship opportunities, and better leads in the form of better educated customers, and through the Dealer Real Time system they could get better tracking of sales, inventory, customer solicitations, their responses, and other communications. The dealers were also able to deepen customer relationships. Further, the partnering dealers got a larger geography than the one allocated by the (concerned) manufacturers. ABT also invested in dealer training and support services to ensure a consistent, high-quality vehicle purchase experience. It hosted over 1,000 customizable dealership websites. Customers were able to arrive at the dealers with their loans pre-approved, their credit verification documents in hand, and the loan paperwork waiting for them. This, combined with firm pricing, enabled dealers to turn prospects into customers sooner.

In February 2001, ABT launched iManager, a multi-functional dealer management system offering consolidation of the multiple lead tracking, customer relationship management (CRM), and reporting systems now bedeviling dealership Internet departments. Developed in conjunction with, and tested by, dealerships throughout the country, iManager helped to improve dealer response time to Internet customer requests, provided dealers with turnkey customer retention programs, maintained databases of customer information, deal status and Internet department performance, and allowed dealers to eliminate several of the lead management systems they employed.

In essence, ABT completely changed the distribution model from a "linear" flow of vehicles from the manufacturer to the customer via the dealer, to a "star" network where all partners were connected. The traditional relationships between customers and dealers and those between dealers and automobile manufacturers stand challenged and changed. The response of automakers such as GM to set up their own online retailing services adds an additional dimension – the contact between the customer and the manufacturer – something that did not exist before. The models are shown pictorially in Figure 5.1.

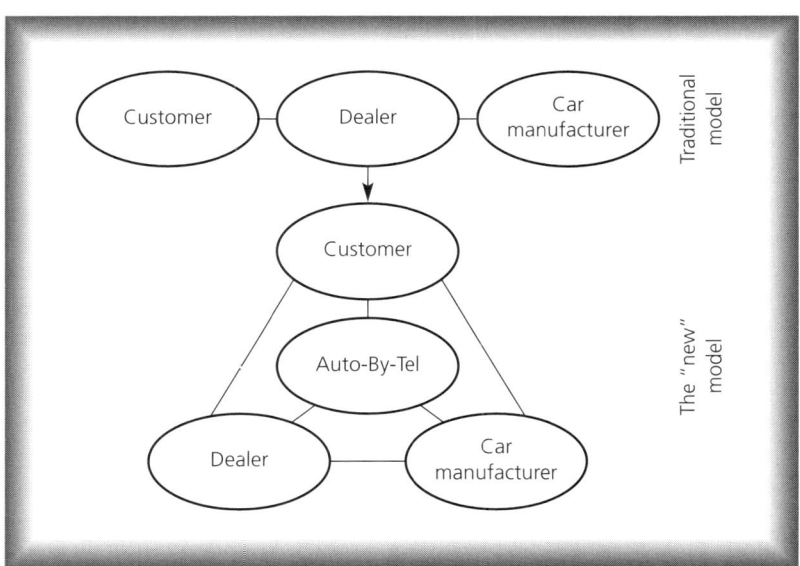

Figure 5.1 Changes in automobile retailing

ABT was over 5,000 dealers strong in 2000 in its dealer referral network. In the same year its revenues stood at $60 million compared to $40 million in 1999. The figures reflected an increasing base of dealers as well as higher monthly fee realization from dealers. The dealers paid a fixed one-time and a small monthly fee and that formed a majority of ABT's revenues. It also allowed some dealers to outsource the closing of the vehicle purchase for a fixed fee, in the range of $100 to $300. By 2000, Autobytel.com had become the seventh-largest generator of automotive sales in the United States, just behind GM, Ford, DaimlerChrysler, Toyota, Honda, and Nissan. Autobytel.com had also been ranked #1 in Dealer Satisfaction with Online Buying Services for three years in a row by J.D. Power and Associates.

Innovative expansion

Access to the ABT website was without charge to the consumer and came without any attached strings – no obligations, no hidden fees, and no clubs to join. ABT eliminated the intimidation often found at dealers, including unpleasant negotiations with multiple layers of salespeople and managers. Links from the ABT site provided easy access to the top automotive information sources such as AutoSite, Kelley Blue Book, Edmund's, and IntelliChoice. Known to provide comprehensive unbiased automotive information, these third-party resources allow the client to query and obtain information on the vehicle of interest. In addition, ABT put out a Weekly AutoMarket Report, which contained advertisements, incentives, and rebates announced by manufacturers as well as articles from top automotive journalists.

Once the buyer was in agreement with the offer or quote made by ABT's dealer, and had consented to its financing options, all the paperwork and other formalities were already completed upon his or her arrival at the dealership and he or she could drive away with his chosen car in less than an hour! Figure 5.2 illustrates the process used at ABT to carry out a sale.

Noted an ABT customer, Michelle V. Goldstein:[7]

> I can't believe this! Yesterday afternoon at 4:15 I found out about ABT – by 7:00 pm I received a call from the dealer and at 11:00 am this morning I picked up the car I really wanted and paid a great price – I don't think I have ever been this satisfied, in the many years that I have been purchasing cars.

"I don't think I have ever been this satisfied, in the many years that I have been purchasing cars."

Ever since its inception, ABT had grown through the introduction of new and innovative services made possible by strategic alliances with partners on and off the Web in the auto industry, achieving an extraordinary growth rate.

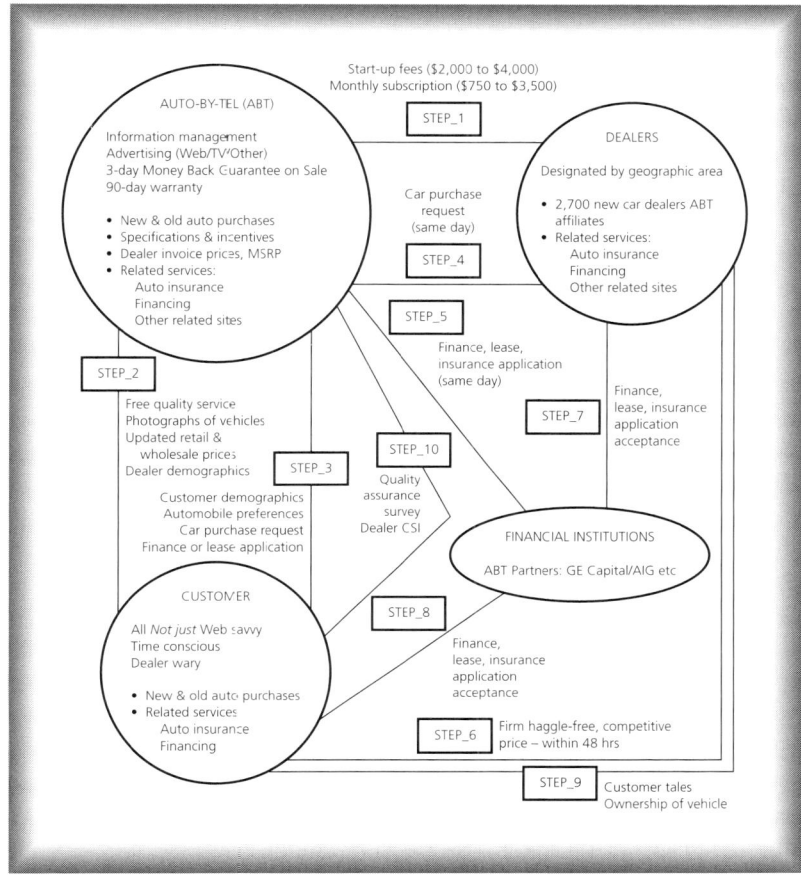

Figure 5.2 Auto-By-Tel's sales process

ABT rolled out its Certified Used Car CyberStore in March 1997. A sophisticated CyberStore search function enabled consumers to find and purchase high-quality used cars by employing geographical area, make, model, price, class, and year of vehicle as search criteria. The CyberStore only stocked used vehicles that had been put through a severe 135-point dealer Certification Program designed to protect consumers. ABT's confidence in the Used Car CyberStore vehicles was backed with a 72-hour 100 percent Money-Back Return Policy and a 3 Month/3,000 Mile Home-and-Away Warranty from its Accredited CyberStore dealers. A travel repair service was available throughout the United States and Canada via the ABT Accredited Dealer Network.[8]

In June 1999, it launched service.autobytel.com to empower consumers with cost-effective and efficient processes for dealing with common service and maintenance issues. It offered accredited service centers and the ability to schedule service appointments online. It also provided an Electronic garage where consumers could store and receive information about their cars and trucks, such as service reminders and lease-related information. Here again, participating service centers had to respond to consumers within 24 hours with competitive no-haggle service prices. It had over 1,500 service centers.

ABT also provided supplementary services such as options for vehicle financing and insurance. Consumers could receive real-time quotes for insurance coverage from InsurQuote Systems Inc. and submit quote applications online. ABT's financing and leasing division, ABTAC (ABT Acceptance Corporation), opened for business in February 1997. Randy Ellspermann, Chief Operating Officer of ABT Acceptance Corporation, added:[9]

> Car shoppers tend to comparison shop the price of a new car, but rarely do they think to do the same with financing. We want consumers to be aware that the cost of financing can greatly impact the cost of the car. At ABT's website, car buyers can shop and compare ABTAC's financing using independent sources to determine the lowest rates.

After researching their vehicle of choice and comparing financing rates with the Bank Rate Monitor, car buyers could submit an optional credit application along with their Purchase Request. The application was then transmitted to the lender whose approval was sent back to both the customer and the ABT Accredited Dealer. A double firewall and state-of-the-art encryption technology ensured system security as well the privacy of the customer's personal financial information. ABT claimed that the pre-approved financing through ABTAC and vehicle delivery at an ABT Accredited Dealer took less than an hour. Peter Ellis described it as:[10]

> What better complement to no-hassle car buying than no-hassle financing. Car buyers want to avoid any frustrations and delays at the dealership level; no one likes to sit around while their credit is being scrutinized. With ABTAC On-line Financing, approvals can come within minutes after the credit application is submitted. It's free, it's easy and the rates are great.

In February 1998, ABT completed the Internet car-buying equation by adding to its repertoire an after-market sales service and an extended warranty program: ABT Platinum Plus Service Agreements. With this announcement ABT filled a gap in easy accessible information about after-market products, including accessories like roof racks, custom wheels, and security systems. ABT research suggested that customers wary of the traditional sales channels for these types of products would be attracted to their new service. Even dealers stood to gain by saving on the sales personnel overheads for keeping these accessories in their product range. Third-party vendors were undercutting dealer prices, thus cannibalizing dealer sales in this segment. With ABT's after-market program, Accredited Dealers would be able to reduce overheads, because the customer was now buying financing and after-market products online without the traditional sales pressure, and thus recapture that customer's business. The ABT Platinum Plus Service Agreement allowed consumers to build an extended warranty product in accordance with their individual coverage and pricing needs – before going to the dealership. In accordance with other ABT services, the consumer was in complete control of the buying process.

Transforming dealership rules

ABT built and worked continuously with its Accredited Dealer Network to transform the traditional sales model. Dealers accredited by ABT established an ABT Department where an ABT Manager, not a traditional salesperson, received the client. According to Mark Lorimer, ABT's Chief Operating Officer, the no-haggle policy among its dealers attracted customers to ABT's website. ABT dealers subscribed to the program (to access what is essentially a customer referral service) by paying US$2,000 to US$4,000 in initiation fees in addition to US$750 to US$3,500 a month. To ensure quality service and top attention to the information-empowered Internet consumer, ABT pre-qualified its Accredited Dealers and provided them with extensive training, including coaching at its exclusive ABT University! Ellis believed much of ABT's dealers' satisfaction was owed to its extensive dealer training programs (21 regional sessions each month) which are designed specifically to educate dealers on reducing costs and passing that reduction on to Internet consumers.[11] In addition, ABT employed a quality assurance application that monitored dealerships for response time and consumer satisfaction. All dealers were required to maintain high CSIs (customer satisfaction index).

ABT estimated that its service cut dealer overhead by US$900–1,100 per car in advertising, staff salaries, and sales commissions. Average new car dealers typically made US$1,800 to US$2,500 gross profit per car, while ABT dealers made just a few percentage points because of their focus on low sale prices.[12] Nevertheless, even though ABT's dealer revenue was assessed to lie only between US$300 and US$500 per car, it implied more profits when lower costs and larger sales volumes were taken into consideration.

> ABT's success can be attributed to several facts:
>
> - Customer orientation: the service and site were designed to respond exactly to what the customer wanted: low cost, hassle free and speed, without salesperson pressure.
> - Innovative, user-friendly, creative sites: while others only used the Web as appendages to the traditional sales process, ABT actually constructed the site so that a complete purchase (including financing) could be realized.
> - Quick deal closing: this came from the Real Time System where all requests were constantly tracked and responded to. This, coupled with the zero negotiation process with very little paperwork for the customer, made him or her appreciate this point.
> - Competitive pricing: lowest prices in the market, coupled with the most comprehensive service – this was easily the core of what the customer looked for in the company he or she chose.
> - Expertise: this came from their dual understanding of both e-commerce and the auto-retail industry. The rigorous training imparted to participant dealerships also played a major role.

Obviously, the issues that formed the foundations of ABT were nothing new. Ellis just saw an innovative solution to these issues in the Internet – something that made the entire process both more effective and efficient. But even Ellis could not have imagined the scope of the changes wrought by the initiatives he started in 1995 in just five years. It is perhaps now time to see how GM reacted to this challenge by an Internet upstart.

General Motors – unbecoming Goliath

GM leads the global automotive industry through the activities of its automotive business segments: GM-North American Operations (GM-NAO) and GM International Operations (GMIO). GM-NAO designs, manufactures and markets vehicles primarily in North America under the well-known brands of Chevrolet, Pontiac, GMC, Oldsmobile, Buick, Cadillac, and Saturn. GMIO meets the demands of the customers outside North America with vehicles designed, manufactured, and marketed under brands such as Opel, Vauxhall, and Holden. While a major portion of GM's operations is derived from the automotive industry, GM also has financing and insurance operations, and produces products and provides services in other industries as well.

Life has not been easy for GM in the past couple of decades. Besides being forced to compete against more agile and cost-efficient Japanese competitors, GM has frequently been criticized for having become big and complacent. *The Economist* magazine had this comment on the challenges facing GM in the late 1990s:[13]

> All empires contain the seeds of their own destruction. The ideas on which they were founded cannot adapt to changing times... Nowadays, General Motors' sole claim to imperial status is size: its 608,000 employees and $166 billion in sales... Today, GM pops up in management books only as an example of what not to do – blamed for not introducing products quickly enough, for poor labor relations and so on... the suspicion remains that the firm's leaders – all GM men practically since birth – still think that the firm is too big ever to lose its dominance.

Against this background, it was not surprising that many experts cast reasonable doubt on the success of GM's attempts to forge a leadership position in Cyberspace. In October 1997, GM surprised many by becoming the first major auto manufacturer to create a consumer-focused online service, called GM BuyPower. The response from GM had come two years after ABT invented online automotive purchasing, in 1995. Though late in adopting the Internet, GM had a long history in technology investment. It was unique in having spent enormous time and money in creating advanced automation systems for automobile manufacturing – so much so it had helped create one of the largest robotics companies in the world, GMF Robotics Corp., a 50-50 joint venture between GM and Fanuc Ltd, a Japanese manufacturer of machine controllers and robots. However, not all of its technology investments had yielded stellar results in work-floor productivity and many of its investments in robotics in the 1980s were later criticized as white elephants. Would GM's forays into the Internet prove different?

GM realized the way it needed to respond – not to ABT but to the opportunity that the Internet was.

GM's BuyPower was initially made available in California, Idaho, Oregon, and Washington. It attempted to put the consumer in the driver's seat. GM BuyPower users could easily compare features of more than 100 of GM's current models and carry out many other customer-oriented services.[14] The purchaser could make his or her own feature-for-feature comparisons between any GM car and comparable models from other companies. This benchmarking by an independent third party added credibility to the information at the site and helped to create trust. From any vehicle detail page, the customer had the ability to locate a Certified GM BuyPower dealer and search its inventory to determine the availability of a specific model. Customers had the option of selecting a specific dealer or could allow the system to select the three closest dealers.

The final step in the GM BuyPower buying process facilitated the face-to-face interaction to actually complete a transaction and deliver a car. Buyers could take a test drive once they had the confidence that they were truly interested in the product. Dealers could focus on providing the best service because the "price haggling" factor was removed from the sales equation.

Things moved rapidly for GM after the online launch. In August 1999, it took the ambitious step of creating e-GM. It was created as the nucleus for the new opportunities. GM had by then realized that it needed to respond not just to ABT but also to the opportunity that the Internet was. e-GM planned[15] to revolutionize the way the world's largest automaker sold vehicles and teach its departments how to work in "Internet time." Mark Hogan, GM's former VP of small-car operations, and e-GM president, noted, "Our goal is to change from an automotive company operating at automotive speed to one that moves at Internet speed."[16] e-GM subsumed GM's BuyPower online shopping site, OnStar in-vehicle wireless technology, and GM Acceptance Corp. online car loan application.

Celebrating the first anniversary of the 150-person unit in August 2000, e-GM president Mark Hogan proclaimed success on many fronts. But he also lamented the considerable obstacles facing e-GM. The biggest problem for e-GM, according to Hogan, has been trying to integrate the unit's dotcom speed with the rest of GM.

> Key strengths of GM:
>
> - The strength of the hard part – existing operational infrastructure, brands, dealer network, and other assets.
> - An early commitment to deploy the Internet and considerable experience in technology investment over the years.
> - New initiatives in collaborative work across partners through alliances.

"We've been working hard on the culture piece. We want everyone in the company to be thinking about what the Internet can do to make us a more effective company," Hogan noted. "We underestimated the importance of the training and integration piece with the traditional business. It's the No. 1 challenge."

Within the constraints, e-GM workers and those at Onstar, GM's mobile roadside assistance program, had compensation packages more heavily weighted toward stock options and other merit-based rewards than other GM employees. And e-GM, though it may not have been operating on the storied "Internet time" of Silicon Valley, did operate much more swiftly than the rest of the company. It forged a deal with AOL in January 2000 in roughly six weeks. "In the old GM, we would have never been able to do that," commented Hogan.

A transformation for sure

As part of a test program,[17] GM introduced seven car dealers in the Minneapolis area to selling Oldsmobile cars and trucks to customers via the Internet. Buyers were able to configure a car, select a dealer, and get a guaranteed price – all via the Web. The system promised to supply such customers with their built-to-order vehicles within 20 days for those buying the Oldsmobile Alero model. Through the normal channel it would have taken 55 to 60 days for delivery.[18] It guaranteed a maximum price,

> "Our goal is to change from an automotive company operating at automotive speed to one that moves at Internet speed."

which was below the sticker price, based on recent transactions in the region and dealer availability. The test program required a dealer to handle the final paperwork. The results of the test was to be an important input in GM's plans to bring the offering to the rest of the United States by the end of 2001. In May 2000, Ford carried out similar tests in Canada for its Windstar, Taurus, and Focus models.

In the context of GM, the most significant part of the "reaction" to ABT, and the online opportunity in general, was that GM did not want to cede control of customers to a third party.[19] It wished to build its direct touch with customers. Its plan for the Internet was to improve consumers' experiences by enhancing what was available to car buyers. The Internet was used to offer a range of goods and services, including order tracking, add-ons such as floor mats and accessories, after-market parts, maintenance and service, and in-car Internet access. Tighter relationships with customers were intended to provide GM with greater cross-selling and up-selling opportunities.

To succeed, it intended to control everything from the point of sale to the production line and more. It was planning to serve as an application service provider for the dealers to minimize the risk of inconsistent image to customers. All dealers do not have either the right resources or the right knowledge to design an attractive web page that contains accurate, well-organized and easily accessible information. They may inadvertently create confusing pages that may damage not only their own, but more importantly GM's brand image. GM's approach would enable it to maintain brand consistency for products and services across all sales channels. It also would give GM control of all opportunities to gather consumer preferences and personalization data, and would avoid discrepancies in price information, which could lead to the loss of a customer to competition. GM's managers thought that repeat customers, especially those who were buying a second car and had already had good experiences with their first GM vehicle, would prefer going through a site dedicated to GM instead of a third party. Ron Clauden Jr. of Valley Pontiac-GMC-Buick in Auburn, Wash., was one of the dealers GM consulted in creating the program. He noted:[20]

> If providing information this way frees up one of our salespeople to focus on selling a car, then it's worth the effort.

GM also started using the Internet to bring innovative facilities for customers. For instance, by 2001 at least 1 million people were using OnStar, and that number was expected to grow steadily to 4 million users by 2003. Originally an expensive option available only on the highest-end Cadillac vehicles, GM has installed OnStar as a standard feature or part of an optional package on 32 of its 54 vehicles for the 2001 model year. GM has also supplied OnStar as an option on 2001 models from Toyota's Lexus luxury division and 2002 models from Honda's Acura division. A one-year subscription to the safety and security package, including stolen vehicle tracking, remote door unlock and diagnostics, as well as emergency roadside services, was $199 per year. A premium package, which added "concierge" services for event tickets, route support, reservations services, and other conveniences, cost $399 per year. Onstar featured the Virtual Advisor, the world's first platform to deliver Internet content into vehicles. Using state-of-the-art and easy-to-use speech technology, Virtual Advisor recognized voice, and read e-mails, news, sports scores, stock quotes, or local weather by simple voice commands. "OnStar is the benchmark in delivering safety, convenience and information services, and this announcement is a natural extension of our intent to maintain leadership in this space," OnStar president Chet Huber commented proudly at the Convergence 2000 conference in Detroit.[21]

In fact, by the end of 1999, GM and other automobile manufacturers had realized the power of the Internet in other areas of the automobile industry, for example in streamlining the design and manufacturing operations. GM and Ford first announced radical restructuring plans for their supply chain in November 1999. "Suppliers will not be coerced into joining the exchange – this will be a 'pull' system … They will see it as the only way to do business," noted Jacques Nasser, Ford's CEO. Harold Kutner, GM's purchasing chief, was more candid: "This will be a requirement for our supply base. For those who buy from us and sell to us … this is the only way we are going to do business." By the end of 2001 GM expected to conduct all of its purchasing through the TradeXchange site while Ford announced the creation of AutoXchange for similar reasons. Interestingly, the two merged in February 2000 (with DaimlerChrysler also joining in) to promote a global supply chain system, called Covisint, for the automobile industry.

Covisint, an online marketplace, was expected to simplify the vast amounts of paperwork and time automakers spent on managing purchase orders and supplier relationships. The automakers that support Covisint (Ford, DaimlerChrysler, GM, Renault, Peugeot Citroen, and Nissan) spend an estimated $300 billion on parts and related expenses at 30,000 suppliers each year. The goal – enabling auto buyers to order a vehicle built exactly to their specifications directly from the factory – is probably five to seven years away. But when it happens, it will enable the automakers to save staggering sums of money – $20 billion per year for General Motors alone, according to some industry estimates. It will also enable automakers to respond much more quickly to buyer demands, which are changing more rapidly than ever before.

> **Buying a car is not like buying a stereo or television. It's much more emotional.**

GM is also looking at the efforts of other automobile manufacturers. For example, Toyota created a portal for itself – Gazoo.com. Of course, this does go the GM way – direct connection with customers – but way farther. "Gazoo.com is one of the viable consumer sites out there,"[22] notes Shu Nung Lee, an auto analyst at Lehman Brothers Japan, "Toyota is well positioned to take advantage of any Internet upside." "We aren't competing with automakers, but with companies like large electronics manufacturers, retailers and (service) providers," added Toyota Director Akio Toyoda. Japan's biggest automaker intended to place terminals, called "G-Towers," which are linked to its Gazoo.com site, in 13,000 convenience stores and 5,500 of its dealerships starting in November, 2000. The terminals, which sell music, concert tickets, travel services, household appliances and even cars, are a way for Toyota to reach young, Web-savvy consumers and boost revenue at Gazoo.com.

Eventually, the company's goal is to create a nationwide network of 30,000 terminals, up from the 1,332 already set up in domestic dealerships. Using Gazoo.com and the G-Tower "is one way to sell cars in a hassle-free, customer-friendly environment," comments Toyoda, noting that some people didn't like the full-service approach used at auto dealerships in Japan. General Motors, the world's largest automaker, on several occasions has said it would like to participate in Gazoo.com to market its vehicles and services in Japan via the Internet. Toyota said it regarded GM's comments as a "voice of support" for Gazoo.com. "We're still considering it, but it's up to our customers to decide whether we should be showing other automakers' models, and how it would contribute to our main business," said Akio Toyoda. Toyota's in-house Web specialist, Jim Pisz added:[23] "The Internet has become our second-largest source of leads, right behind inbound telemarketing."

Issues

In spite of the race to embrace the Net, most automakers have only started the journey to adopt the Net. Many of the early attempts were feeble and constrained by legacy mindsets. For example, when in early 1997 Chrysler inaugurated its Get a Quote website, accessible initially only to buyers in California and Maryland, the website was not seen as a sales tool, as noted in a company statement:[24]

> We see the Internet at this point as a channel that allows us to make contact with customers we might not have access to otherwise and put them in contact with our sales channels. But we do not see the Internet as a direct sales tool. Buying a car is not like buying a stereo or television. It's much more emotional. It would be very difficult to dispose of a trade-in vehicle on-line. Or, for that matter, to test-drive a new vehicle.

However, as the case studies about Auto-By-Tel and GM demonstrate, the industry is slowly but surely being changed by the Internet. In the automobile industry the trigger for innovation came from a new entrant (ABT), but the innovation was absorbed and improved upon by GM and others. The case studies show how legacy companies can adopt Internet-based business activities, on the condition that they can develop the appropriate mindset to innovation. While we do not want to explore at length at this stage what this requires, we just want to point out that GM had to change its organizational culture and had to learn to treat its customers in a very different way.

Interestingly, GM and ABT have come together for a novel initiative. In March 2001,[25] the two announced they had selected the Washington DC area and the Chevrolet brand to conduct a 90-day test of the locate-to-order business model announced by the two companies a month ago. The test program would combine the independent all-makes, all-models capability of Autobytel.com with a new GM locate-to-order vehicle inventory model. The test was designed to help GM and its dealers learn how to create an effective online locate-to-order system that displayed a market area view of available inventory and enabled consumers to purchase selected vehicles at a dealer-set online e-price. Vehicle buyers would not only be able to find a Chevrolet car or truck they wished to purchase, but also select a preferred Chevrolet dealer to complete the sales transaction. "Testing this new locate-to-order model on the Autobytel.com site will help us determine the best way to sell Chevrolets to online vehicle buyers," noted Gerry Ryan of Sport Chevrolet.

So David and Goliath are teaming together to possibly reshape the industry yet again. There is a lot of potential for innovation. And a lot remains to be done. Auto manufacturers have still a long way to go in utilizing the richness of the information interface via the Internet with customers and linking that to their operational infrastructure. There is little integration of customer preferences and requirements into product design processes and production planning schedules. Most are only starting to move up the Internet learning curve.

Notes

1. "Who will deal in dealerships," *Economist*, February 14, 1997: http://www.economist.com
2. "Who will deal in dealerships," *Economist*, February 14, 1997: http://www.economist.com
3. http://www.arktimes.com/022098coverstory.htm
4. http://www.autobytel.com/index.cfm
5. http://www.popularmechanics.com/popmech/auto2/98CBG/98CBGFBM.html
6. From 10-K field with the USSE commission and provided on www.autobytel.com
7. http://www.autobytel.com/backgrounder.cfm
8. Auto-By-Tel press release, Washington, DC, April 28, 1997, www.autobytel.com/april28.cfm
9. Auto-By-Tel press release, Irvine, CA, June 9, 1997, http://www.autobytel.com/june9.cfm
10. Auto-By-Tel press release, Irvine, CA, June 9, 1997, http://www.autobytel.com/june9.cfm
11. *Software Magazine*, December, 1997 – Electronic Commerce, http://www.sentrytech.com/97issues/Dec97/sml27f6.htm
12. Auto-By-Tel press release, Corona del Mar, January 15, 1996, http://www.autobytel.com/jan15.cfm

13. "The decline and fall of general motors," *The Economist*, October 10, 1998.
14. www.gmbuypower.com/cgi_bin/setframe.pl?about
15. Based on the report by Rachel Konrad, "e-GM sputters with mixed reviews of its first year," CNET News.com August 2, 2000.
16. Wilder, C. "GM forms unit to boost electronic-business effort," *Information Week*, August 16, 1999.
17. Luening, Erich (2000) "GM gassing up test program to sell cars online," CNET News.com, September 18.
18. "GM runs trial of online ordering for custom cars," *Bloomberg News*, November 17, 2000.
19. Adam Sarner, Garter Analyst (2000) "Commentary: GM firmly grips the e-wheel," Special to CNET News.com, May 18.
20. http://adage.com/interactive/articles/19970915/article2.html
21. Konrad, Rachel, (2000) "The next Java Frontier: your car," CNET News.com, October 16.
22. "Toyota drives Gazoo site with fleet of net terminals," *Bloomberg News*, September 26, 2000.
23. http://www.popularmechanics.com/popmech/auto2/98CBG/98CBGFBM.html
24. http://hpcc940.external.hp.com/Ebusiness/october/index_auto.html
25. www.autobytel.com

Learning from the past

Innovation: lessons from the past reinforced? 6

Bookmark

Sure, the case studies do not pronounce "all is new." Amazon invested in major warehouses while Barnes & Noble.com drew upon the resources at its parent company to offer "out of print" books. Walmart.com only reiterated its commitment to the long-standing Wal-Mart policies on customer care and service. Similarly, there's nothing unusual about the role of leadership in organizational transformation – good fortune has very rarely successfully transformed organizations – vision and leadership have always been central to transformational changes.

But there is more. There is far more in the case studies that may be common with the past. Some lessons from the past about innovation have been reinforced in the case studies. Let's explore.

A treasure chest of experience

What is at play in the three sets of case studies? Is there anything common across the firms in the case studies? Indeed, there is one – the application of the Internet in their businesses is not of the ordinary kind. They have gone far beyond digitizing their product catalogs on the Internet. They have intervened to innovate their business context and in most cases to transform the guts of their organizations. They have countered the emergent competitive pressures by innovative business models that promise higher value creation.

Before we proceed to elaborate upon the lessons from these case studies, we need to see whether what we observe today is really unprecedented. Have similar things happened before in business history? In other words, what are our past experiences about changes in competitive dynamics following a major disruption in a technological trajectory? For instance, the changes at the beginning of the twentieth century in the automotive industry, or in the 1950s with the introduction of transistors. Let's take the automobile industry.

The lessons learned by nineteenth-century entrepreneurs may actually be a treasure chest for today's entrepreneurs.

By most reckonings, between 1895 and 1905 there were more than 2,000 start-ups in the automobile industry in the US alone, and putting "Motors" in your company's name immediately increased the attractiveness of your company to investors. However, by 1910 the entire automobile industry had gone through a shake-out and only a few dozen companies remained afloat. It sounds familiar, doesn't it? Indeed, it is not the first time that we are confronted with a major disruption in technological trajectories. The lessons learned by nineteenth-century entrepreneurs may actually be a treasure chest for today's entrepreneurs. Can we learn something from these past experiences? At the same time we should be open-minded and ask ourselves whether there are any new imperatives, and opportunities, in the emerging digital-economy.

We argue that the answer is yes to both of the above questions. There are many similarities with other moments in business history where we had discontinuities, but there are also some interesting differences, which create new challenges for the management of innovation in the digital era. This chapter will dig out the similarities. The next chapter focuses on the differences and the subsequent chapters (8–11) discuss the new imperatives in detail.

> Two quick insights
> - Not everything we observe in the Internet environment is "new." We have witnessed in the past other moments of technological discontinuities and incumbent companies can learn from these experiences about how to better manage the integration of the Internet into their business strategies. Be humble.
> - A discontinuity in technology is the occasion to redefine the boundaries of an industry. Incumbents have often a real or purely emotional stake in "their" industry and this holds them back. But the "wiser" ones quickly accept the eventuality and work to cut out the slice of the new cake that should belong to them. They actually speed up this transformation. Be wise.

There is a very comprehensive body of knowledge about how we've managed innovation in periods of technological discontinuities in the past. As a consequence, there is a rich body of extrapolated prescriptions for navigating through periods similar to the one we are experiencing today. Summarizing all of that is obviously beyond the scope of this book. And perhaps even irrelevant, because some of it is quite technology specific. We've chosen to focus in the following sections on four questions that highlight the major issues and associated lessons developed from the literature on the management of innovation and technological discontinuities:

1. The Internet creates a discontinuity in the management of information and communication. **What do we know about management of discontinuities?**
2. Internet-driven innovation is mainly about service innovation (about providing solutions rather than "products"). **What do we know about the management of innovation in service environments?**
3. The Internet is a new technological infrastructure. **What do we know about innovations made possible by new infrastructures?**
4. Any innovation runs into resistance against change. **What are the main drivers of resistance to innovation?**

Management of discontinuity: the technological life cycle

To begin with, Abernathy and Utterback's[1] model may be the best framework to understand the issues in the management of discontinuity. This model, which goes back to earlier economic models, proposes a *technological life-cycle model*. The model is depicted in Figure 6.1.

PART THREE LEARNING FROM THE PAST

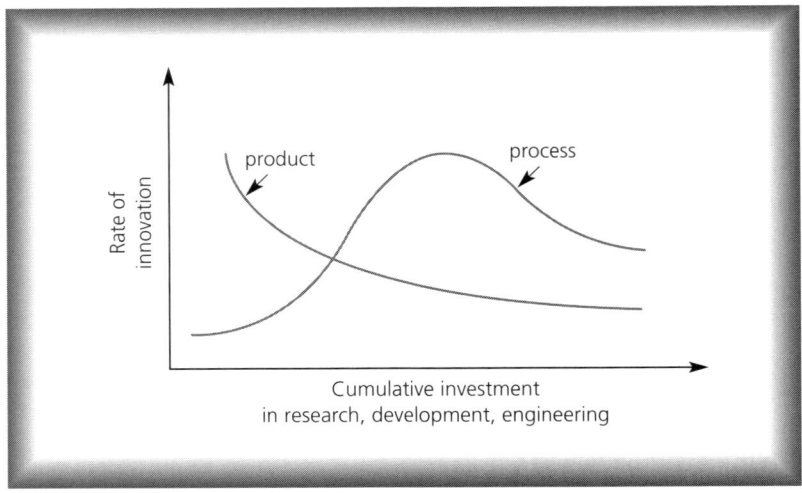

Figure 6.1 Technological life cycle

The unit of analysis of this model is a new technology, or a new combination of existing technologies. In other words, the model takes a particular new technology as the cause and then explores the effects of the same on business dynamics. Typically, the analysis is not limited to a particular firm, or product; it develops the evolution of a set of firms, which apply the new technology or the new combination of technologies. For example, the model could be applied to study the impact of any of these technologies: digital watches in the early 1970s, personal computers in the second half of the 1970s, genetic engineering techniques in the early 1980s, and, yes, Internet applications in the early 1990s. Genetic engineering was perhaps a scientific breakthrough, while the personal computer was not really a new technology, but an innovative combination of existing components such as a keyboard, a microprocessor, a simple monitor, and input/output devices.

Experimentation is key in the fluid phase.

Figure 6.1 describes a qualitative model for the rate of innovation as a function of human and capital investment in research, development, and engineering. The model argues that you can distinguish four phases in the development of new technology. The first phase, the *fluid phase*, is characterized by a spurt of activities in product innovation. The goal is to learn about the true needs of customers – often a complex process of experimentation given two contextual factors: low barriers to entry and the difficulties of conducting market research in an emerging market.

Why are the barriers to entry typically low in the fluid phase? Well, in this early phase, there are no firmly established brands or market structures. Customers who are the pioneering adopters are typically more interested in new or enhanced functionalities and performance. Cost is not of prime importance and expensive capital investments to obtain economies of scale in production are not mandatory. For example, a user of a PC in the late 1970s did not demand system compatibility or complain about high costs. The major concern was to get the latest new system hardware and software that would enhance the capabilities of his or her PC. And the production of those PCs was simple: a garage to assemble freely available components seemed to be enough. The same can be said about the Internet applications in the late 1990s: customers had no preconceived idea of what the Internet should enable them to do, but looked all the time for newer and more exciting sites. And many websites did spring up – frequently in garages and bedrooms.

And why is market research so difficult in this phase? Largely because the customer does not have a clear idea about what the product can do and how much to pay for it. The product's functionalities are not obvious and the customer is searching for both knowing what is technologically possible and how those possibilities can be used to satisfy or redefine needs. Ask yourself what you expected in 1996 from the Internet, and your mind probably goes blank. Worse, you might not even have developed a real interest in its existence then.

The emergence of the dominant design changes the nature of the competition completely.

This fluid phase usually ushers in what is commonly known as a *dominant design*. It has been variously described in the literature, and it may be seen as a particular variation of a product, out of all the variations available, that gains most popular acceptance as the de facto definition of the product features. It is sort of a milestone in an industry's evolution. The product variant that becomes the dominant design embodies the requirements of many classes of users, even though it may not perfectly match the requirements of a particular group of users. It is different from a standard, because in many instances standards are not necessary, and the dominant design itself may allow a lot of small variations around it. However, it does impose, very often, a standard. The breakthrough of the IBM PC with MS DOS as the operating system software is a typical example; the look of a digital watch with its recognizable black plastic housing is another one.

The emergence of the dominant design changes the nature of the competition completely. From competition based on the functionality of the product, one moves to competition based on cost and quality. The challenge is not anymore to define your product, but to offer a product similar to the one from the competition at a lower price and at a higher quality. That requires usually heavy investments in automation, business reengineering, and an efficient organization. This is a period of intensive *process innovation*. Finally, there is a fourth phase in the technological life cycle, when innovation, both in process and product, becomes less relevant to survival in the competitive arena. In this phase, the competition moves to creating *complementary and supplementary value propositions* around the product to create new differentiators.

> Important insights from Abernathy and Utterback's model of the technological life cycle:
> - The first phase of "fluid" innovation requires a learning-driven strategy. A flexible organization is needed to support the search for value-creating opportunities.
> - The fluid phase sows the seeds of the design "coalition" as the quasi-standard starts becoming evident. This leads to the second phase where the dominant design gets established. It requires a good "technology watch."
> - The third phase of process innovation is one of efficiency drives, productivity improvements and other process innovations. Producing the dominant design at a lower cost and higher quality is the goal in this phase.
> - In the fourth phase, the competition moves to creating complementary and supplementary value propositions to create new differentiators.

Technology life cycles in the Internet too?

You may already have guessed correctly that the technology life-cycle model was originally developed for hardware products, and is probably most appropriate for complex assembled products. But the model can, with relevant adaptation, be applied to understand the process of innovation in different segments of the Internet world too. For example, we can see that different segments of the Internet industry are in different phases of the technological life cycle. For example, in the case of Web browsers we may already have something close to a dominant design. It is no surprise

Different segments of the Internet industry are in different phases of the technology life cycle.

then we are seeing a shake-out in these sectors and an increasing emphasis on efficiency and effectiveness. The market for B2B portals is still in the fluid phase and a dominant design is yet to emerge. All kinds of experiments are on – from Freemarket's real-time online auctions for selected suppliers, to incumbent-driven exchanges such as Covisint and eBay's "all-in-one" online marketplace. Many public B2B portals have gone down in the business graveyard and 2001 is witnessing the birth of a range of private B2B marketplaces. The search for a dominant design is in full swing.

If we accept that the technology life-cycle model applies to the Internet world, four observations from the past seem to be particularly relevant to the management of Internet-enabled innovations by incumbents:

1. The "fluid" phase of innovation requires a very flexible organization. Competition is based primarily on the intrinsic functional values you can offer to customers and only trial and error can help: you have to offer a bundle of functionalities to customers, observe how they react, and adapt your product offerings accordingly. We observed this in the portal market in the initial years where companies such as Yahoo! offered several beta versions of their products/services – frequently more than once a month – and then quickly adapted their products/services to customer feedback. This need for quick reaction is further enhanced by competitive pressure. Entry barriers are low and new entrepreneurs constantly join the competitive arena. They offer new ideas and new features. You not only have to react quickly to customers' opinions about your products, but you also need to react to these competitive challenges. This ability to react requires significant organizational agility, and thus entrepreneurial, organic structures.

2. The fluid innovation phase can also be seen as a phase of definition of new industry boundaries. The period after the discontinuity is a period during which the borders of sectors become fuzzy. Sectors are redefined, and the dominant players in the sector are challenged. Was Amazon.com in book sales, and thus a competitor for Barnes & Noble? Or was it actually honing a distribution system, which could be used for distributing other products – such as lawnmowers? As Amazon.com pulled away from selling books and CDs, it entered into direct competition not with traditional bookstores but with mainstream retailers such as Wal-Mart. As this book goes to print, can we define with certainty the competitive boundaries of Amazon.com's business? Is Bertelsmann a competitor of Amazon.com in the book publishing business? Is Sony a competitor of Amazon.com in the music publishing business? Where does retailing end and the media business begin? The boundaries are being redefined.

3. The fluid phase requires a learning-driven strategy as opposed to market- or competitor-driven strategies. Every step a company takes must have a strong learning component. Incumbents are specialists in competitor-driven strategies. But you cannot successfully navigate the fluid phase by matching competitors. You are probably simply not sure about the right competitive set. As we saw in Chapter 3, it took Merrill Lynch a costly few years to realize that Charles Schwab had become its prime competitor. Charles Schwab's success is not the result of a brilliant design, but rather of radical experimentation. Tomorrow, who are the prime competitors for Charles Schwab and Merrill Lynch? E*TRADE? Or Yahoo!? Or yet another "unknown" company? Amazon's concept was not the consequence of a grandiose initial design, but evolved out of continuous innovation based on the daily feedback from customers. The willingness to listen, to experiment, and to learn from these experiments is what led to its success. Customers have to see and experience what's possible to be able to ask for specific products. Incumbents who want to succeed in the Internet world will have to develop the ability to learn quickly.

> **The art of the possible is being constantly redefined by the science of technology.**

4. The fluid phase also sows the seeds of the design "coalition" as the quasi-standard starts becoming evident. A dominant design is rarely the outcome of the action of a dominant player. It may have been the case for IBM when it defined the PC. But even the PC became dominant only or rather precisely because IBM, in contrast to Apple Computer, had the bright idea to open up its design to all its competitors. This open design, which was also strongly advocated by Microsoft at that time, created de facto coalitions to promote the PC concept, and has helped to define the PC as a dominant design for a desktop computing "instrument."

The other phases require a different approach of management, one that is perhaps closer to what established incumbents excel at. The second phase is the one where the dominant design gets established. It requires a good "technology watch," i.e. an analysis of the trends that may lead to the emerging dominant design. The third phase is one of efficiency drives, productivity improvements and other process innovations with more or less stable value propositions. Traditionally, larger and more established organizations are very good at that. Business history is replete with instances of incumbent companies buying up innovative but cash-strapped start-ups and then superimposing their efficient organizational structures and processes to commercialize the innovative new products. One could argue that this strategy underlies Microsoft's success. It rarely innovates itself, but has a great capability of spotting the moment when a dominant design emerges. Once that design is spotted, it captures it through acquisitions, or imitates it rapidly. With its excellent engineering and marketing skills it is then able to roll out that dominant design at high speed and at a relatively low cost.

However, we do stress that we have to exercise caution in applying lessons derived from the technology life-cycle model to the Internet world. The online world consists of many segments and the life cycle is probably evolving differently in each of these segments. Further, the Internet is a wonderful new infrastructure whose capabilities are being constantly enhanced by new technologies and applications. Thus the art of the possible is being constantly redefined by the science of technology. But the model does provide useful insights into broader imperatives for incumbent companies. The need for flexibility, the need to implement a learning strategy, the need for coalition building around the dominant design, and the consolidation that happens when that design emerges are recognizable in the developments in the Internet world in 2001.

The earlier one enters an emerging business the greater the chances of success. Every emerging sector or application of new technologies goes through a phase where "anything goes": barriers to entry are low and entrepreneurs work through trial and error to find out what customers want. An early entry – before the emergence of the standard – allows a firm to buy time in order to experiment with new products in a period in which demand is still volatile, both in volume and the features required.

Moreover, the earlier a company experiments, the easier it will be to create externalities out of complementary assets, e.g., build brand image, develop special competence, etc. and thus create barriers to entry for others. The early entry of Amazon, in the distribution of books, gave it an advantage over Barnes & Noble and other latecomers. This doesn't mean that these barriers cannot be overcome, but it requires significant resources and commitment! Witness how Wal-Mart has used its muscle to power-back its entry into e-tailing.

The successful incumbents will be those that take the plunge early in the innovation game.

An early entry is probably more important in Internet-driven applications than in the traditional hardware world. In the Internet world, more than anywhere else, the "Winner takes it All." And the reason is simple: pure Internet applications are hardly confronted with capacity problems. In traditional businesses, successful innovators are usually constrained by capacity limits and cannot completely fulfill the market demand. This leaves a window of opportunity for imitators who, with a copy of the innovator's product and some production capacity, can capture a part of the market that in fact should market that in fact should have been captured by the innovator. In pure Internet applications, capacity is only limited by the response time of your server, and perhaps the size of your telecom pipe. But both are very light constraints: servers can easily be added and bandwidth is abundant. So if you have a good value proposition, and the customer can be made aware of it, the limit is literally the sky.

Beside capacity, is there any other relevant driver? Well, in many Internet applications networks count: your service becomes more attractive if more users are connected. The more users you have, the more attractive your service becomes and the more users you will attract. eBay, the pioneering auction company in the US, is an interesting example of this. Everybody should be able to organize auctions of products over the Internet. But its early entry has given it such a large number of users that more than 90 percent of auctions go through its site. To be the winner it helps to be one of the first. And of course you need to be excellent too!

Service innovation: the real face of innovation on the Internet

The Internet is an information tool. A tool that can be used for increasing the amount of information exchange between a firm and its customers. As we will argue elsewhere in the book (see Chapter 8), the Internet is making customers co-creators of the products they want. Innovating by exploiting the advantages of the Internet is essentially innovating in the service component of a value proposition. We have seen that in all the case studies. For example, in the GM and Auto-By-Tel set of case studies (Chapter 5), we saw how the automobile sector is moving beyond the simple act of a customer buying a car to a reconceptualization of the process from conception to crusher. Therefore, there is probably something to be learned from how the service industry has traditionally conceived innovation.

The service management literature always has had a bit of a conceptual problem with the definition of a product innovation. Why? It usually argues that process and product are identical in services. Think about the educational services. The product is as much determined by what the teacher has to offer in terms of content as by how he or she goes about delivering that content. In a first-class restaurant we appreciate the food as much as the way we are treated in terms of overall service and attention. All airlines deliver the same product: transport from point A to B with basically similar physical planes. But we know that airlines are all different – they are each different in the way they take you from point A to B, Airbus or Boeing notwithstanding. How a service is delivered is as important, if not more important than what the service consists of. Innovation in services is thus very often the consequence of innovations in the process or the way a service is delivered.

One could even argue that new technologies do not strictly generate new services, but only drastically improve the process of delivery. This may be true at a purely conceptual level. It may be argued that railway systems did not bring a new service, but simply a different response to a deeply ingrained human need to travel, or to transport goods. But we all know that this is a bit theoretical. Railways or airborne transport drastically changed the product offered in terms of travel and transport services. The Internet is also bringing about "new services"; Schwab's online "full-service" brokerage offering is one example.

Conceptually, a technological discontinuity can make changes at three levels in a service:

1. It can alter the place of delivery: very often it enables us to move the delivery from the point of production to the point of consumption. Home banking or financial services à la Charles Schwab bring the transaction from the branch office or the financial adviser to your desk. Distribution of books or other goods via the Internet enables you to make choices at home, and to discuss the merits of a product, through a chat group, again via your computer at any location convenient to you. Internet-based retail has interesting side effects. Many people use it to shop at their convenience, i.e. late at night when the shops are closed. You can also shop for groceries from another continent. Services such as the one offered by houra.com for the French Cora group enables one of the authors to do his grocery shopping in a quiet moment from Singapore, in preparation for his arrival in France three days later. No time lost upon his arrival in France in filling up the fridge. Or you can make your choice of an apartment through a well-equipped real estate agent who can show you the facilities that he or she has on offer via a webcam. One of the major constraints of service providers, i.e. that they were geographically limited, is suddenly disappearing.

2. It changes the qualitative nature of the service: very often it enables the service provider to offer more choice, more flexibility, and at the same time more transparency. The Auto-by-Tel case makes this point – more choice and the possibility of bundling the car with financial services, insurance, after-sales maintenance, add-ons, etc. And just think about the difference between a customer who visits a traditional hypermarket, e.g. Carrefour or Wal-Mart, and one who orders over the Net. The moment you enter a hypermarket, you almost commit yourself to believing that the particular hypermarket will offer all desired products at the best prices. The online buyer does not have to make such an assumption and can easily compare the offerings from different suppliers and buy products from different retailers. And all this probably in less time than he or she would use to go shopping in a traditional supermarket.

3. It can drastically change the relationship between the service provider and the customer. Amazon's electronic bookstore is an excellent example of this. In a traditional bookstore the shopkeeper is in many cases an informal adviser and the customer is basically in charge of the logistics, i.e. selecting the books and transporting them. The electronic bookstore redefines this relationship completely. Chat groups and billboards with readers' comments replace partially the advisory function of the bookseller. It is the fellow reader – "colleague" – who provides the advice, not the librarian.

This last point deserves further elaboration. Traditionally we use a very simple picture to describe the design of a service operation. This is shown in Figure 6.2. Three components are important: the customer, the delivery system, and the support services. In retail banking the service delivery system would be the branch office and the teller window. The support services would be the back office, the information systems of the bank, etc. In education the service delivery system is the classroom. In the hospitality industry it is the hotel room or the restaurant. The support services in education include a library and the kitchen in the case of a restaurant.

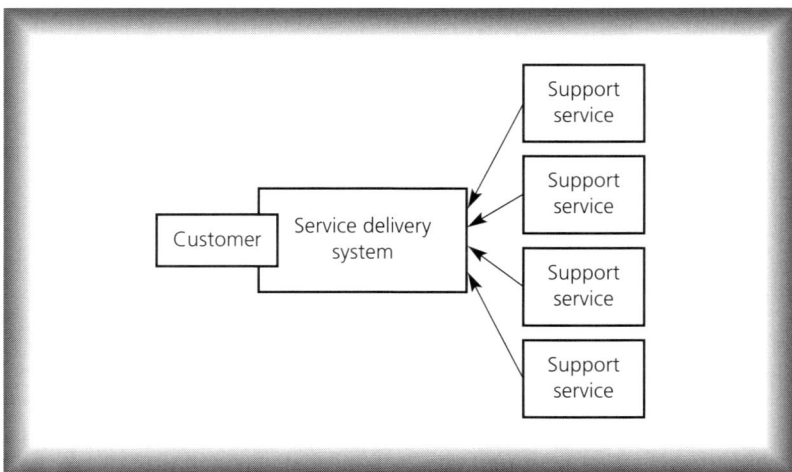

Figure 6.2 Design of a service operation

Services differ from normal production systems because of the overlap (or interaction) between service users (customers) and service providers. In a traditional production system we can separate production from consumption. That implies that one can build a quality control or inspection system in between producers and users. In services there is always a moment of interaction. Even for the smallest bank branch transaction, there will be a direct exchange or "overlap" between the person behind the teller window and the customer. Even in the most boring lecture the student has to listen to the professor in order to "obtain" some education.

One of the most important design parameters of a service system is the degree of "overlap" between customers and the service delivery system. The way an airline treats a tourist flying a charter flight and a first-class passenger is very different. A lecture and a case discussion are two different levels of interaction and two different modes of education. In both cases the difference in service is the reflection of a difference in the degree of "overlap" (or interaction).

A major avenue for experimentation and innovation is the degree of interaction between the customer and the firm.

Innovation in services is often the result of a dramatic change in the overlap between the service provider and the user. Self-service in shopping was a major innovation. It was also a major change in the way a shopkeeper and the customer "overlapped" with each other. E-learning is another innovation: it moves some learning initiatives from instructor-led learning (in a classroom) to resource-based learning (in remote settings).

> Conceptually a new technological infrastructure enables us to make changes on three levels in a service:
> - the place of delivery;
> - the qualitative nature of the service;
> - the relationship between the service provider and the customer.
>
> One of the most important design parameters of a service system is the degree of "overlap" or interactions between customers and service delivery system and this is the area to watch. Generically, there is nothing right about the overlap increasing or decreasing due to a specific technology in a given service.

The Internet infrastructure provides us with many more degrees of freedom in the design of service delivery systems. Interestingly enough, the change can take effect in both directions: an increase or a decrease in overlap! Online trading is an example where the overlap is reduced to the essential (i.e. the customer does much more on his or her own) as compared to the overlap in branch-based stock brokerage. Home banking is another example of reducing the overlap. On the other hand we see that the electronic bookstore, as designed by Amazon, actually increases the interaction. In a normal bookstore you may perhaps have a short chat with the store salesperson and pick up your books. Through Amazon you can contribute to the reviews of the book, understand how the book is related to other publications, learn more on the author, get advice on what other books you should read when you are interested in a particular topic, etc.

Celebrity Sightings,[2] a site for teenagers that combined the fan clubs of several teenage stars from well-known TV series for youngsters in the United States, increased the overlap between the teenage customer and the teenage star, as compared to a fan magazine. One can organize real-time chats with teenage stars, something that was impossible through the published magazines. And the reaction time of the magazine is much longer. A magazine has a regular publication schedule that may not coincide with the high moments of a star's life. A website can inform its fans on a daily basis. Or even faster! A star can carry a webcam and the fan can "live" with the star for part of the day. The Internet offers in these cases many possibilities to play with the degree of overlap between the service delivery system and fans/customers.

Implementing innovation in the Internet world offers many opportunities to experiment and innovate with the overlap between customers and service providers. And the interesting aspect of a new technology like the Internet is that it offers a great opportunity to create major changes in the way we interact with customers. Conceiving and accepting such a different interaction is not an easy task for incumbents: you are probably confident that the way you do it today is the right one. One retailer told us: "You must be mad as a retailer to sell through the Internet. You give up all the advantages that a supermarket has built up. In a traditional supermarket the customer does the picking and transports the goods home. When you sell through the Net you have as a retailer to do the picking yourself and you have to bring it to the customer's home. And that in the knowledge that in a city in Europe more than half of the customers will not be home, and you may have to go a second time. In a sector where our profits are razor thin it is sheer madness to do that." A similar set of emotions can be witnessed today in educational institutions where many professors are skeptical of the effectiveness and benefits of e-learning.

Nurturing technology: innovation through a new infrastructure

We must also look back at some specific discontinuities that bear a close resemblance to the current source of discontinuity – the Internet. The Internet has perhaps little to do with discontinuous innovations in product technology such as the replacement of vacuum tubes with transistors, or horse carts with automobiles. There seems to be greater similarities with what happened when infrastructure-based innovations such as the railway systems were developed. Other examples that bear resemblance are the development of the current hub and spoke system for air transport and the implementation of telegraphy.

When you think for a moment about these examples you will realize that all of them started as an innovation in infrastructure, entailing many product and service innovations later. Steam-powered machines existed before railways were developed. But it was the installation of an infrastructure that enabled these machines to run with low friction and thus in an energy-efficient way. Once the system was installed, railway companies could start innovating with different types of services, and develop special travel arrangements such as holiday packages, overnight sleepers, mail services, etc. Many have argued that the emergence of a telegraph network in the middle of the nineteenth century has had an impact on the world similar to the one we currently observe with the Internet. Before the telegraph, long-distance communications happened through horse courier services, e.g. the Pony express, or with ships. But the immediacy of telegraphic communication enabled companies to change the way business was done on an international basis. Similarly, online database services existed before the Internet was put in place. Compuserve has existed since 1985. But it was the breakthrough of a worldwide Net and an effective communication network that made these databases and online services popular – and that is supporting many innovations.

Typically when an infrastructure is put in place, one can observe a *reverse product life cycle*.

Does the analysis of these specific instances help us develop a conceptual framework about how to manage innovation in the e-era? Typically, when an infrastructure is put in place, albeit gradually, one can observe what Barras[3] has called a *reverse product life cycle*. Life cycles are a common concept in management – the marketing product life cycle is a well-known concept. Barras proposed a somewhat different life cycle that consists of three phases. In the first phase the application of the new technology and the technological infrastructure that it enables are designed to increase the efficiency of the delivery of existing services. In the second stage, the technological infrastructure is enhanced to improve the quality of services. In the third stage, the technological infrastructure assists in generating wholly transformed or new services.

Let's look at a specific example. The sequence of these three stages is what we have seen during the creation of the hub and spoke approach in the airline industry. The early hub and spoke systems were indeed first aimed at improving the cost efficiency of airlines. But soon it enabled passengers to have greater choice, more flexibility, and perhaps increased clarity in the structure of routes. Therefore the quality of air transport improved. More recently we have seen a number of innovations in the airline industry through the linking of these hubs in regional or global alliances. The integration of the Charles de Gaulle airport in Paris with the high-speed train system in France, Belgium, and the UK has enabled companies to sell door-to-door solutions for long-distance transport. And the pooling of hubs by several airlines in global alliances such as the Star Alliance provides the traveler with a new product of integrated traveling. The hubs have also been an innovation in distribution. Airports in Europe used to derive the little attraction they had from duty-free sales. With the creation of the European market these duty-free advantages have disappeared. But hub airports like Schiphol, Copenhagen, and Heathrow have developed into full-fledged shopping centers. The busy traveler who transits through one of these airports has a need to be entertained. Shopping is a solution for that. In fact, spending time in an airport, something that used to be a dreadful experience, has in some cases become pure entertainment!

As we saw in the cases presented in previous chapters, we are witnessing a similar evolution with respect to the Internet. Indeed the survey that we discussed in the introductory chapter suggests that a number of incumbent organizations are organizing transactions on the Internet, and are thus improving the efficiency and perhaps the quality of their relationships with customers. Very few are engaging as yet in the transformation of their business propositions. The similarity in evolution to other innovations based on a new technological infrastructure is obvious. Increasingly, the issue is how can we speed up that evolution.

Riding the cycle from efficiency improvements over quality improvements to new or transformed product offerings is perhaps something that cannot be avoided. There may be no short cuts on that journey. But what an incumbent may have under its control is the ability to speed up that journey. Legacy firms need to experiment with that *sequence* of efficiency improvement, quality improvement in innovation, and transformation in business processes.

Riding down the reverse life cycle: yes, but how?

Speeding up the evolution from efficiency improvement to the development of new business models requires us to reduce the friction that prevents customers from adopting the innovations. What kinds of friction or hurdles exist for innovating in services? Here again, past lessons can guide us. But let's make a little detour into theory first.

> Traditionally, in innovation we have two types of hurdles for innovators:
> - adoption hurdles (e.g. price/performance hurdle), and
> - realization hurdles (e.g. resistance to change).
>
> Adoption hurdles slow down the firm in the rollout of the innovation. Realization hurdles prevent the user from getting the full benefits of the innovation, even after adoption of that service innovation.

Traditionally, in innovation we have two types of hurdles for innovators: adoption hurdles and realization hurdles. Adoption hurdles are hurdles that slow down the firm in the rollout of the innovation. Typical examples are:

- The price/performance hurdle: Is the change in value for the customer sufficient to compensate for the higher or different price structure? Is the value of shopping online indeed higher than going to the store? Is shopping for books via Amazon.com a better price performance proposition than browsing in the bookshelves of Kinokunya, Borders or FNAC? And how much can an industrial buyer save by doing all the purchasing though a B2B portal?
- The risk attached to the investment to be made by the firm: Will the service work? Concerns about the security of the online use of credit cards illustrate this aptly. Will consumers trust the payment system provided? How can you assure the quality of the products ordered through the Internet? eBay, for example, had this problem when it initially launched – how to guarantee that the buyers and sellers participating in its auctions are honest in the description and delivery of goods and payments?
- The ease of use of the innovation such as user friendliness and the availability and quality of service: Anybody who has compared a few Internet sites will have noticed that some sites can be great, but that they can be found next to the bad and the ugly. For example, even today there are large differences in the user friendliness of the sites of different online bookstores. Try buying a PC online. You will have different experiences on the sites of the major PC manufacturers – not to mention on the sites of the different PC retailers.

Adoption hurdles tend to be correlated with the size of the discontinuity in the technology. The more the service innovation differs from the past, the greater the amount of friction and delays.

Realization hurdles are the barriers faced by the users of the innovation in realizing the benefits of the innovation. They prevent the user from getting the full benefits of the innovation, even after the adoption of that service innovation. Typical examples of realization hurdles or barriers are:

- The market structure of users: An oligopolistic market of users usually does not see an advantage in "rocking the boat." Innovations can be tiring and when a cozy group of users can together decide not to exploit the possibility of an innovation, there will be no competitive disadvantage for the members of that group. Fragmented markets usually lead to faster adoption of innovations. There is always somebody who wants to try the innovative approach and get an advantage over peers.

- The lack of potential opportunities created for the trend-setting innovative adopter over the laggards: A student who buys a book over the Internet and has to wait for several weeks has no advantage over his colleague who buys the same book at a similar price from the cooperative store of the university.

- The resistance to change of the user: Using the Internet requires us to change our habits. Many industrial buyers like the cozy atmosphere of a negotiation and a handshake and may not like the efficiency and immediacy of a portal for purchasing. Some Asian managers, who often pride themselves that they get so much done through their informal networks, find Internet-based transactions quite threatening.

Let us explore these issues further in the context of the Internet. Looking at the adoption hurdles, it's obvious that the demand for services based on great innovative ideas will be slow if the price/performance relationship of the service does not provide an attractive change for the user. Many Internet shoppers have given up on online purchases after they realized that while they indeed could order from the comfort of their homes, they had to wait several weeks for the delivery and that the total cost (including delivery) was not cheap. Interestingly, the early innovators in the Internet sector were able to find ample resources in the financial markets to develop new services and price them below or at cost, so that the price/performance relationship remained reasonable.

The breakthrough will only come when a consumer with a problem will first think of the Internet, before looking for other possibilities.

The usability of Internet innovations is relatively good. Sites can be designed quite creatively and software for site design has become user-friendlier. And with the rapid (though uneven) spread of Internet access points and support from governments to enhance computer literacy, accessibility, and ease of use are not the biggest hurdles.

A significant source of friction in the growth of the Internet probably has to do with inducing sustained changes in customer behavior. How can the consumers be seduced into changing their habits? How can industrial buyers and sellers be convinced to use B2B portals? Purchasing two books from Amazon and buying stock for $5,000 via the Internet may be fun experiments, but do they really change the consumer's behavior? The breakthrough will only come when a consumer with a problem will first think of the Internet, before looking for other possibilities. Such a fundamental change in behavior will not come through a few excellent but isolated applications. Consumers may only fully convert to online services if the range of services they find is sufficiently wide and of the right quality so that their risks are minimized. Why would I shop for my groceries online, if in the end I still have to go to the supermarket because my Net-grocer cannot supply the complete range of my needs or products with the right quality assurance?

The solution may well lie in providing comprehensive solutions as described further in one of the later chapters (see Chapter 8). Successful innovation may require the development of bundles of related services and value propositions. The success of Auto-By-Tel is partially due to the comprehensiveness of the services offered. Not all of these services came from the same supplier. To the contrary, the service gave easy and transparent access to a wide variety of service providers related to the acquisition of a car.

Thus what do we know about adoption and realization hurdles? It may make sense for incumbents to go through the six types of hurdles we have pointed out and ask themselves to what extent they will influence the success of innovation in their markets. But there is need for an honest analysis. It is too easy simply to assume that customers will be resistant to change, or that your market is oligopolistic.

The hurdles may also differ from one industry to another. The risk hurdle is perhaps higher in banking than in shopping for fast-moving consumer goods or the sale of industrial products. The immobility of the consumer may be higher for the sale of life insurance (where a relation of trust between suppliers and buyers appears to be a key success factor) than in the trading of shares. And oligopolistic markets will in general move more slowly than fragmented markets.

Action points

1. Try to position your firm using Abernathy and Utterback's technology life-cycle model (Figure 6.1). What evidence do you have to justify your perceived position?

2. If you are in the fluid phase of the technology life cycle, how good is your firm in learning and experimentation? Can you point to successful experiments that have contributed to significant changes in your online strategies in the recent past? Are there any commonalities across these experiments?

3. Do you see any dominant design emerging? What are some key parameters of this dominant design? How much learning does your firm have to do to master this emerging dominant design?

4. The creation of a dominant design usually requires a coalition of partners. Can you identify these partners for your firm? Will they want to partner with you? How will you ensure the success of these partnerships?

5. Identify the components of the service operation system for your firm (Figure 6.2). Explore the impact of increasing or decreasing the amount of overlap or direct interaction with your customers. Should you aim to redefine the nature of the interactions with your customers? And would you improve your competitive position by changing that overlap?

6. Can you position your firm along Barras' reverse product life cycle? Are you satisfied with the speed at which you are moving down the reverse product life cycle? What kinds of barriers are you facing in your journey?

7. To what degree have your customers successfully adopted your Internet-enabled innovations? What kinds of hurdles do they face to adopt these innovations? What can you do to ease the adoption process?

Mantra

The past has given us four useful lessons: the technological life cycle, the concept of innovation in services, the reverse life cycle in infrastructure-based services, and a typology of hurdles for the adoption of innovation and the realization of innovation benefits.

First, our previous experience with technological discontinuities reminds us of the fact that we need more flexible organizations, a willingness to question the existing industrial organization, and the need to build coalitions and communities of partners in order to create the quasi-standard.

Second, the Internet is a great tool to get drastic changes in the design of the overlap between service providers and customers. Mind you, that drastic change can go in two directions: increasing or reducing the overlap! Explore the implications of each carefully.

Third, we know that the implementation of a new infrastructure will enable efficiency improvements, followed by quality enhancements and finally new services. The challenge is to run faster through this sequence.

Fourth, we are convinced that the three major elements of friction in the adoption of new Internet-based business models by the customer will be in the price–performance relationship of the value proposition, the quality of the interaction and delivery process, and the comprehensiveness of the set of services that will be offered to the user.

Notes

1. Abernathy, W. and Utterback, J. (1978) *The Productivity Dilemma*, Johns Hopkins University Press.
2. De Meyer, A., Dutta, S. and Demeester, L. (1997) "Celebrity Sightings," INSEAD case study.
3. Barras, R. (1986) "Towards a theory of innovation in services," *Research Policy*, vol. 15, pp. 161–73 and Barras, R. (1986) "Interactive innovation in financial and business services: the vanguard of the service revolution, *Research Policy*, vol. 19, pp. 215–37.

Innovation as strategy 7

Bookmark

Hopefully, reading the last chapter was reassuring. Not all is new! Many continuously strive to improve their competitive position and seek new opportunities. And there are others who are among the leaders in their industry and yet actively reach out for all opportunities to consolidate their positions. Apparently, and happily, there are a lot of new opportunities.

We observe a new design in the actions of companies as they seek these opportunities. We call this new design – "innovation as strategy." A new design where innovation is not derived from corporate strategy, but rather one where innovation is the corporate strategy.

Let's briefly revisit the cases to see what's new under the sun as far as opportunities for innovation are concerned.

A new design: innovation as strategy

In the previous chapter we explored how some existing concepts about management of innovation also apply to the Internet world. Some of what is described in the three case studies in previous chapters can be explained by what we know from the past about managing innovation. Remember, for example, all of the cases involve service innovation where they let the customers decide the exact nature of the service demanded by letting them do a great degree of "self-service" at their convenience (searching for specific experiences on products, online from home, for example). We saw that Wal-Mart has continued to do what it always did: highest level of customer satisfaction. The "10-foot attitude," lower prices, and the sundown rule all still hold as true. But more is clearly visible.

> **In fact, the Internet may just be another name for innovation.**

We observe some designs in the actions of the companies in the cases that are fundamentally different from having a great "innovation strategy." We have chosen to call those new designs "innovation as strategy." It is epitomized by innovation as a way of life, innovation as the common thread running longitudinally, as well as latitudinally, in an organization. While the two terms, "innovation strategy" and "innovation as strategy," appear similar, the essence of the two cannot be more different in our usage. Innovation strategy is used to represent the sectoral strategy for innovation; the agenda for innovation as derived from corporate strategy. Typically, it's very closely associated with Research and Development (R&D) in products and processes and embodied in an R&D budget and a department. On the other hand, innovation as strategy is used to represent innovation as **the** corporate strategy. Within innovation as strategy, all departmental strategies, such as marketing, human resources, and operations, emphasize innovation as the key deliverable.

One of the simplest manifestations of innovation as strategy is that innovations need not always be "big" in terms of their scope. Many times, small steps prove to be the proverbial "a stitch in time saves a dozen." Back in 1994, when Jeff Bezos started Amazon.com, he hadn't thought through all the details. He did know though that the Internet was slow – people had taken to calling it the "world wide wait." So to sell anything online, Bezos decided he was going to have to make the buying process appealing by offering a value that was way out of proportion to the wait.[1] The defining value Bezos ultimately hit upon was customer care. Its website was built with the visitor's experience in mind. But what really sets it apart is its ability to innovate – to come up with novel ways to service customers and thereby leapfrog its competition. As we saw in Chapter 4, many of these innovations are small individually – but cumulatively they define innovation as the strategy at Amazon.com and help to set it apart from other e-tailers.

A world of twists and turns

Back to the cases! The actions of GM, Barnes & Noble, Amazon, Charles Schwab, and others prove that the world has changed. The cases emphatically indicate that the assumptions behind business models are being questioned and in many cases are being turned upside down. For example, why would products exist in catalogs with definite specifications when it is now possible to tailor the products to individual customer specifications? Similarly, why have prices cataloged in a price list, and "final" when you can offer tailored prices for tailored products? That's where the trials being carried out by GM and Ford become significant. A buyer will be able to configure a car and get a guaranteed and customized price – over the Internet. Why not encourage customers to spread the word for you in the communities they are a part of and gain from their word-of-mouth advertisement of your products? While Amazon.com is an obvious example, Auto-By-Tel's Certified Used Car CyberStore also thrives on the high-quality cars that are posted for sale on the site by Auto-By-Tel's community of users.

The cases are full of decisions reflecting some new dynamics. The pricing strategy of Schwab, for example, may seem simple enough but carries some significant pointers. First, it's unheard of in a competitive industry, like discount brokerage, to drop prices by over 75 percent in one shot. The underlying economics had changed due to the Internet. Second, retaining market leadership in spite of the lack of first-mover advantage and pricing at twice that of E*TRADE's level raises some interesting questions. What do Schwab's customers find in Schwab?

We saw how Auto-By-Tel totally changed the way cars are bought – the time required, the process, the pricing, choices of models and colors, transparency – everything changed, and how GM followed suit. Further, Auto-By-Tel completely changed the distribution model. From a "linear" flow of vehicles from the manufacturer to the customer via the dealer, Auto-By-Tel has used the Internet to create a whole new web of relationships threatening traditional links between customers and dealers and those between dealers and automobile manufacturers.

Charles Schwab,[2] Co-CEO, Schwab, captures some of the new thinking as he says, "Everything we do starts with the question, 'Is that useful to the customer?' We don't start out with, 'Can we make money at it?' That part comes later." Precisely, if the new business model is "profitable" for your customers, it will be profitable for you too. Revenue (and profits) is actually incidental to appropriately serving customers. At GE, Jack Welch is prepared to bend his ironclad rule[3] for financial services, a highly fragmented industry. "Being No. 1 or No. 2 is not as important as being big enough to control your own destiny," says Michael D. Frazier, head of the GE Capital consumer unit building gefn.com, GE's new consumer finance company. Is GE making an undesirable exception? Not necessarily. GE may only be reasserting its leadership – as long as it can "control its destiny" to design and implement its businesses in the way it wants, it feels firm footed.

> We see a clear movement toward value being rotated 180 degrees – customers are moving to the beginning of the value chain.

Broadly speaking, we see a clear movement toward value being rotated 180 degrees – customers are moving to the "beginning" of the value chain. Companies are taking instructions from them! The transformation at Merrill Lynch and GM is a step in that direction. And suddenly the quality of customer interfaces is becoming an important determinant of success. Wal-Mart had undertaken two major revamps of its website in about ten months. And that involved way more than a great design of the website – it called for a new perspective. While revamping its site Wal-Mart was very clear that the website was not to be a leading-edge application of available technologies. It was to make things simple – to make the shopping experience easy. Away from an inside-out perspective to an outside-in perspective, i.e. maximizing the effectiveness and efficiency for customers as much as for the organization itself.

We saw how Auto-By-Tel thrives on the information base that it has developed. Physical players like dealers and financiers act on the information resource of Auto-By-Tel. This separation of the physical and information value chains has proven to be a powerful source of advantage for Auto-By-Tel. E*TRADE displays a similar strategy for online scalability. In order to "empower people" – to help them manage their money better – it has moved from being a broker to a bank, a virtual credit union and an owner of ATM networks. Apparently, it is complementing the online scalability with appropriate offline assets.

Needed: an open mind

Through the case studies we also see how three critical industries – retailing, brokerage, automobile – have dramatically changed in a matter of a few years. Retailing has changed in two significant ways. First, online resources such as customer communities and accumulated knowledge about customers have become critical for growth. Amazon's assertions about not being a book or music company but being a customer company comes from that context. And that's how it became the leading online music store and video store within three months of their respective launches. Second, "click and bricks" is the retailing mode for the future – retailers will have to make the best of both worlds. We know how Amazon has invested heavily in developing a robust and modern warehousing and distribution network. Wal-Mart discovered that the online store enabled the "real" stores to improve shelf-space utilization. And at the same time it helped the online store avoid the "silly stuff" on its site – to obviate situations where it was "spending $9 to ship a 19-cent lip pencil."

> Quick insights
>
> 1 While we can learn from the past we need also the courage to see that a new paradigm is emerging, … even after the dotcom world appears to some to have become a deadcom world. Information and telecommunication technologies can enable us to develop radically new business models and implement them quickly.
> 2 But the new business models call for embracing a new mindset about how an organization works. Culture, organizational structure, people management, partnerships, and technology deployment will have to change.
> 3 The new dynamics in the business environment has its own demands. There is a need to manage a process of continuous transformation and adaptation. Further, organizations are increasingly being designed around knowledge. Knowledge is dynamic and cumulative and requires continuous change and rebuilding of the organization.

The brokerage industry too stands completely redefined. As happened to Schwab, there's no discount broking anymore. It's all one industry now – no regional or discount broking; all are "full service." To an extent we can also see that the brokerage industry itself may be seeing its boundaries getting blurred – remember what E*TRADE and Merrill Lynch are up to! Schwab, for example, is really a full-service brokerage firm again. But a different kind of full-service brokerage firm – the customer is in control, as opposed to the broker. The customers seek assistance if they want – Schwab is in the business of educating and empowering them so that they can help themselves.

PART THREE LEARNING FROM THE PAST

The automobile industry is already witnessing a change in industry dynamics that may be the most significant one after the 1920s assembly line invention. The industry seems to have finally galvanized around its traditional pot of gold – distribution. Distribution is at the center of revolutionary changes this time.

Shift the focus of scalability from physical assets to information assets.

While manufacturing is also undergoing commensurate changes, the automobile industry is an interesting example of how the traditional core processes of an industry are not at the vortex of change as the industry witnesses a metamorphosis.

The story with many other industries is different only in degree. We expect that the Internet will let loose a new "gold rush" – the rush to innovate. In fact, the Internet may just be another name for innovation. And, in spite of what happened to the Nasdaq in the second half of 2000 and 2001, expect it to reach for greater heights in the medium term when incumbents start harnessing the Internet for innovative business models. What meets the eye today is probably a fraction of what the Internet will deliver over the next few years.

Apparently, a whole new opportunity set is up for grabs if you have an open mind about having a close look at your existing business. New opportunities abound which cannot be captured by just restructuring your existing businesses. Traditional strategies built around getting a bigger slice of the same cake are a wrong start. The opportunity is not only to take a bigger slice but also to greatly enlarge the cake. The new business model is about breadth, about stretch. Scalability, not efficiency, is the key word. Efficiency is only a necessary and not a sufficient condition for growth. But there is a catch. The mechanics of securing scalability stands changed. Scaling up a business always meant a commensurate commitment of new investments in physical assets; scaling up business has always been financially intensive. It mostly required capital investments in operational infrastructure. In the emerging scheme of things, however, the opportunity is to drastically reduce the financial intensity of scalability – to innovatively scale up without adding much to your operational infrastructure.

How to scale up the business manifold on the back of existing operational infrastructure (or small incremental investments)? Shift the focus of scalability from physical assets to information assets. Indeed, the essence of the emerging business model is the vision to effectively leverage information resources online. The two relevant online resources are: knowledge about customers and online operational process knowledge. These are the two important dimensions for innovating. Leveraging customer knowledge is about benefiting from

Nobody knows your customers better than you do.

offering better product customizations and creating enhanced customer value; or simply putting more products down the product pipeline to customer communities. Leveraging operational process knowledge is about gaining from integrating the physical operational infrastructure and increasing its connectivity with customers.

We have a word of advice about innovating business models: actively redefine the scope and vision of your current business operations. Again, we have seen this happen in all of the previous cases. In fact, each of the case studies has illustrated how firms have redefined their industries. But how do you do it?

For a start, simply put your current business strategies, processes (and revenues) aside for a while and rework how you would ideally want to conduct your business so as to increase customer satisfaction and maximize profitability. Then go ahead and implement your "ideal" way to conduct business. If a strategy seems logical on paper, it's probably implementable on the Internet. The Internet provides a seamlessly flexible infrastructure backbone that can implement the most imaginative of strategies and processes.

While the Internet can be deployed for making your existing operations more effective and efficient, the real opportunity is business (re)modeling – redefining the scope of the current business model. And how would you redefine the current business model? To repeat – just do what you think is best for your business. Inventing new business models is going to be the most important opportunity for innovation.

Keep in mind that there is nothing inherently right or wrong about a chosen business model. The best business model is business just the way you want it to be. Nobody knows your customers better than you do. Who then best knows how you can maximize your top line and bottom line? The opportunity is to dream your business model. More importantly, if you did not create your business model you will not be able to adapt it along the way – for you'll never fully understand and appreciate the assumptions that went into the design of the business model in the first place.

The four imperatives

Years from now, we may wonder why once we were so skeptical about the impact of the Internet. The changes around us are loud and significant – they're impacting the way we've gone about our lives all these years. But why are we still apprehensive about its role in our lives? Perhaps we're evaluating the new technological changes in the existing legal, commercial, behavioral, social, and personal context. We're not reinventing business models significantly yet! And what do you need to do? We've classified the new opportunities and imperatives for innovation in four broad categories. We briefly introduce them in the following paragraphs and then describe them individually in detail in the following chapters.

> New innovation opportunities can be categorized in four domains:
> - Co-creation: roping in your customer to lead the innovation process.
> - E-nfrastructure: creating the right organization to exploit the unique processes enabled by the Internet.
> - Perpetual metamorphosis: leading the process of continuous adaptation to the changing environment.
> - Institutionalizing knowledge – both customer facing and operations intensive – to stimulate innovation.

The first imperative is how to rope in customers to tell you what to innovate and how to innovate – the involvement of the customer as both a supplier of ideas and the consumer of that ideas-turned-service. We call this co-creation. This is about finding ways to integrate customers into the "operations" of the organization, to open up opportunities to listen to them and educate them about how they may maximize the value being sought. Fortunately, the Internet brings totally new opportunities in customer interface design and implementation. At the same time, pricing is a more strategically serious issue in co-creation than in mass production so that in most orders, if not all, the price realized remains higher than the cost (of production). This is also about building communities of users to serve your customers better.

We saw many examples of co-creation in the earlier case studies. For example, we read how Amazon and M.J. Rose made publishing history as her book *Lip Service* hit the street to become the first self-published novel discovered online; how Toy Quest invited kids to design and create their dream toys. Similarly, behind Wal-Mart's online initiatives is the urge to bring far more choice into the selection available to its customers – to slowly induce co-creation capabilities. From the day it pioneered online trading, E*TRADE's motto has been simple and constant: to empower people, to help customers to help themselves! Co-creation is in full swing. Are you in play? Chapter 8 will help you to develop some winning strokes for this game.

Organizational infrastructure is becoming ever more important in the quest for excellence and innovation. In our view, three elements of the infrastructure – organization, partners, and information technology – provide a highly fertile substrate for growth through innovation. We call this potent combination the e-nfrastructure. Chapter 9 dwells in detail on the vital ingredients of a firm's e-nfrastructure.

INNOVATION AS STRATEGY

We mentioned earlier the uniqueness of the technology infrastructure enabled by the Internet. While technology can create the necessary infrastructure for cross-functional integration, it can't make the infrastructure deliver – it takes people to do that. People, both as leaders and executors. Yes, people structure and culture form the core building blocks of an organization. You may remember the way Schwab and Pottruck took the very hard decision of taking Schwab online. Schwab's leadership position is literally a reflection of the leadership provided by the two. Jeff Bezos and his visionary zeal is of course the energy behind Amazon.

What happens when technology allows organizational boundaries can be reworked quickly, comprehensively, and effectively? Organizational boundaries become a new source of significant innovative opportunities and sustainable competitive advantage. As organizations extend themselves to reach out to their partners, resellers (dealers), and suppliers, they create collective enterprises that tap deeper into collective knowledge and competencies. For example, Auto-By-Tel has its Accredited Dealers connected through a proprietary Dealer Real Time Communications System, enabling instantaneous communication and a quality assurance that monitors dealerships for response time and consumer satisfaction. Life becomes more interesting, doesn't it? Read Chapter 9 for more insights into the emergent e-nfrastructure.

We believe that the Internet fundamentally presents two kinds of opportunities to firms: they can use the Net to make their existing processes more effective and efficient (e.g. banks can reduce cost by moving transactions online) or they can exploit the Internet to redefine the scope and vision of their business operations (e.g. Amazon.com redefined retailing on the Web). While we do not wish to undermine the importance of the first option, it's the second opportunity that's the more interesting one. It's about the need for continuous change. Perpetual metamorphosis is the term we chose for this: the act of undergoing a slow death for rebirth – achieving a break from the past body and soul in order to build a new one. However, having the humility to recognize failures and then metamorphose into yet another stage of experimental evolution is all part of the process of perpetual metamorphosis. If you are ready to metamorphose yourself, read Chapter 10.

Perpetual metamorphosis is not really new. Many leading firms have transformed their guts and core businesses several times over the last decades. IBM is a good example. It was incorporated in 1911 to manufacture and sell commercial scales and industrial time recorders, meat and cheese slicers, and of course, tabulators and punch cards. During the 1940s and 1950s it evolved into an office automation company. Looking at IBM today, it is more of a software company than anything else and one would be hard pressed to find traces of its original roots in its current businesses. The case studies also illustrated some dramatic transformations. In the case of Schwab we have seen how the company evolved by completely changing tracks twice in the past two decades. In 1975, when many brokers increased their commissions, it significantly reduced commissions and gave birth to discount broking and dominated that segment. In 1998, it gave birth to the first "click and bricks" broker and has successfully maintained its leadership in that segment. As you can expect, perpetual metamorphosis is nice to read about, but extremely painful and difficult to execute. Chapter 10 provides you with some guidelines for managing this pain and reducing your risks.

> **Years from now, we may wonder why once we were so skeptical about the impact of the Internet.**

The last imperative is about the role of knowledge in the management of innovation. While innovation sometimes is the result of serendipity,[4] more often than not, it is the result of a systematic focus on collecting, refining, and applying knowledge. Knowledge lies at the root of innovation and innovation creates new knowledge. In fact, there is a strong synergistic relationship between knowledge and innovation. The Internet provides a unique infrastructure that enables successful scope and scale for knowledge institutionalization within organizations and thereby makes it possible for firms to initiate and sustain the knowledge–innovation cycle. Knowledge management is becoming an integral part of the process of managing innovation. Do you know how to master the knowledge–innovation cycle in your firm? Chapter 11 lets you in on some critical secrets.

The knowledge–innovation cycle is probably most explicitly observed in the customer interfaces. The greater a firm's knowledge about its customers, the better the organization's ability to innovate and create new products and services. This is amply evident in all previously described cases, including Schwab, E*TRADE, Amazon.com, and Auto-By-Tel. Of course, knowledge exists in every nook and cranny of a corporation's operational processes and thus firms have to be masters at identifying and leveraging the right knowledge elements. Chapter 11 describes best practices in the knowledge–innovation cycle in two firms – Xerox and Arthur Andersen. Over the last decade, Xerox has built a successful knowledge management system for its customer sales engineers by effectively combining new Internet technology with a clever redesign of the relevant organizational context. Arthur Andersen has spent decades in trying to master the knowledge–innovation cycle. It has probably one of the most well-developed holistic systems for knowledge management across the global corporation and spanning a large range of knowledge elements.

The menu to come

Yet, the whole point will be missed here if these imperatives are looked upon discretely. They blend into each other. They reinforce each other. No firm can sustain innovation by focusing on any one imperative in isolation. The new discontinuity has sharpened the focus of innovation.

Firms now need to work on multiple fronts. The focus of innovation is both inside and outside the organization. Innovation can no longer be defined solely in terms of resource utilization efficiency and effectiveness of production. Innovation is the entire company's business. Innovation is everyone's responsibility. Innovation is the strategy. Innovation as strategy is the new motto for the firm.

The next four chapters explore the above themes and provide the essential substrate for formulating your action agenda.

Action points

1. Think carefully about the phrase "innovation as strategy." What are its implications for your organization? Can you imagine a scenario where your firm has truly embraced "innovation as strategy" as one of its core values? How does your current firm compare with the one in the above scenario?

2. Reflect on your core business processes. Can you identify the information assets related to customer knowledge and operational process knowledge? How effectively are you leveraging these information assets online? What can you do better?

3. We have briefly identified four imperatives in this chapter. The following four chapters detail our views on and suggested action agenda for these four imperatives. Before you start reading the next chapters, answer the following questions for each of the four imperatives:

    a. How important is the imperative for your organization?

    b. What are the strengths and weaknesses of your organization today for this imperative?

    c. What action recommendations would you have for your firm for the imperative?

4. Would you add any imperative to the four that we have chosen to highlight in this book? If yes, try explaining why you think this is important (and send us an e-mail with your response!).

Mantra

Innovation as strategy is the new mantra for corporations. Assumptions behind current business models are being challenged and most sectors find themselves in the initial fluid phase of the technology life cycle. Experimentation is the order of the day. Experiment not in isolation, but in close cooperation with customers. Customers are moving to the beginning of the value chain.

Traditional strategies about taking a bigger piece of the pie (of benefits) are not necessarily correct. The trick is to redefine the scope of your business so as to greatly enlarge the pie. This is not possible without cleverly leveraging the unique operational infrastructure provided by the Internet. The focus of operational scalability has to move from physical assets to information assets.

Continuous change is becoming a way of life. The correct organizational form has to be designed to support this. Leadership becomes central to success, as always! Knowledge has to be recognized as being key for innovation. Knowledge of all types, including customer-facing and operational process knowledge, has to be integrated into the innovation cycle.

Notes

1. See Brown, Eryn (1999) "Selling to customers," *Fortune*, May 24, p. 123.
2. www.Schwab.com
3. Moore, Pamela L. and Smith, Geoffry (2000) "GE catches online fever," *Business Week*, August 28, pp.144 A2–A4.
4. Serendipity refers to the occurence and development of events by chance in a happy or beneficial way. Its origin can be traced back to 1754: coined by Horace Walpole, suggested by "The Three Princes of Serendip," the title of a fairy tale in which the heroes "were always making discoveries, by accidents and sagacity, of things they were not in quest of."

Defining the imperatives

IV

Co-creation 8

Bookmark

The nineteenth-century industrial revolution made a significant impact on business in more than one way. Of course, the most important one was that it enabled mass production. And in the past 150 years mass production has changed life on earth. And what is the Internet up to? Undoing all that! And going back to the pre-industrial order – customized products – but with a difference. The Internet is fueling and facilitating the realization of a fundamentally new way of life – pumping value in individuality – putting a premium on being dictated by our heart rather than a production line!

What does this mean to your business? Customers have to be helped to move out of the audience and on to the stage. Organizational policies, processes, and practices have to change to let customers uncover, for themselves, new possibilities – create most value for themselves by exploring, redefining and choosing what makes best sense for them. How do you get to this? Rope in your customers and then innovate, and innovate! Read on to get some insights into what are some of the innovation opportunities and build on them.

Something new?

Says Rob Vandermark,[1] president and co-founder, "Seven Cycles (www.sevencycles.com) exists because you have asked for more from your cycling. We understand, for we too are devoted cyclists. We are a team of skilled craftspeople – designers, engineers, machinists, welders, and service professionals – whose love for cycling fuels a single-minded desire to build the world's finest bicycle frames and accessories. We want to create the best bicycle you have ever ridden. Let us build the bike you have always dreamed of." Never before had a bicycle company embraced customization so completely. Many said it couldn't be done. But in three years (1997–2000), by reaching deep, and entirely rethinking long-entrenched ideas about design, materials, and the very art of manufacturing, Seven has become the largest custom builder of cycles in the world. From the beginning, the cycling press heralded the Seven as "the best I've ever ridden," "my favorite bike ever," and even, "the perfect bike."

A Seven Cycles customer voices a consenting tone. Mike Tierney,[2] 51, a Canadian fireman and cyclist who rides more than 100 miles a week, took to the Net to search for his dream bike and settled for Seven's "Sola" (a $2,500 titanium frame). He added another $2,500 worth of hand-picked components such as hubs, spokes, etc. to complete the bike. But the cost was offset by the attention Tierney got from Vandermark and his 19 employees. Tierney corresponded regularly by e-mail with Vandermark and he also checked – up to six times a day – on Seven's "Where's my Frame?" web page. Tierney was so pleased with his finished Seven that he posted a photograph of it on his personal homepage. Added Vandermark, "When the customer sends an e-mail, they get an answer from the bike's designer." He also adds, "Part of our success is that we're tied to a business model that includes the Internet." An industry with $5 billion retail sales in the US, cycle manufacturing has been declining there. But Seven is reversing that trend, and perhaps pointing the way to the future of manufacturing.

Do you see something new in the interactions between Tierney and Seven? We think that the level of collaboration between the two is not representative of one between customers and producers. Tierney was a welcome "participant" in the production processes at Seven. In fact, Seven has developed a unique production system specifically for upholding the true meaning of "custom": made to order. However, if you prefer greater simplicity, you can still enjoy the superior quality and benefits of a handcrafted Seven by choosing from their extensive Signature Sizes^{TM}.[3] These, too, are built to order; allowing you to specify any number of custom features. Importantly, building frames to order isn't something Seven does on the side; it's all it does. And

> **The era of individuality has arrived.**

no less important – it does not charge extra for a custom, and all Sevens are priced comparable to other frames in their class. And remember: what did the collaboration manifest itself in? A pleasantly possessive Tierney. Are you wondering, "Why wouldn't I have a frame made to order?" You should.

You may not anymore accept products "as they are." Though you always intended to buy solutions to your specific needs and likes, you ended up with "products" – the closest substitutes to your needs and likes. Going back to Seven's example, if you had a voice in your frame's creation[4] – in its performance, fit, and comfort – wouldn't you be sure to get what you want? You deserve to get the performance, fit, and comfort (and the style, of course) you need in your cycle. The Internet will enable you to be listened to in whatever affects you. The Internet has indeed heralded a major revolution in the very definition of products, and major innovative possibilities are sweeping the design and delivery of products.

The most important manifestation of the same is the growing "destination-bound" capabilities – a product is made for a given destination (customer). To take another example, Dell lets you "customize your Dell system" – choose your monitor, digital camera, power protection, ready ware, software, etc. for each of the models. The PC that you will ultimately get would be made for you – against your order and as per your needs. Similarly, the shopfront you visit at Amazon is not the same as the shopfront that your friend visits. Amazon uses its detailed knowledge of your likes and dislikes to customize a shopfront which is uniquely designed to give you the best shopping experience. Similarly, you can customize your mouse pads, Post-it Notes, polo shirts, mugs, etc. at iprint.com. But how is all this new? You customized your mugs and polo shirts in the past too.

> **There is a cost of customization for customers too and there is thus a trade-off.**

Customization is getting redefined in some simple but important ways. Simply put, you will be able to customize most of the products and services that you need. Customization is becoming real and simple – there would be no great virtue for a vendor in claiming to offer customized solutions; each one of them will customize for you – just ask for it. Customization will be the standard – you'll not usually pay premium for customization "efforts" and it wouldn't take extra days/weeks. Moreover, earlier firms claimed to have customized solutions but in reality only had a few "standard" variants of their products. Look at the whole theory of market segmentation. Most firms have worked for decades with little more than half a dozen market segments for a given product. Today, such a view seems woefully inadequate given the benchmarks being set by online pioneers such as Amazon who customize storefronts and selling approaches to each individual customer – all 25 million of them. The era of the individual has arrived.

Customization is becoming a major vehicle of value delivery to customers and a natural corollary of the same is that we'll be continuously creating products that never existed before. This is not to imply that each one of us will seek to customize every product we buy. There is a cost of customization for customers too and there is thus a trade-off. While customizing a product may increase its value to us, we will have to decide the details of the customization and perhaps occasionally audit the progress of the customization. Deciding the details is not an easy job because:

- It takes time and effort to think and lay down the customized specifications for a product. You may only invest the necessary time if the product is important or if you are really discriminatory about product usage. For example, it would take a while to think of the different breads one may want for the different days or occasions in a particular week – the shapes, sizes, amount of sugar, salt, kind of packaging, softness, white or brown, etc. You may just decide not to seek customization of the breads that you buy – not worth the time spent! Or you may just customize only in the weeks when party schedules are heavy and definite.

- There is also a search cost associated with finding an appropriate source that will be a trustworthy creator of the customized products at an acceptable price. It takes time to figure out the most appropriate source for getting a customization because a particular company can profitably customize only within a given range of specifications. And if the customization specifications change in a way that the current supplier can not address the requirements adequately then one has to either live with the current choices or invest time to find another supplier!

- There is an element of uncertainty about the appropriateness of the price being charged for a customized product because the prices for customized products will not be on a price list, and there may not be any benchmark to compare with. This could scare away people from seeking customized products. It would take time and effort to figure out the most competitive price band for given customizations.

Thus, only some customers would be demanding a specific customization in a given product. But whenever a customization is sought, it will be a win-win situation for both – customers and producers. Each contact with a customer is worth all that there is for the producers. It provides them a unique opportunity to learn – to learn to create a uniquely defined "new" product and to learn more about the customer's specific needs. The latter is an important source of profitable exchanges with customers.

> **Quick Insights**
>
> **1** Information exchange will allow you to avoid the most difficult exercise of having to second-guess the customer. The customer can think, design and work for you.
>
> **2** In a world where ultimate customization for the individual becomes possible we need to develop a radically different approach to pricing. True value pricing can become the dominant form of pricing.
>
> **3** Once you have a hotline to your customer you should exploit that capacity to its utmost. What else can you push through the communication line? How can you optimize the capacity utilization of that customer hotline?

The contrast

But the contrast between the above scenarios and current business practices could not be starker. You just have to recollect the last time you bought anything. When was the last time that you found something that was exactly what you were looking for? Take detergents, for example. The department store you visited probably had a well-stocked collection of detergents. But it's likely that none of them precisely met your needs and the detergent you ultimately purchased represented a compromise. You might have been looking for a packaging that combined detergent tablets, liquid detergent, and the standard detergent powder that together weighed 750 grams, your monthly detergent need. But you might have ended up purchasing 500 grams of detergent powder and another 500 grams of liquid detergent because the department store didn't offer the mix of the three you needed. This may be a trivial example, but the compromises only increase as we move toward durables like music systems, cars, and watches. Companies typically produce fixed product lines with some tailoring at the point of purchase. However, even that small set of tailoring is fixed long before customers come into the picture. As a customer, you end up mostly making sub-optimal choices from a limited set of products.

To be sure, however, companies should be undertaking the necessary change very happily. The current push technology of production, for example, is sub-optimal for producers. Notes Charles Fine,[5] from the MIT Sloan school, "If companies could make cars and add options to order, not only could they charge full price, they could satisfy the customer – people will pay more for what they really want. Predictions of future demand, no matter how well grounded, are inevitably inaccurate. The result: all these "unhappy sales." Frustrated retailers and manufacturers spend tens of billions of dollars in discounts every year to help dispose of merchandise that isn't moving the way they thought it would. There is a lot less waste if you know exactly what your customers want." And in fact, you may not even have to invest in working capital, because the consumers will pay up front exactly for the product that they want.

So how did a system that's bad for both customers and companies hold sway for over a century? Historically, there hasn't been an alternative. The Internet has changed all that. Customers today can design their own computers with Dell's online configurator, create their own dolls with Mattel's My Design Barbie, assemble their own investment portfolios with Schwab's mutual-fund evaluator, and even design their own golf clubs with Chipshot.com's PerfectFit system. So, you could almost exactly know what you need to produce. But there is a learning curve for companies because managing a variety of customer experiences is not the same as managing variety in products.[6] The realization that product attributes could be subordinate to experience will require managers to change their traditional perceptions and mindsets.

> Managing a variety of customer experiences is not the same as managing variety in products.

And it's happening at the real big ones too. Ford and GM are neck to neck on this initiative and ahead of many of their competitors. Many people are skeptical that they can transform themselves into a build-to-order manufacturer from being among the world's biggest build-to-stock operations. But they seem to be fairly committed to the vision of co-creating their vehicles with their customers. For example, GM's experimental "modular" assembly plant in Latin America is expected to help develop a "plug-and-play" capability that will ultimately reduce production to some 30 bigger sub-assemblies from over 3,000 parts.

Moving center-stage

Customers have moved out of the audience and on to the stage. A major revolution in customer lifestyle is waiting. We are entering an era where customers will be enabled to uncover, for themselves, new possibilities – they can create most value for themselves, by exploring, redefining, and choosing what makes best sense for them.

Are you excited? There can not be a better recipe for innovation in business. Product ideas will be free; consumers will be giving their best inputs for free. To the extent that they will be paying a "premium" price for customized products, they will be giving money to producers to experiment. There will be limited risk of over-stocking, rejects, etc. To top it all, customers will want to be loyal and be retained; you can only throw them away. As already discussed, there is a personal cost of customization for the customer and thus, given satisfactory service, customers are less likely to move to competitors.

We have long been talking about "competing as a family," but that included only suppliers and alliances with other companies. Customers were largely ignored and not treated as part of the "family." The Internet is finally correcting the situation by initiating consumers as an integral part of business processes. Consumers are defining and auditing the value they want in a transaction. We're entering an era where perhaps the greatest value-creating virtue is to enable customers to give wings to their imaginations. Consumers are becoming a new source of competence for companies – and perhaps the most defensible source of competitive advantage.

Prahalad and Ramaswamy put the issue in perspective by pointing out that the concept of competence as a source of competitive advantage originated in studies of the diversified firm.[7] Managers started to conceive of the company as a collection of competencies rather than as a portfolio of business units. Managers eventually came to realize that the corporation could also draw on the competencies of its supply chain partners. During the past decade, managers have extended the search for competencies even further; they now draw on a broad network of suppliers and distributors. Over time, then, the unit of strategic analysis has moved from the single company, to a family of businesses, and finally to what people call the "extended enterprise," which consists of a central firm supported by a constellation of suppliers.

But the recognition that consumers are a source of competence forces managers to cast an even wider net: competence will now be a function of the collective knowledge available in the whole system – an enhanced network of suppliers, partners, investors, and customers. eBay is a great example of harnessing "customer power" to run its site. In fact, buyers and sellers primarily run the site – very much like a physical marketplace.

Consumers are becoming a new source of competence for companies.

New as it is, co-creation is a major innovation opportunity for most companies. They should be devising new ways of taking the dialog with customers to its logical end – no end – retain customers in an ever-evolving dialog. However, we do not even remotely imply that it's an easy task. It's complicated enough for a large company like Ford to understand its internal competence base, let alone the competencies of each of its top 100 suppliers. And you can easily imagine how difficult it will be for Ford to understand the competence base of the millions of heterogeneous individuals who are the automaker's customers. But that's the challenge.

Specifically, the formal induction of customers in the "extended enterprise" fundamentally alters the value creation mechanisms. We already argued in Chapter 6 that the Internet changes the qualitative nature of the service and can drastically change the relationship between producers and customers. But how do you start? And what do you start with? The subsequent sections discuss four sets of issues to help you to do it:

1. Destination bound: Every product and service has to be designed for a very special destination – its customer! How can your organization build destination-bound capabilities?

2. Efficient interfaces: How to increase the efficiency and effectiveness of conversations with your customers? How do you manage a dialog across multiple channels?

3. Value pricing: Every product will have a different price for each customer; in fact, the same product can have a different value to different customers. This is normal as each customer is unique. How to innovate using value pricing?

4. Comprehensiveness: The imperative is to gain more opportunities to serve customers in the most comprehensive manner possible. How to achieve your goal?

Destination bound

Ironically, one of the more effective vehicles for innovation is to stop thinking for your customers! Stop anticipating what your customers may want. We saw in Seven Cycles that all production processes are initiated for specific customer orders. Customers are the destination; they're the reference point! Look at your products as being specific solutions to your customers' needs and imperatives. No initiative is small if it links up with the imperatives of your customers. In GE, for example, the generators division sells spare parts online. No innovation apparently, but a great value for its customers; getting the right spares at the right time is a highly valuable service for the customers – because customers buy the generators not for the power the generators produce but for the power as a means to ensure effective delivery of their products to their customers. Initiating innovation could not be simpler! Millions of ideas for innovation are very much in your "front-yard" – with your customers.

One of the more effective vehicles for innovation is to stop thinking for your customers!

A significant example of what the destination-bound capabilities are going to usher in is the GE Power System division. Customers can use the Internet to watch their turbines being built in GE's manufacturing plants from anywhere in the world. They can thus monitor, all by themselves, the status of various activities and phases in manufacturing and point at appropriate changes during manufacturing itself. This ensures that the turbines and customers are "made for each other" and the cost of corrective changes for GE is minimal. A typical turbine has over 10,000 components and thus early detection of deviation from customer expectations is very valuable. Of course, there are similar processes for pre-sales and post-sales periods too. A turbine's engineering designs could be exchanged and manipulated over the Web and the actual performance data of the turbines are monitored through the Turbine Optimizer, again an Internet-based system. Not a thing of the future, it's the ultimate destination-bound capability. Clearly, the Internet is the necessary infrastructure for any sincere destination-bound capability.

Destination-bound capability is a win-win situation. It brings increased features and convenience to customers and reduced cost for companies. For budget airlines such as easyJet (www.easyjet.com), more than 70 percent of its passengers already book via the Internet and the company is moving to Internet-only booking. This may sound simple but it's tremendous empowerment for travelers, for they will face no gatekeepers, no additional/special options hidden away, and all information accessible online. A "fully" informed decision about destination, route, cost, facilities, timing, etc. will follow and that by itself is a very gratifying event. The ownership of the decision will entirely rest with the traveler and the post-purchase dissonance will be less – a great start for happy travel.

The airline promotes ticketless travel, giving travelers a reference number instead. Eventually the company plans to allow customers to exchange their ticket for a different flight or even transfer it to someone else online. "This would free our call center staff to concentrate entirely on customer service," says James Rothnie, easyJet's communications director,[8] about going to Internet-only booking. And add to this the savings that accrue due to far better planning and execution of activities due to much better knowledge about what to do (after the customers have indicated what they want). The Internet allows what one vendor[9] refers to as "one and done," the ability to service a customer's needs on first contact, regardless of the medium the customer is using. With a highly integrated virtual contact center, companies can achieve results that weren't possible just a few years ago. An airline, for example, might push its most frequent fliers to the front of the calling queue.

It can take numerous forms. Landsend.com, for example, offers a feature called Your Personal Model™, a 3D modeling application that lets users "try on" clothes suggested for their body type. "Customers are using the tools to answer their needs. We don't look at the expense, but just the benefit that it causes," says Tracy Schmit, e-commerce business manager for Lands' End.[10] Schmit also hopes all of this extra effort will keep the need for returns, currently averaging at about 15 percent, to a minimum. Similarly, Polymerland, GE's plastics distribution business, has used the online interface to reduce the time to deliver products from two weeks to two days. More importantly, this is despite a high level of customization. Customers have much more information about the product, real-color online screening of the pellets, and various other customizable services.

Destination-bound innovative opportunities for some would mean creating customized supply chain windows for organizations. For instance, Western Geophysical[11] uses e-marketplace solutions to cut transaction costs, simplify its global purchasing, and speed delivery of supplies to employees at home and in the field. Whether at Western Geophysical's Houston headquarters or in the middle of the Indian Ocean, Western Geophysical employees can order everything from oil filters, ropes, crankshafts, and magnetic tape to computer parts directly from suppliers, with approval, custom pricing, tracking, and reporting all accessible from their desktops. More than 10,000 purchase orders have been processed through the system from suppliers representing 75 percent of the company's total maintenance, repair, and operating supplies (MRO) spend. The company plans to process 80 to 85 percent of its purchasing through the Internet-based system. Among the benefits are:

- The transaction costs are getting closer to single-digit figures from the earlier levels of around $100 per order and the time is also reduced to hours.
- The Western Geophysical procurement staff is no longer bogged down processing transactions and now focuses on strategic sourcing opportunities such as negotiating preferred supplier deals.
- Real-time pricing and inventory management and better control over purchases are possible.

But there is one significant assumption in getting destination bound: that customers know exactly what they want. More often than not, post-purchase dissonance is a reality for most consumers because they cannot really decide all by themselves. Information has no face – the comfort level with information increases if it's backed up with some personal experiences too. Is there a way out? How you could be destination bound while your customers happily take ownership of their choices? One possibility is to actively promote customer communities. Communities are to the online world what markets are to the offline world and more. Communities are going to be the owners of the spaces where individual customers will be exploring and firming up many of their wants. Thanks to the Internet, customers are finding it easier to form, on their own, self-selecting virtual communities. The growing influence of such communities lies in the speed with which they can be mobilized and the ease with which large communities could organize their affairs.

> How to sharpen destination-bound capabilities:
>
> - Stop thinking about what a customer may really want. Wait, watch, and customize.
> - Increase convenience and facilities for customers.
> - Strengthen customer communities to help individual customers take ownership of their decisions.

Most importantly, these communities will have a major branding power – individual members will trust and listen to the experiences of their fellow community members. Creating and nurturing a loyal community is thus a very critical task for companies. And great innovative possibilities exist in creating and nurturing communities not only because they aggregate somewhat similar needs but also because no two communities are alike, by definition. Nurturing communities pays off because long-term customers buy more, take less of a company's time, are less sensitive to price, and bring in new customers.

Communities are going to be the owners of the spaces where individual customers will be exploring and firming many of their wants.

Communities can indeed be harnessed to maximize destination-bound capabilities. Customer communities[12] bring far more resources to individual customers to easily customize a product to their individual needs. Linux is an example of a product developed out of customer competence – innovative use of customers in product design and development. It is available as open source code, meaning that it is not only freely available but also developed by a virtual community of system developers who want to see an operating system that matches their imagination. If you use Linux, there is a world of people working for you.

But how do you build vibrant influential communities? There are only a handful of examples that come close to being influential communities. eBay and Amazon are the two best-known ones. And, not surprisingly, they are among the online leaders. They've powerfully harnessed the community's word-of-mouth. They have created an environment where the lateral communication among members of their customer communities has some bearing on certain decisions of the members. The essential characteristics of that environment are:

- a set of online tools to facilitate effective lateral communication, which must reflect the peculiar nature of the community in focus;
- organization of the communication database for easy accessibility and quick search;

- appropriate incentives for members to contribute;
- enforcement of a code of conduct and behavior; and
- continuously expanding the scope of sharing and involvement, and thereby increasing the stakes of each one of them in the community.

But how would you possibly measure the reciprocation by a community? The return on community investment? Where do you stand in the pecking order of the service providers that are servicing a given community? There are several indirect indicators to measure this:

- the growth in the number of members;
- the average number of visits per member per unit time (days, weeks, months, year) on your site;
- the number of suggestions for changes or improvements in tools or databases;
- the demand for new tools or databases or changes in the objectives of the community;
- the perceived reasons of the new members for joining the community.

However, reconciling community focus and personalization for individual members at the same time will not be easy. Communities exist because they bring value to the members, and value that is meaningful to each individual member. While a given community will have a predominant agenda, no two members of a community will have completely overlapping expectations from membership of the community.

Efficient interfaces

When co-creating products, "conversations" with customers will become the norm. Customers sign off your production schedule – you have to produce what they want and when they want. The stakes are high on both sides, of course. Such conversations are double-edged weapons – the cost of ill-managed conversations is very high. A lot depends on the efficiency of the means of conversation – customer interfaces. Customer interfaces have been subject to a lot of innovation at all times. We've already mentioned the interfaces like Schwabline, Equalizer, and StreetSmart that Schwab developed before the online interface. Similarly, Wal-Mart developed SAM'S CLUB as a members-only warehouse club, Supercenter for one-stop family shopping convenience, besides the usual discount retailing offering a wide variety of general merchandise. But the Internet brings a totally new opportunity in customer interface design and implementation.

Amadeus Global Travel Distribution has innovated a new interface that analysts say will give the company a clear advantage over its competitors. It will be using a new search engine that integrates low-fare searches with seat availability, booking capabilities, and an "intelligent" interface. The new application has several advantages over existing models. It is a one-stop engine that allows for multiple queries – a different airport, a different date, or even a shorter layover along the way – with just one request. At the same time the interface is "intelligent" – as the interface works like a travel agent; it is the first e-commerce travel application that integrates all the disparate data involved in a fare search.[13] Initially available in the domestic Internet travel portals driven by Amadeus in the US, such as Wal-Mart Stores Inc.'s Internet travel service, it will be made available to a much wider audience.

While the Web provides a whole new customer interface, we think that the more significant impact is that the traditional interfaces are undergoing a major metamorphosis as they get interconnected seamlessly. Herein lie great opportunities for innovation – for making traditional interfaces closer to customers. Integration of customer interfaces to the backend as well as to all other interfaces will make customers' lives far more convenient and pleasurable. The super-normal profits fetched by the 7-Eleven retail chain in Japan are also attributable to the information warehousing that it maintains about the profiles of its customers. Each time you buy from the store, the counter-person punches in your apparent biographical profile such as age and sex. The records of all the customers in any store are then analyzed to store the right kind of products so that the goods turnover is much higher and they always find what they want.

At the heart of making efficient interfaces is the facilitation of the overlap between the service providers and customers. Bringing the showroom into the customers' living quarters is just one example. AOL's LiveProducts is an interactive product demonstration facility to allow online shoppers to experience many of the more popular consumer electronic items from the comfort of their own homes. LiveProducts enables Shop@AOL customers to simulate the look and sound of the real products, or watch animated walk-throughs of the product features.

By simply clicking on one of the products displayed, shoppers can easily test the ringer on a cell phone or click on the phone keypad and digits will appear on the phone's screen; they can maneuver the features of a digital camera; or even learn how to program a VCR before deciding whether to make a purchase. If shoppers then want to buy the product, it's only one click away. In addition, LiveProducts stores the complete owner's manual for each of the products to enable users to quickly find all the information they need.

The Internet can strengthen the process experience – the experience associated with the entire buying process – planning, choosing, ordering, and using the product rather than only the actual consumption of the product. The power of the Internet to seamlessly connect disparate and distributed customer databases is an innovators' dream laboratory. This connection could be used to change the process experience significantly. The Internet is not just another medium to reach customers but an infrastructure on which you can build your dream interface(s). The lesson: look at the processes in your interfaces. Innovate them continuously – maybe in small simple ways. Innovate till you could make available personalized processes for each of your customers irrespective of the chosen interface – a far more evolved version of personalization available in many of the leading websites like Amazon, Schwab, Auto-By-Tel, etc.

Increasing customer convenience could be one easy focus for innovating the interfaces. Some "gift" sites reduce considerably the required effort from customers. Camdens' site (a high-end gift retailer) is one example of enhanced physical convenience as the site touts various features to make gift-giving easier. A "recipient's choice" option allows gift-givers to select several items, which are then presented to recipients to choose from; a "gift manager," which sends the gift-giver frequent e-mails about gift availability and delivery status; and "Camdens mail," which informs recipients via e-mail about their gifts – and the company's services. Similarly, Amazon has a feature called Gift-Click. Just enter the recipient's e-mail address and Amazon will take care of obtaining the mailing address and wrapping and sending the gift. Amazon is trying to make things as easy and as personalized as possible and be receptive to customers' needs.

Convenience is a very potent area for innovation. Just re-look at the mundane activities that we engage in day in and day out to identify points of intervention to innovate. PayPal.com is among the world's first e-mail-based payment services. PayPal allows you to send money instantly and securely to anyone with an e-mail address. You can also send personal bills to a friend or group of friends, who can then pay you quickly and easily online. PayPal makes sending and collecting money as easy as e-mail. PayPal integrates seamlessly with existing financial networks, allowing you to beam money to friends from your credit card or bank account. Equally important, you can now accept credit card payments from anyone. You can use PayPal to buy and sell items at online auctions, classified sites, and personal websites. And unlike checks, which can take days to clear, PayPal transactions clear instantly. Some examples of what you can do: pay a coworker back for buying your lunch or collect money from friends for buying rounds of beer.

> Make your interfaces efficient:
>
> - Connect the traditional "offline" interfaces and the online interface.
> - Fine-tune the processes associated with each of the interfaces.
> - Get a complementary mix of online and offline interfaces. Consider what is best for your customer community.
> - Ensure that the quality of the interaction and fulfillment is seamless across the interfaces.

Similarly, getting a complementing mix of the online and offline interfaces is open to creative inputs. But you may not decide at all – let customers tell you the mix required. Says A. Guenthard, VP SwissAir, "We're seeing customers we did not expect to see online. Initially, we thought that bargain hunters – the 25-to-35-year-old crowd – would be the bulk of our visitors. However, it turned out to be a different story. The biggest segment of online users happens to be frequent business travelers who are accessing the Web site and booking and paying for tickets online. We're selling a major percentage of business-class tickets online. What's even better is that the average ticket price online is actually higher than the average ticket sold face-to-face or on the phone. Everyone initially talked about the Web driving down prices, but we're seeing just the opposite here."[14] Actually, that's not so surprising. Business travelers are saving money by buying online and being able to reschedule their travel itineraries on their own. And they're passing on a part of value thus generated to the airlines. A win-win situation for both.

The travel industry has been a leader in the Internet revolution. Yet, the industry has actually thrown up little innovation in increasing the utility of its services to customers. That also explains why the travel agents in the industry feel so threatened by the alliances of the airlines in the US and Europe to offer online ticketing. They would not have felt threatened if they had been using the physical contact with travelers to make them get more out of a trip by helping them with individual attention and knowledge inputs. The ability to create the appropriate mix of offline and online features in your products will be rewarding and another great source of innovation in business modeling.

However, the mix decision is not a "corporate" one. It could vary by products, customers, divisions, or geography. Uniglobe Travel International[15] – the largest single-brand travel agency in the world, with 1,100 branches in 20 countries – is pursuing a promising online strategy. Uniglobe is combining the better of the two worlds – human touch and reach. It discovered that out of its different operations cruise booking is the one most unlike air travel or hotel booking. The issues that need answers are far and many. It provides cruise travel specialists who can be contacted for online chat all the time. It promises response to e-mails within 20 minutes and there is a 24-hour help line. Besides, you have complete information on around 100 cruise ships. Thus, its mix of offline and online services for cruise and hotel booking is different. Cruise has far more online support compared to others.

What's the potential of the online interface? Customers may actually start customization from the familiar channels – retail outlet or direct salesperson – and then later move on to customize through the Internet. Or it could be the other way around. Eventually, they would be customizing at their convenience and that means from any of the interfaces. However, the Internet is likely to emerge as the dominant channel for exploring customization. Individual customers may find it the preferred channel because they can explore far more and at leisure. They will also be able to access their past customization details, read the experiences of fellow customers, and perhaps get a visual feel of the product before ordering. And of course, the psychological advantage of being in control of customization if they do it online. Anyway, even the online interfaces are providing real-time chats and telephonic conversations with customer representatives to give the offline "comforts." David Pottruck,[16] Co-CEO, Schwab, puts the point in perspective: "people should enter their life style and they should be able to get appropriate product features or possibilities to service that life style."

Customization through the Internet saves a lot of manpower cost and effort, reduces errors in interpersonal communication, and predisposes customers to seek word-of-mouth from others. It also leaves open the possibility of reaching customers again through offline channels in case a customer does not get adequately convinced of the customized solutions. But companies will have to greatly upgrade their online channels to let customers decide the level of involvement they want in creating a product. Since the level of customer engagement can not be predetermined, companies will have to give consumers as much choice and flexibility as possible in the communication and design of products.

It also makes all the more sense to encourage customers to seamlessly use all the interfaces. Border Books is a good example of an incumbent that did not dilute its offline thrust for the online foray. It integrated the two very thoughtfully. Its customers can search for the books in the store or on the in-store Internet terminals. They can chat online or read reviews online or talk to the attending personnel at the store. But a key challenge will be to ensure that the quality of the interaction and fulfillment is not very different across the interfaces.

Value pricing

For mass customization to be profitable to producers[17] the price realized by them should be higher than the cost of customized products. But under conditions of mass customization both the price and cost associated with a product vary from order to order, unlike mass production. Thus, pricing is a more strategically serious issue in mass customization than in mass production so that in most orders, if not all, the price realized remains higher than the cost. Consequently, strong customization ability without a robust pricing strategy could be dangerous. Pricing decisions will become increasing complex – many parameters will have to be tracked for the pricing of a single order. Typical price–customization matrices will be beyond manual calculations.

But the flip side of complex situations is always bright – they always represent great opportunities too. Those who can manage the pricing matrix deftly will reap rich profits. The opportunity has its origin in the following critical asymmetry: the cost of providing a particular custom feature in a product to a producer, and the value of the same to a customer (measured by the level of perceived benefits), are rarely the same.

If the asymmetry could be managed in such a way that cost is less than the value, profits are assured. This is mostly possible. For there is nothing absolute about the value of any product or specific feature. It's all perception; it's contextual. It is possible to increase the perceived value of the features in the eyes of the customer by exploiting a better knowledge of the customers' value drivers. It becomes far easier then to initiate a dialog with customers which starts with due education of the customer about the specific benefits of the features in his or her context. More importantly, the dialog will also prompt specific questions on how the feature could be more useful.

> **But the flip side of complex situations is always bright – they represent great opportunities too.**

Pricing decisions would require a closer watch at the top. GE, for example, is leading the pack in upgrading its pricing manager's role and position. The group has launched an initiative in which a pricing manager in each of its 40-odd divisions reports directly to the chief executive. A chief pricing officer who reports to Jack Welch then coordinates the initiative across the divisions.[18]

Gary Reiner,[19] CIO, GE, illustrates the spirit, "GE's web approach is three-pronged: buy side, where GE interacts with suppliers; sell side, where GE interacts with customers; and make side, where GE interacts within its own operations. In all three areas," says Reiner, "we see huge opportunities in productivity, for ourselves and for our customers." On the buy side, GE now negotiates with many of its suppliers by holding reverse Web auctions where pre-qualified suppliers bid for GE business. "We are getting price deflation that we never had before," says Reiner. Each organization will have to look into the inefficiencies in the entire value chain to maximize value.

What's the innovation opportunity here? Unlimited. The innovation opportunity here is one of applying the knowledge of customers to help figure out better applications of products/specific features. There are many innovation opportunities because the more one understands the possibilities about one's own products/features and the applications of the same for fulfilling customers' needs, the better one can project.

Being innovative in pricing policies is also going to be strategically important. Soon price comparisons will lose force because products will not be exactly comparable. Internet-based auctions and bidding have actually been shown to result in better prices at times. eBay, for example, is not the cheapest marketplace. And rightly so – being a global marketplace, people from all over make bids based on the particular value that they expect to derive from the products on sale.

But the pricing issue is nothing all that new. The airline industry has for long applied it. However, the transparency is missing in airline ticketing and product differentiation is minimal. For the past 20 years, "revenue management" in the airline industry has required the most powerful computers to crunch the pricing options for flying from point A to point B. Complex mathematical models are routinely applied and continuously monitored. The new thing is that it will become an imperative for all!

No company can be all things to all people even in a narrow product category. And thankfully not anymore, because it need not. A company will not only have a global customer base to achieve scale economics but also have the exact knowledge to know who wants what and why, and thus may not make products for "assumed average customers." Every company will find some customers it's better off losing. It would be more profitable for companies to secure positive word-of-mouth about the products that they wish to be known for rather than dilute their position in the minds of their prospective customers. Focus will be important and profitable too.

Pricing strategies will continue to be a challenge for all organizations. It is important to note that:

- There is always a critical asymmetry in the cost of a product and its perceived value to a customer. If costs are managed below perceived value, profits are assured.
- An in-depth knowledge about each individual customer is needed to make the most out of the asymmetry.
- Nothing need be free in the e-era! Customers will pay a premium when seeking customized products.
- A portfolio of pricing strategies will be a must.

We have already discussed how GE uses the Internet for innovative pricing practices. The Internet does create unique pricing challenges and opportunities, and eventually, a great innovative window. Pricing strategies will require creative inputs. We're already seeing "name your own price" pricing; auctions of various types such as "starting at $1," "reverse auction;" "everyday lower prices" pricing. We'll see many more as pricing gets linked to value derived from a particular product by a particular customer.

The Internet creates unique pricing challenges and opportunities.

Potentially, each producer–customer dyad and interaction could result in a unique pricing situation. There are many pricing dimensions that are greatly underutilized today. For example, discount level, payment schedule, credit period, interest rate for the credit period, delivery schedule and cost, packaging type and cost, discount on related or other items, degree of professional assistance during shopping, cash-only or credit card – the list of factors, besides the cost of the "core product," that closely influence the price of the core product is limited only by our imagination. Most of these pricing factors, however, require an in-depth and quickly accessible knowledge about customers to be appropriate. The Internet promises to fill the gap. Buying will not be the same ever again.

The dotcom "phase" has created a misplaced notion about emerging pricing strategies. The Internet, at one point, was turning out to be synonymous with free and price was assumed to be the dominant product feature. And wherever it wasn't free all the way, it was expected to be "falling prices" – bottomlessly – even below the actual cost of production. And as it happened, that didn't really help customers. Organizations have to create wealth to continue to serve their customers. A correction of sorts is already under way and customers are duly encouraging it. Buy.com, for example, discovered that the traffic on its site and buyer behaviors have changed for the better since it changed focus and started reducing the items sold at cost or below cost. Even advertisers are more interested in the site now. While it had only 100 advertisers in 1999, it had over 200 advertisers on its site in 2000.

There is in fact an important corollary to pricing innovation – an organization should have a portfolio of pricing strategies. Priceline.com was one example of being indiscriminate about pricing policy. Priceline applied its "name your own price" to sell everything – grocery, long-distance call times, airline tickets, and mortgages. And it steadily landed itself in trouble. What went wrong? Apparently, "name your own price" works best for the travel industry. The very nature of the travel industry makes it work. For instance, the level of transparency in airlines is low and thus a customer can never know if he or she got a good deal. Further, prices vary by season, date, route, and many more ways. And only airlines and travel agents know about the price structure at any point in time. Another peculiar aspect of travel tickets is that they perish if not consumed by the due date. But all these are not true for many other products like mortgages and groceries. Thus, an organization must adopt different pricing strategies for different products.

We mentioned earlier how Buy.com's top line is doing better as it moved away from "at cost" offers on its site. IstUP, an ISP (Internet service provider), is experiencing a similar phenomenon. Based in San Francisco, it made its mark for a simple reason: it provides Internet access free of charge. And it's doing pretty well. It took AOL ten years to sign up 3 million subscribers.[20] IstUp, a company with no brand, no advertising, and a 25-year-old graduate of Stanford University as its prime driver, did it in eight months. Yet, even IstUP admits that free doesn't suit everyone. It unveiled its own private-label subscriber service for those who're willing to pay a little to avoid advertising. Indeed, Steve Case, AOL's Chairman, insists that he will never offer a free service in the US. It has a number of weapons in its arsenal to keep its 23 million subscribers paying. Its chat rooms are hugely popular communities. It has the best line-up of alliances with other product and service providers. Thus, you no longer have to worry about falling prices. Just keep focused on the value delivered – the utility derived by customers.

Comprehensiveness

The possibility of direct access to customers should be wonderful news for most companies. The smarter among us will not only increase the size of their pie but also enlarge the cake. They'll redefine their goals in terms of market space and focus on the "whole" customer. The imperative is to gain more opportunities to serve customers in the most comprehensive manner possible. How could you effectively serve more needs of your existing customers? How do you understand their broad categories of needs? What incentives do you offer to them to seek more services/products from you?

The essence of comprehensiveness can be best understood through an analogy. If the relationship with a customer is seen as a pipe, then comprehensiveness represents the opportunity to increase the capacity utilization or throughput of the pipe. Amazon's zShops is a simple example of innovatively addressing the issue of comprehensiveness of service to a community – more than 25 million-odd Amazon visitors. Yahoo! is another example of comprehensive service to its community – it's just getting bigger and bigger! Nomura Securities, the biggest securities firm in Japan, added a new dimension to comprehensiveness: it is providing an

> **The relationship with a customer is like a pipe. The opportunity is to increase the capacity utilization or throughput of the pipe.**

unusual brokerage service – online stock trading to the owners of Sega enterprise's Dreamcast video-game consoles. Nomura is thus creating another channel for the convenience of its customers. Dreamcast consoles already have Internet connections.

But one of the strongest supports for comprehensiveness as an innovation mechanism comes from Toyota. As described in Chapter 5, Toyota Motors' website gazoo.com was launched in 1998 and it's one of the most successful sites in Japan. It sells a whole range of goods such as cars, books, CDs, videos, household utensils, and games. Toyota believes that gazoo.com has the potential to generate 600 billion yen ($5.5 billion) in sales by 2003, when it expects to have 4 million consumers registered as gazoo.com subscribers. The site is so powerful that GM has been eyeing a tie-up to sell GM cars over the Internet, in Japan, through the gazoo.com site. To top it all, Toyota is now mulling over the idea of offering online brokerage services through the site, among other services! The lesson: the cost of online scalability is low. But the key thing is to think about the products that would appeal to the community on your site.

Forrester Research[22] analyst Evie Black Dykema notes that examples set by HomeRuns, Amazon.com and others who have found that selling CDs and other products offers a chance to insert higher margin products into the mix without the need for additional warehouse space. "Smart firms view this as an early step toward using their infrastructure pipelines to deliver a range of household goods," commented Dykema. Every business is potentially a mall on the Internet. Once the visitors are anyway on the site, they could be offered a host of other products alongside. This is a new opportunity. Earlier you had to think of a mall, design it, build it, and then operate it as a mall.

Comprehensiveness in servicing customers is a major opportunity. It can be realized in the following ways:

- See the relationship with your customer community as a pipe. Then focus on the capacity utilization of the pipe.
- Add depth and breadth to the services currently provided.
- Create a web of alliances to service comprehensively.
- Comprehensiveness implies profitability from a bundle of services and not necessarily from each individual service.

Comprehensiveness is also an interesting route to add depth in your product portfolio. Thanks to a new service in Sweden, called YadaPrice, consumers can use their handsets to compare prices of CDs and, soon, other products at participating retailers on the Web – right at the shop where they are shopping: an instant price transparency that would otherwise take hours of window shopping or surfing on the Internet. Consumers call up the local number for YadaPrice, punch in the product's so-called UPC/EAN code (the number below the bar code on the product), and receive an instant message on the display of the phone that lists the three cheapest prices of the product available at participating retailers on the Web. Mobility, by itself, is adding a very useful dimension in innovating comprehensive services. For example, reserving movie tickets used to be a cumbersome process because one had to go to the theater at least half an hour before the start of the show to buy the ticket. But with mobile phones one can book and pay simultaneously because the bank is also linked with the mobile.

Trying out new ideas and products is not easy in the offline mode but fairly easy online. Putting up a new product for sale does not come at the cost of shelf space of others and may remain transparent for most. For example, all leading online recruitment businesses are bent upon making money in the traditional way – charging fees to employers for making available suitable candidates. But do they not realize that there are tens of other revenue possibilities once job seekers start visiting their sites? Once on the site, they should be attracted toward a host of other services to ease their career transitions.

How would you expect a gay and lesbian site to make money if it's not for comprehensiveness? Being a gay and lesbian site is after all only an "excuse." It's all about life ultimately and you will see all the familiar things on the site. The first gay and lesbian website, PlanetOut of San Francisco, succeeded in raising a third round of funding at a time (year 2000) when most investors had abandoned B2C start-ups and content plays.[24] Two major backers, Mayfield and AOL, are repeat investors. PlanetOut targets a gay and lesbian population of 17 million US Web users that wield $450 billion in buying power, the company claims. More importantly, once gays and lesbians choose a company to patronize, they generally stick with them, noted COO Susan Schuman. "This market is extremely brand-loyal," she added, citing American Airlines, American Express, and Absolut Vodka as companies that targeted gays and lesbians and continue to get their business. Significantly, PlanetOut is indeed edging out other gay and lesbian-focused websites because the site serves not only its core audience but also the friends and relatives of gays and lesbians. Did you get the economic significance of getting non-gays and non-lesbians in!

How will comprehensiveness be sustained? Through a network of alliances. Alliances in day-to-day transactions were not the natural choice in the past as it was not easy to coordinate such operations effectively and efficiently. But the Internet is changing all that. Inter-organizational interface costs are getting comparable to intra-organizational interface costs. Simply put, it is getting easier to "get work done" from a third party as from another department in your organization. And this is potentially an opportunity to build a very powerful portfolio of businesses – a great source of business model innovation. More details on this are provided in the next chapter.

Action points

1. Analyze how often in the past you discovered that your organization had made false assumptions about customer needs. What would it take to open up a hotline to a group of leading customers and involve them in your thinking, to let them do the thinking for you? What more can you do to let your customers drive your innovation agenda?
2. Working with all customers individually may be impractical for your firm. You can probably apply a 20/80 rule in this case: who are the 20 percent of your customers that can contribute 80 percent of the innovative ideas? Do you know them? And how do you reach out to them?
3. Is there an effective community of customers out there for your organization? Note that a community implies that your customers are communicating *with each other* and not just back with your firm. Does your organization realize the appropriate benefits from these customer communities?
4. Pricing is always a challenge. Can you analyze how you communicate the value of your service to the customer, and how that influences the price the customer is prepared to pay? Are your firm's pricing policies geared up to support customized pricing?
5. Are you being sufficiently comprehensive in servicing your customers? What other customer needs can you satisfy? Who can partner with you to satisfy these needs?

Mantra

Customers are becoming an integral part of organizations – far more inside than outside. They are, in fact, moving to the starting point of the value chain rather than the end. Your organization has to be ready to welcome customers in.

Destination-bound capabilities will become important – a product made for a given destination – its customer. However, not all customers may know exactly what they want. Engage in co-experimentation to discover what adds value. Educate customers. Help your customers to educate themselves by creating and nurturing customer communities.

Millions of ideas for innovation are very much in your "front-yard" – with your customers. You only need to have a continuous dialog with them. Effect innovative changes in the customer interfaces to make conversations easy with your customers. While the Web provides a whole new customer interface, the more significant opportunity lies in interconnecting the Web and other traditional interfaces seamlessly.

Re-look at the processes in your customer interfaces. Specifically pricing is a strategically serious issue to master as you create your own destination-bound capabilities. Strong customization ability without a robust pricing strategy can be dangerous. Focus on how to reduce costs while increasing the perceived value of your products and services to your customers.

The imperative is to gain more opportunities to serve customers in the most comprehensive manner possible. A web of alliances is critical to enhance your ability to service your customers more comprehensively.

Notes

1. Based on material from the site www.sevencycles.com
2. Valigra, Lori (1999) "Why seven cycles is racing ahead: The net," *Business Week*, June 22.
3. Based on inputs from www.sevencycles.com
4. www.sevencycles.com
5. Andrews, Fred (2000) "GM aims to build cars the way Dell makes computers, *International Herald Tribune*, 27 January, p. 11.
6. Prahalad, C.K. and Ramaswamy, Venkatram (2000) "Co-opting customer competence," *Harvard Business Review*, Jan/Feb, pp. 79–87.
7. Based on the article by C.K. Prahalad and Venkatram Ramaswamy (2000) "Co-opting customer competence," *Harvard Business Review*, Jan/Feb, pp. 79–87.
8. Shillingford, Joia (2000) "Flight reservation," *Financial Times*, September 14.
9. Cisco uses the term for its ICM software.
10. Solomon, Karen (2000) "Getting to the land of no returns," September 15, www.cisco.com

11. www.intelisys.com
12. Unless otherwise mentioned, communities refers to customer communities.
13. Johnson, Keith (2000) "Amadeus expects fare search engine to boost web plan," *Wall Street Journal*, February 18–19, p. 24.
14. "Taking flight online," Interview with Guenthard, Swissair, www.cisco.com
15. Diba, Ahmad (2000) "An old-line agency finds an online niche," *Fortune*, April 3, p. 93.
16. www.ge.com
17. The term "producer" is used generically to represent product or service providers.
18. Simon, Hermann (2000) "Pricing turns into a science," *Financial Times*, October 31.
19. Rudnitsky, Howard (2000) "Changing the corporate DNA," *Forbes Global*, July 24, pp. 99–100.
20. Upbin, Bruce (2000) "Free for all," *Forbes Global*, May 1, pp. 78–9.
21. Shirouzu, Norihiko (2000) "GM seeks to market cars on Toyota website," *WSJ*, February 21.
22. Macaluso, Nora and Regan, Keith (2000) "Webvan on collision course with Amazon" *E-Commerce Times*, June 6.
23. Macaluso, Nora and Regan, Keith (2000) "Webvan on collision course with Amazon" *E-Commerce Times*, June 6.
24. Based on Mathew A. DeBellis, (2000) "PlanetOut is in with VCs," *Redherring.com*, September 25.

E-nfrastructure 9

The last industrial revolution galvanized on the back of the railways. The retail revolution led by Wal-Mart happened because of the easy mobility afforded by the automobile. In fact, infrastructural discontinuities have played a significant role in initiating and consolidating significant innovations around us.

Would you consider co-creation a significant source of innovation in our lives? Wonder what's the underlying infrastructural discontinuity? It's the e-nfrastucture. Discover how Oticon built and exploited an e-nfrastructure. What did it mean to Cisco and Schwab? What are the significant components of the e-nfrastructure and how might you go about making co-creation real for your customers?

As you read, keep reminding yourself that e-nfrastructure refers to more than the technology platform. It encompasses the entire organizational system – people, processes, and partners – necessary for excellence and innovation.

Damn the middle path

Over the past century, the Danish company Oticon has carved out an outstanding reputation for the quality and technological superiority of its advanced hearing solutions. Oticon is the oldest surviving hearing instrument manufacturer in the world and presents a fascinating exploration of how innovation can be enabled and sustained within a mature organization. Building on the theme of customer focus outlined in the previous chapters, Oticon admits that its professional starting point has been audiological rather than technological. It does not develop technical features unless they reflect actual customer needs. As you might expect, Oticon is a world leader, with its hearing aids being sold in 100 countries, and 95 per cent of its turnover generated abroad.

Its most recent innovative hearing solution is DigiFocus – the world's first 100 per cent digital fully automatic hearing instrument that adjusts to different situations dynamically. It supports many advanced features: advanced feedback management, in-situ assessment of the customer's most comfortable listening range, two separate speech processors for the vowels and consonants, and self-adjusting mechanism for group conversations. Essentially, Oticon stole a lead over its competitors by going a step beyond the obvious customization: real-time customization of hearing aid – constant adaptation to the environment. The hearing instrument "learns" how customers tend to adapt to their changing needs. This real-time customization radically changes the hearing experience because hearing depends not only on the degree of deafness but also on the sound characteristics. The latter are greatly influenced by the immediate environment of the listener.

How does Oticon manage to be so innovative? Strong focus on research and innovation is the answer. However, the research and innovation at Oticon are not all technology; the context of the technology is an equal participant. Oticon is a good example of how the design and implementation of operational infrastructure and practices becomes a great enabler and source of innovation, how leadership influences innovation, and how culture stimulates radical if not revolutionary innovation. In the previous chapter, we discussed how Internet-enabled co-creation opportunities could obtain a win-win situation for both customers and organizations. This chapter takes us to the logical conclusion – what infrastructure is needed to make the most of the new opportunities. In other words, how can the changes in the infrastructure be used to induce and sustain innovation?

Perhaps unexpectedly, Oticon, the "old-timer," is considered to be the "ultimate flexible organization."[1] It all started with Lars Kolind, the previous CEO's, resolve to "think the unthinkable, and…do something out of the ordinary" to excel in an industry dominated by global electronics companies such as Siemens, Philips, and Sony. His key strategy was to move "from products being fundamentally technology-based to becoming fundamentally knowledge-based." His chosen option? "It is impossible to change a traditional machine-like organization into building in that level of flexibility and ability to advance knowledge by any means other than revolution." His role? "not a captain who steers the ship but a naval architect who designs the ship."[2] Oticon under Lars Kolind became a role model for knowledge organizations where innovation is a way of life.

From a traditional hierarchical company in the 1980s, it transformed itself over the 1990s into a fundamentally different company. For example, departments and titles were eliminated and all activities became projects initiated and pursued by volunteering individuals. Each employee decided where and how to best apply his or her competencies – they got to choose how to best contribute! Oticon has a flat organization with a minimal structure. Employees work within the framework of one or more project groups for different periods of time. They may be developing a new hearing instrument, a new generation of software for fitting hearing instruments, or a marketing campaign directed toward users of hearing instruments. Although employees spend most of their time working in one or more project groups, each employee belongs to a specific professional area so that there is active accumulation of knowledge in identified professional areas for future product development. Obviously, middle-of-the-road organizational attributes cannot support the demands of the emerging opportunities.

Evaporating boundaries!

However, is the creation of an advanced product like Digifocus all out of the "ultimate flexible organization"? How did Oticon define what parameters needed to be adjusted and how to adjust them in Digifocus? It did collaborate with many others outside its organizational boundary. Oticon relied on an active network of employees, customers, and hearing aids professionals to innovate and create value. It says that it does not believe that the quality of a hearing aid can be measured in a laboratory. Clinical measurements may provide guidance and valuable information, but the only way to determine the success of a hearing aid is by listening to the experiences of the user; by finding out how he or she copes on a daily basis with the hearing aid. To that extent, Oticon's core objective is also different. It's not to deliver the smallest, cheapest, or most advanced hearing aids. Its goal is to deliver solutions that improve the quality of life for its customers.

Oticon particularly emphasizes that it views its suppliers and distributors as cooperative partners rather than adversaries. It also holds that its primary objective is not to become the largest company, but rather be one that can retain its autonomy and freedom of action. And it hopes to achieve that by being the company that creates the largest value for customers – for each one of them. Thus its organizational culture and infrastructure reflect the flexibility and adaptability necessary to create unique customer solutions. The network of suppliers, distributors, knowledge providers, producers, and customers together take the responsibility to maximize value creation. Bart Victor and Andrew C. Boynton call, in their book *Invented Here*, the capability to produce such a network as co-configuration.³ They add that co-configuration interestingly never results in a "finished" product. Instead, a living, growing network develops among customers, products, and producers and leads to a new way of innovating.

> Business will be more like experimental theater, where everyone and anyone can be part of the action and the script evolves during the play.

To use an analogy, business would no longer be like a traditional theater show where the actors (i.e. producers, suppliers, and distributors) have clearly defined roles and act according to a script, and customers sit back and watch passively. Producers, distributors, suppliers, and customers will no longer have a script that defines watertight roles. It would be more like an experimental theater; everyone and anyone can be part of the action and the script will evolve during the play. But all this would not be uncoordinated. Innovating to the tune of the customer will be the coordinating force for all.

The shift away from watertight roles is already visible in many partner relationships. Consider the experience of Cisco. By the mid-1990s, the competitive pressure in the networking industry had reached a point where Cisco realized that an innovative strategic intervention was needed to reassert its leadership. It was also important that the intervention did not worsen industry profitability and thus affect other participants adversely in the medium to long term. The solution that Cisco hit upon was to network its suppliers, resellers, and customers. To accomplish this, Cisco identified four primary tasks: outsource manufacturing to key suppliers, create a "single enterprise" with suppliers through information sharing, involve strategic suppliers in new product introductions, and ensure that the entire supply chain worked off one central demand forecast. Manufacturing Connection Online (MCO) is Cisco's window to its Globally Networked Manufacturing Environment. Employees and suppliers use it as a single point of access to manufacturing applications, reports, tools, and information. Cisco's suppliers continuously upgrade their technology and processes in close cooperation with Cisco. Often they initiate technology and process innovations that go on to improve the overall efficiency and effectiveness of Cisco's fulfillment cycle.

Result: Cisco reduced its inventory levels by 45 percent over the past six years and decreased the time to market for its products by as much as 12 weeks. "Virtual manufacturing" saves Cisco upward of $175 million in annual operating costs. A significant proportion of products is shipped directly to the customers; new product designs take fewer iterations and less time per iteration, with fewer engineering change notices, allowing for quicker and more cost-effective product introductions. Its credo is,[4] "The most expensive box of anything is the one sitting still. Forget Just in time. We're managing inventory in real time." The same is true for its resellers who use Cisco Connection Online (CCO) to interface effectively between Cisco and its customers. Partners are getting closely integrated into the operational infrastructure of individual organizations, creating an extended network of firms.

In fact we've seen such a thing operating at a completely different level too. Think about the "Wintel chain" or the Microsoft–Intel dominated value chain in PCs. Motorola, for example, could not beat Intel as the dominant microprocessor maker because it was competing against an entire value chain driven by the collective "Microsoft–Intel" enterprise and not Intel alone as a chipmaker. It was competing against a whole chain of partners around the operating system and microprocessor architecture of Microsoft and Intel respectively. The new aspect is that such competitive scenarios will become increasingly commonplace. It will not be enterprise versus enterprise but a network of firms against another network of firms. Consequently, the quality of the integration across organizations in a network will become critical for success.

The rising star

Information technology (IT) is the rising star. Evidence is piling up by the day that success today requires the innovative use of information technology in order to create the new operational infrastructure. Operational infrastructure is being recast to enhance flexibility for maximizing customer value. Oticon's employees work in an open office environment, relying on information technology for the backbone support of their daily activities. Notes Christian Jeppesen[5] from Oticon's IT department, "One of things I like best about being here is that we try to use IT the way it should be used – as a tool to support the whole organization." He adds, "It's an important role, because in the end, we depend upon IT in order to function."

At Cisco, over 80 percent of all support questions are answered by a quick visit to the Web. Internet-supported customer-care solutions across the company saved Cisco $270 million and increased customer satisfaction by 25 percent in the year 2000. More than 90 percent of the software components of products are downloaded from the network, saving $2.5 million a year in logistics cost. The company uses the Internet to enhance its ability to close out inquiries with one customer interaction. No more fax, e-mail, voice mail, documents, etc. from different non-communicating departments. Its Intranet helps to merge all the different islands, e.g. manufacturing, design, logistics, customer support, etc. into one seamless organization. It has drastically pruned goods return costs by developing online configuration tools so that the field and customer/partners can order accurate configurations online – and thus guarantee 100 percent correct orders (99.55 percent now as compared to 98 percent some years ago).

UPS Logistics Group, a subsidiary of United Parcel Service, is helping Ford Motor Company to reengineer the Ford transportation network of rail and haul-away carriers to optimize speed, precision, and reliability. "We are coupling lightning-speed, web-based technologies with leading-edge distribution network design and execution to deliver cars and trucks to customers faster," commented Frank Taylor, vice president of material, planning, and logistics, Ford Motor Company. "We are reengineering the Ford delivery network – introducing new management practices, eliminating bottlenecks, minimizing delays, and providing information technology systems that greatly improve the monitoring of vehicles across the entire journey to the customer," noted Dan DiMaggio, CEO, UPS Logistics Group.[6] "When the optimized network is complete, Ford customers can expect the same on-time delivery reliability they get from UPS."

Three elements of the infrastructure – organization, partners, and information technology – provide a highly fertile substrate for growth through innovation.

Among the benefits of the same are a 40 percent reduction in the time required to deliver vehicles from Ford plants to its dealers and customers and a significant reduction in Ford's multi-billion-dollar vehicle transportation, distribution, and inventory costs. Jerry Reynolds, Ford Dealer Council chairman and general manager of Prestige Ford in Garland, US, stated, "This is a win-win-win for Ford, for dealers and most importantly, for new vehicle buyers." The network is being launched in phases beginning in March 2000. The network is expected to be fully operational in 2001. Eventually the tracking tool will be extended to customers. "Ford customers who shop online for cars and trucks will be delighted to learn that they soon will be able to use the Web to track their vehicle delivery as well," added Taylor. Information technology is dramatically enhancing organizational ability to serve customers better.

What is the conclusion? Organizational infrastructure is becoming ever more important in the quest for excellence and innovation. The three elements of the infrastructure that we observed – organization, partners, and information technology – provide a highly fertile substrate for growth through innovation. We call this potent combination the e-nfrastructure. The three are the subject of discussion under the titles indicated below:

- A naturally innovative organization: People, structure, and culture should be reorganized for innovation. But how to undo the present?
- Collective enterprises: Extend your organization to your suppliers and resellers. A lot of competence and knowledge about better serving your customers lie there. How do you partner with them effectively to continuously innovate?
- Technological savviness: The people versus machine dichotomy is meaningless now. How to integrate the two seamlessly to create new value?

A naturally innovative organization

Let's start with analyzing what we observed at Schwab (in Chapter 3) – it's a rich source to understand the organizational setting of an innovative organization. Certain organizational behaviors displayed by Schwab do stand out for their sheer intensity and underlying convictions. The leadership style at Schwab, for example, is uniquely driven by a strong vision and comfortable acceptance of uncertainty in the environment. We also see how swiftly it acted to create the online trading solution development team. Indeed, organizations will have to act on customer needs and demands in real time. Necessarily, the level of cross-functional integration required for e-success is an order of magnitude higher than was necessary in the past.

While technology can create the necessary infrastructure for cross-functional integration, it can't make the infrastructure deliver – it takes people to do that. People, both as leaders and executors. Human capital is finally mightier than the greenbacks. You must also have noticed that Schwab's entry into online trading has quite been bottom-up – a very important reward for effectively managing the knowledge flow and content within the organization. In fact, we see something more in Schwab – an emotional energy commensurate with the logical designs – an organization culture that actually sustains the strategic initiatives and induces consistent behaviors by employees. Behaviors consistent with the expectations and assumptions of the strategic intent.

By implication, it also illustrates why a vast majority of the companies will find that their organizational legacy is quite a mixed bag – an advantage as well as a burden. While they have got leaders, skilled human resources, and a culture good enough for their existing business context, many of them will find the transition to an Internet-supported infrastructure to be costly and risky. Schwab was always an e(ntrepreneurial)-incumbent – an unencumbered incumbent – and yet it wasn't easy at all for Schwab to take the plunge.

Carly Fiorina, CEO, Hewlett-Packard (HP), has been exhorting employees to "aspirational performance"[7] and asking them to commit "your hearts, your minds and your souls" to her mission. HP, she says, "must be known as much for its strength of character as it's for the strength of its results." The first outsider to take the reins in HP's 60-year history also has used what she calls "well-placed shocks" to goad the technically accomplished but slow-moving manufacturer into the Internet age. For all her pep talks, Ms. Fionira's firm demands for improved performance have taken a personal toll at the company.

Several executives protested that employees weren't ready for a major reorganization.[8] Some executives fretted that managers wouldn't wield "real" authority if they couldn't control both product development and marketing. Consternation rippled through the ranks. Managers who had long aspired to run their own autonomous units, known as P&Ls, short for profit and loss, suddenly saw most of those jobs disappear. "The feeling was, here was Carly, who wasn't long time in the H-P culture, who doesn't understand our business and the H-P Way, and doesn't understand our strengths, particularly in businesses that were viewed as so successful for so long," said one of the top executives. "It initially felt like a big disempowerment." Even HP found the going tough.

So what should be the organizational agenda to secure effective transition to an innovative company? We believe that there is not much of "generic how-to" that can help managers to effectively develop innovative capabilities. Organizational issues are all-encompassing and there's little proven theory-at-work. It's a lot about situational expediency given an organizational context.

It is only natural that organizations are paranoid about remaining attractive to the best talent.

Noted Jack Welch,[9] "Seeing reality today means accepting the fact that e-business is here. It's not coming. It's not the thing of the future. It's here. Reality today means, 'go on offense.' One cannot be tentative about this. Excuses like channel conflict, or 'marketing and sales aren't ready,' or 'the customers aren't prepared' cannot be allowed to divert or paralyze the offensive. Moving aggressively raises some thorny issues with no clear and immediate solutions, but the challenge is to resolve these issues on the fly in the context of the new Internet reality. Tentativeness in action can mean being cut out of markets, perhaps not by traditional competitors but by companies never heard of 24 months ago." Obviously, proactively seeking change is hard. It calls for sincere commitment and committed execution. It also involves effecting necessary changes in the organizational context to create an enabling environment.

Welch may just be doing the right thing given GE's industry leadership in most of its businesses. In his book *The Innovators' Dilemma*, Clayton Christensen has advocated that ironical as it may sound, industry leadership has often been behind the fall of some of the great companies. These companies responded to "disruptive technologies" with sustaining innovations – improving their products – to serve their customers better. He also adds,[10] "If you go back in history, some of our economy's most powerful, successful companies today were once disruptors" – Intel, Wal-Mart, Toyota, Sony, the telephone companies, and Cisco. The only precondition (for getting the key resources to respond appropriately in these situations) is a CEO who has the self-confidence to make an intuitive bet that this is a business that is going to be real. Tomorrow's world will be shaped in the boardrooms and not in the technological laboratories! CEOs will have to be excellent in both conceiving the most appropriate deliberate organization and translating the same into effective structures for implementation. Recall from Chapter 3 how both Christos Cotsakos of E*TRADE and Charles Schwab and David Pottruck of Schwab each bet their respective firms on the Internet by having the guts to take and sustain bold innovative positions.

But how do some leaders galvanize their employees more than others? The incentive system they introduce is one of the important reasons for the difference. In fact GE has taken the whole concept of sharing, collaboration, and team play to great length. Says Dennis D. Dammerman,[11] CFO, "we wanted to become what we call boundaryless, to incentivize rather than discourage sharing, learning, working together across functions and businesses and levels within the company. We kept the bonus, but made it volatile only to a range of about 20 percent on whether you, individually, have a good or bad year. But we overshadowed it with a stock-price-based compensation – stock options." In that process "serious money" could lie in the overall company performance.

Are you surprised now why employee stock option plans (ESOPs) may be one of the common denominators in many innovative companies today? ESOPs allow employees to become co-owners of the business – a novel situation for many incumbent managers. A bottom-up pressure develops for innovation. A knowledge organization, where many employees have stock options, can be compared to an organization that moves from a dictatorship to an oligarchy. This means that many business organizations will become managed in ways similar to the way consulting firms (with partnerships), hospitals, or even universities are managed. A tough call but an innovator's paradise – replace the vertical structures by lateral ones.

What about the ESOP owners? The employees? In Silicon Valley, people have always been the key resource – it's not a recent truth. The unique fit of entrepreneurship and intrapreneurship is at the heart of the success that the Valley is. That's exactly the idea that Bill Hewlett and David Packard had in mind when the two young engineers met to form their company in 1937.[12] The minutes of that fateful meeting went on to say, "The question of what to manufacture was postponed." In fact the whole founding concept of the company was not so much what, but who. After World War II, they hired a whole batch of fabulous people streaming out of government labs, without anything specific in mind for them to do. Packard grasped the subtle truth that a great company will always generate more opportunity than it can handle, and that growth is ultimately constrained only by the ability to get enough of the right people. And Packard's law stills hold, even in today's economy: growth in revenues can not exceed growth in people who can execute and sustain that growth.

> "A great company will always generate more opportunity than it can handle."

Noted John Chambers,[13] "I will put my jobs anywhere in the world where the right infrastructure is, with the right educated workforce, with the right supportive government. I can do that today with the technology we have, but I can't do it socially. I don't know how to manage it yet." He added, "We had realized early on that a world-class engineer with five peers can out-produce 200 regular engineers. That's what the start-ups do so well in Silicon Valley."

Further, people as the key resource results in an organization that can respond to customer stimuli in real time – a very desirable value for any customer. Because customers get best served in the processes – emotionally and objectively. Incidentally, the value of emotional gratification that comes due to prompt attention has always been underestimated, but let's not forget that it's all about perception and the latter has good emotional content.

Why may all this be a tall order for many companies? Dawn Lepore[14] plumbed deep into her experiences to add a caution, "To inspire change, you have to know and emphasize what does not change. For us, that is our commitment to our vision of providing the most useful and ethical financial services in the world, and our values of being fair, earning trust, striving hard, and working as a team. When we emphasize these things, and make sure that our employees understand that changes are happening inside of these principles – then they begin to see changes as urgent in order to fulfill our commitment to that vision and those values for our customers. Constantly communicating to your employees how and why your move to electronic commerce is consistent with your company vision will go a long way towards ensuring your success." And she added, "And it's our vision that drove us to the Internet – because we fundamentally believe that the Internet is good for customers." Her remarks are critical for understanding innovation in successful organizations.

But incumbents have to be extra cautious in planning and implementing the induction of the online operations. Says David H. Komansky,[15] Chairman and CEO, Merrill Lynch, "What took us, frankly, so long to respond was not a recognition that it was real, that we had to change our business plan. What took so long was how to do it without blowing up what we had."

But is this avoidable? Can we do without these changes? Dawn Lepore had the answer,[16] "The Internet is a democratizing force – imperfect to be sure, but it does de-centralize power in unprecedented ways. Don't kid yourself that things can stay the same – your employees are becoming increasingly empowered consumers, and that sense of control carries into the workplace." She added, "And there is a compelling business reason for getting rid of the old command and control – the problems are so complex and the need for speed to market is so great that everyone's intellect counts." She continued, "In a sense, the internal reflection of your brand is your culture. If your company does not have a history of innovation or moving quickly, your transition to the Internet will be more difficult." The Internet has unleashed a run-away one-way train – organizational cultures have to change and become more conspicuous to be recognized as an important complement to the formal organization. The winners have already boarded the train and some of them are firmly in the driver's seat. GE is one in the driver's coach.

Welch argued about GE: "It is not unique in the diversity of its businesses. There are other large multi-business companies. It is not unique in its size. There are a handful of companies around the world as large or larger. It is not even unique in what we call its culture of learning. There are a few companies whose cultures thrive on learning. GE is unique in that it is all three: a very large, multi-business company with a learning culture that has transformed the diversity of its businesses and its size – from what is sometimes perceived as a handicap – into a tremendous competitive advantage."[17] Indeed, a happy marriage of the formal organization and informal organization holds the key to the "new-age" organization.

This boundary-less learning culture killed any view that assumed the "GE way" was the only way or even the best way. The operative assumption today is that someone, somewhere, has a better idea; and the operative compulsion is to find who has that better idea, learn it, and put it into action – fast. Selflessly sharing good ideas while endlessly searching for better ideas became a natural act. It purged NIH – not invented here – from its system, creating a company with an insatiable desire for information. All this was done the hard way, before the arrival of the Internet. Today, with the Internet, information is available everywhere to everyone, and a company that isn't searching for the best idea, isn't open to ideas from anywhere, will find itself left behind with its survival at stake. Another management concept that served GE very well over two decades was the belief that an organization that was not only comfortable with change but relished it – saw it always as opportunity, not as a threat – had a distinct advantage in a world where the pace of change was always accelerating.[18]

To create a naturally innovative organization:

1 Focus on people – both as leaders and as executors. People are infinitely more important than both bricks and clicks.

2 Build an emotional energy in the organization commensurate with the logical ambitions. You need a tailored organizational culture to sustain the strategic initiatives by inducing consistent behaviors by employees.

3 Let ideas, capital, and talent circulate freely across your organization – processes and structures notwithstanding.

And the barriers? Not all is gold that shines, and a real-time flexible organization may be difficult for employees. The creation of a flexible organization will impose psychological and emotional traumas on employees. There is a limit to an individual's elasticity. There is a reason why start-ups have fewer problems in pushing the frontiers of established business practices than established firms do – its easier to start something new than it is to change something old. So, too, will the ability to attract – and retain – the right employees. In an era when the pace of change keeps accelerating, the only way to stay ahead is to hire people who are self-motivated to change. The new frontier for managers is to create the future by harnessing competence in an enhanced network that includes customers.

Collective enterprises

The ability to adapt oneself quickly and precisely to emergent situations has always been a source of great innovative possibilities and opportunities in personal life. Such ability is very difficult, however, for organizations. The legacy of competencies, resources, organizational culture, and strategic commitments puts a leash on what's possible in a given time frame. In other words, organizational inertia limits competitive agility and innovative pursuits. What happens when organizational boundaries can be reworked quickly, comprehensively, and effectively? Organizational boundaries become a new source of significant innovative opportunities and sustainable competitive advantage. As organizations extend themselves to reach out to their partners, resellers (dealers), and suppliers, they create collective enterprises that tap deeper into collective knowledge and competencies.

And the ability to create (and re-create) collective enterprises is steadily taking up the center stage of strategy. Oticon, Cisco, and Wintel (Microsoft and Intel) are living testimonies of such collective enterprises. However, all three have gone their own way in designing and implementing the same. Oticon has not given a top-level structural frame to its collective enterprise but the structure is formal. Cisco has formalized the collective enterprise closely around itself in a top-level design. Wintel has no top-level or formal structure but the collective works together in close cooperation. There is no one right way of creating collective enterprises.

Collective enterprises have to be opportunity-driven and adaptable.

Obviously, collective enterprises have to be opportunity-driven and adaptable. Cooperation and collaboration will be far more dynamic and specific to customer clusters or solution clusters. The growing demand for more in less time has stimulated the creation of this new operational architecture. But even otherwise, to service increasingly global and mass customization demands, collective enterprises need to be able to reconfigure and assemble the right complement of resources quickly. The concept has variously been described and one of the popular names given to it is *virtual factory*.[19] A virtual factory represents a group of organizations that interacts as one to create and deliver value to a specific target customer(s) or product(s). No two virtual factories will be similar. Their revenues will also be shared among them in a complex way – specific to the contribution made in each of the executed customer orders.

You'll have to tailor your virtual factory in your own unique way. You'll also nurture it in your own unique way to get the most out of it. Fortunately, it's not that hard to do as it used to be. The Internet has brought about a fundamental change in inter-organizational interface costs.

As mentioned in a previous chapter, the latter are reducing steadily and are soon expected to be close to intra-organizational interface costs. Sew up your dream virtual factory and the Internet will deliver it. Do you now see the virtual factories as innovative factories too?

HP and Oracle provide a good example of reaching out to each other to develop new competencies in serving customers. By using Internet-enabled technology from both companies, Oracle's and HP's sales environments will be linked via the Internet, allowing the companies to collaborate on joint sales opportunities to expand the market potential for both companies. "HP and Oracle are expanding the CRM market by taking the notion of partnering to a whole new level," said Ellison of Oracle. "By using Internet-enabled Oracle CRM products to link HP's and Oracle's sales forces, we can get an incredibly detailed view of joint opportunities and can act quickly to close deals that give our customers what they want. This is the prototype for a whole new sales model."

"Customers want less complexity, better integration and faster implementation of their Internet solutions," noted Carly Fiorina, CEO, HP. "They want industry leaders like Oracle and HP to do a better job of delivering a total customer solution that exceeds customer expectations." With the new systems in place, every HP and Oracle salesperson will be able to collaborate and share information in real time over the Internet. At the same time, both management teams will have instant access to a greatly expanded view of the pipeline and an even more detailed, up-to-the-minute global sales forecast.

A Xerox–3M alliance is another good example of pooling complementary assets for innovation. In 1999, Xerox Corporation and 3M came together to bring to market Electronic Paper – a digital document display with the portability of a plain sheet of paper developed at the Xerox Palo Alto Research Center (PARC). Like paper, it is user-friendly, thin, lightweight, and flexible. But like a computer display, it is also dynamic and rewritable. Xerox looks to establish a means by which the electronic paper material can be manufactured in the volumes necessary to meet market demands and to make the development of a wide range of supporting applications commercially viable. This initiative combines Xerox's leading-edge technology with 3M's extensive manufacturing experience, representing an ideal pairing to establish a market-leading technology.

As described in Chapter 4, in August 2000,[20] Amazon.com and Toys"R"Us.com decided to partner together to do what they can each do best. Amazon manages the online presence and handles the customer management from order receipt to shipping. Toys"R"Us purchases and maintains the inventory in Amazon's warehouses. Noted an industry analyst, "each company's strengths will compensate for the other's glaring weaknesses." Amazon has now a similar tie-up with Border Books too.

You can do even better. You can create virtual factories that can effectively network a far bigger number of organizations together. There would be a number of digitally connected specialized and efficient participants in a collective to provide a given product (or service) to a customer. Each activity in the collective will have to produce the best value possible for customers. If the participants in a value chain can not provide the best value to the customer being served by the value chain, that value chain will disintegrate. The participants in a value chain will, by themselves, strive to choose the best fit participants because the overall performance will be determined by the weakest link in the supply chain.

Expectedly, outsourcing as a broader competency is at the heart of a virtual factory. Online collaboration is enabling a complex but very efficient web of outsourcing arrangements. It's creating not only horizontal structures but also vertical or hierarchical structures. ImageX.com,[21] a printing e-procurement services provider, is an example of an intermediary securing supply chain innovations built on a network of players. Its system enables organizations to modify, proof, order, and manage custom-printed business materials directly over the Internet. The service is innovative in many ways. For example, it lets your remote offices place orders, yet manage their release into print production from the corporate offices. You can combine multiple orders together to take advantage of volume pricing. And when you make changes, a proof is instantly available on-screen and can be printed to your own desktop printer.

But the more interesting innovation lies somewhere else. ImageX outsources its manufacturing to a network of partners, who through its proprietary software, receive production-ready digital files directly from the customer. At each point there are a number of partners to provide a large number of service options. No less significantly, ImageX's manufacturing partners achieve increased efficiencies because the proprietary system serves as the common standard backbone for the processes of file preparation, prepress, and transfer. This results in greater file consistency, fewer errors, and higher quality, as well as simplified tracking and reporting processes. Thus a number of vertical links get added at different points on the horizontal chain to create infinite operational possibilities for innovatively servicing customers.

Ever thought of a European Airlines Ltd? A new entity that would sell the tickets of all airlines in Europe? Loads of innovative opportunities now become possible among bitterly competing firms by establishing new cooperative structures. How? Air France, Lufthansa, British Airways, Swissair, and KLM have come together to form an alliance to provide one-point customized travel solutions. These five airlines are, in fact, the leading participants in at least four existing global airline alliances such as Star

Alliance and One World, and are bitter rivals. Actually, ten of Europe's largest airlines, including these five, are negotiating the launch of a joint travel agency. One of the first pan-European bodies after the European commission itself? Perhaps. Thank the Internet for it. They are planning to launch an Internet travel portal.[22]

The initiative follows a similar venture, Orbitz, declared in November 1999 by four big airlines in the US – Delta, United, Northwestern and Continental Airlines. In January 2000, eight other US carriers signed on to the project, along with 15 foreign carriers. All have agreed to sell discounted Internet-only fares on the proposed site. While Travelocity and Expedia have been successfully navigating cyberspace for some time, other brick-and-mortar travel agencies are not so happy – this initiative will bring about a fundamental change in their businesses.

Obviously, the expected change is hugely disruptive for the travel industry. The American Society of Travel Agents (ASTA) has formally requested that the US Department of Justice (DOJ) block the sale of airline tickets by 27 US and foreign carriers on an industry-wide website. "This joint site is a clear attempt on the part of the airlines to lure consumers onto the Web with lower prices and drive all their competitors out of business, resulting in complete and total domination of the public airways," noted Joe Galloway, CEO, ASTA. The key lesson from this example is that collective enterprises will cut a lot of processes and cost in any existing value chain. And innovatively applied, it represents a very strategic opportunity for first movers.

Andy Grove,[23] Intel's chairman, adds a new dimension to the competitive impact of innovation when he says that Napster may mean Intel is about to waste $80 million a year. He is referring to the $80 million a year, for five years, that Intel is going to invest in internationally expanding the capacity of its internal network and wide-area network. He says that Napster is like "a reversion of a large portion of traffic back to some modern equivalent of local-area networking rather than wide-area networking. It doesn't have to be music or video. It can be corporate data." He elaborates, "My worry about building up of the networking infrastructure that is costing us $80 million a year is that we're going to build that infrastructure just when the usage pattern is going to a much more peer-to-peer-based orientation." The peer-to-peer networks that the Internet is enabling are a new possibility and open up a whole new world of very innovative opportunities. A thing of the (near) future, but one that is worth exploration to steal a march over competitors.

Collective enterprises are:

1 Opportunity driven and adaptable – a collective enterprise reconfigures rapidly to assemble the right complement of resources.

2 Like virtual factories – a company's virtual boundaries are redefined to include not only itself but also all partners in collaboration with whom it creates and delivers value.

3 Value maximizers – each activity in the value chain to produce a given product should represent the best value possible for the customer.

Technological savviness

New technologies bring new possibilities. The Internet is hardly an exception. In fact, in the case of the Internet such possibilities are limitless. For the Internet is hardly a technology, it's a construct – more logical than physical. The possibilities are truly immense. The comprehensive integration of processes – across all online and offline channels – is the new innovation platform. Successful companies have been creating additional value by going beyond creating an efficient customer interface (such as online order entry, order status tracking, and links with customer service centers) to integrating all customer contact channels, seamlessly, to the relevant backend participants such as product development and manufacturing, services like finance and legal departments, and external partners such as suppliers. Emphasized Stuart Hamilton,[24] innovations director of Axon, an SAP software implementation consultancy, "If it ain't integrated, it ain't e-commerce. The aim is not to connect customers to your web site, but to connect them to your business."

> "If it ain't integrated, it ain't e-commerce. The aim is not to connect customers to your web site, but to connect them to your business."

Flextronics, a leading global high-tech (contract) manufacturer, has a network of global manufacturing facilities located in key markets of the Americas, Europe, and Asia. It services original equipment manufacturer (OEM) customers by offering them a world-class manufacturing infrastructure across the globe. It is a good example of what a truly integrated operational infrastructure creates – unique value creation and delivery opportunities. Flextronics's innovative use of IT has greatly increased the effectiveness of its manufacturing services, leading to enhanced flexibility and speed of its services. It has completely reorganized its processes and implemented an enterprise-wide IT infrastructure that includes a unique array of processes for services such as customer order processing, fulfillment, support, and product repair. Flextronics can even provide customers with a website to collect data from sales channels to facilitate order processing; thus, effectively extending its manufacturing process into its customers' intranets.

Flextronics has implemented an ERP business solution to achieve the highest level of standardization within every department of the company. Every operational phase, from materials pricing to order processing, is exactly the same in China, Hungary, Silicon Valley, and at every other Flextronics facility, making it possible to efficiently shift production to the lowest-cost manufacturing areas for its customers. It has also created a global network of Product Introduction Centers (PICs), located near OEMs. The PICs provide an environment in which OEM and Flextronics engineers work concurrently to achieve specific design goals to reduce development, production, and delivery cycles.

An IT-enabled and IT-intensive enterprise architecture is rapidly emerging as a major organizational imperative. The need for a "design" behind the operational infrastructure was never more urgent; the need to create flexible operations by getting the right marriage of IT and physical processes never more important. But IT can do more than merely support a business process. It can be the real enabler of creativity. Technology-based processes can be the trigger for innovation, a great platform to unleash creativity.

Dell has taken its own processes right into the manufacturing processes of its main suppliers; process innovations are being used to blur traditional boundaries between supplier and manufacturer and customer. One of the simple applications at Dell is the Scoreboard where its suppliers can score their performance against key Dell metrics. The metrics have been set for each supplier to provide the highest quality and reliability to customers, and it helps drive quality at the component level. Each supplier can see its own score on the metrics and compare how they're doing compared to other suppliers in the same class. The innovative use of IT enables transparency in performance.

Teloquent, a leader in call center platforms, for example, provides an innovative e-business customer interaction platform. Teloquent's unique value proposition is the ability to direct incoming requests to the right agent – the person who can best serve that particular customer at that moment in time, regardless of how the request came in or where the agent is located. Integrated with leading CRM systems, it delivers to this agent not only the call/request, but also the information necessary to prepare the agent to respond. Their solutions enable companies to bring one-on-one human interactions – via telephone, e-mail, web text chat, web callback, pushed/shared web screens or VoIP (voice over IP) – into their business infrastructures in a way that maximizes satisfaction for customers and minimizes cost.

The Teloquent platform ensures consistency across all points of contact since one agent application can handle voice over the public switched telephone network (PSTN) as well as e-mail and Web-based contact over the Internet. One set of business rules and customer information drives interactions across all media and locations. One point of management can oversee multi-site and even virtual call centers and teleweb centers dispersed across the country or the world. One set of reports can be generated across the entire operation. And the best part: Teloquent solutions can be "dropped into" existing telephony and data networks, without the need to modify existing infrastructures or make them the same from site to site.

Indeed, a sustainable value creation is obtained by creating interfaces among complementary technologies – and thus alliances between companies. Collaboration among technological partners, in many cases, is now one of the architectural requirements for innovating new products. Integration holds the key to major innovations in value creation. Increasingly, software is becoming the more important vehicle for integration. Significant innovation capabilities could be secured by acquiring or developing appropriate software complementing the physical processes. Siebel's Web-based business solutions provide, for example, enterprise-wide support for internal sales, marketing, and customer service organizations and extends that support throughout the entire extended enterprise, seamlessly uniting third-party resellers and service providers, business partners, and customers into a single information system.

A good beginning in the innovative pursuit of technology applications is simply to address the problems at hand in the most logical way – a solution is always possible. Google, the well-known search engine, is one such example. Its search service is what it should ideally be; not an edited, limited directory or a list of results that have been auctioned to the highest bidder, but a thoughtful method of organizing the Internet according to the Internet's inherent structure. And it took all these years after Yahoo! Google has revolutionized searching on the Web with its PageRank technology. This link structure automatically democratizes the Internet. It eliminates hierarchy and enables information and ideas to flow unimpeded from site to site.

The PageRank method uses the Internet's vast link structure as an organizational tool. In simpler words, Google interprets a link from page A to page B as a vote, by page A, for page B. Google assesses a page's importance by the votes it receives. But Google looks at more than the sheer volume of votes, or links; it also analyzes the page that casts the vote. Votes cast by pages that are themselves "important" weigh more heavily and help to make other pages "important." Google's complex, automated search methods preclude human interference. Unlike other search engines, Google is structured so no one can purchase a higher PageRank or commercially alter results. A Google search is an objective way to find high-quality websites, easily.

In this way, PageRank is Google's general indicator of importance but it does not depend on a specific query. Rather, it is a characteristic of a page itself based on data from the Web that Google analyzes using complex algorithms that assess link structure. Of course, important pages mean nothing to you if they don't match your query. So, Google uses sophisticated text-matching techniques to find pages that are both important and relevant to your search.

But we need to be careful in this technology push. Tony DeLuca, CTO of electronics components distributor Avnet Inc. comments: "My job has become business process design. We recognized that the focus and the energy is really on process and less on technology. It's not because IT is less important. But from an IT-consolidation standpoint, we've gotten that reasonably down to a science. More and more, the focus of the IT staff working with the business community is on business process, business process, business process."[25]

A competence in Information Technology is critical because:

1 The boundaries between technology and processes are disappearing. Information technology, especially the Internet, does not create another channel. It should be the channel – the backbone for the entire operations.

2 Collective enterprise cannot be realized without it. Thank information technology for making inter-organizational interface costs comparable to intra-organizational interface costs.

3 The opportunity is to let customers help themselves. That means combining your offline (bricks) and online (clicks) channels and linking the two to your operations. And this isn't feasible without information technology systems.

Technology adoption is not a purely technological issue. Chambers,[26] CEO Cisco, remembers that customer service was at the top of his list. He also looked for other groups that could benefit from going online – and was open to a new approach. "Engineering and sales were my most independent and headstrong groups," he recalled. "If I had led with them, I might not have been successful." Instead Chambers started pushing other divisions, namely, manufacturing, customer ordering, and finance, to network their operations more fully. And it worked and the rest is history. Chambers has other lessons too: the first company to capitalize on an innovation reaps the greatest rewards and most improved operating margins. When competitors start to use the same technologies, "your competitive advantage or differentiation, or your effect on margins, gets commoditized." Then it's time to move on to the next new thing. But wait too long and "you get Dell'd or Amazon'd, or Cisco'd or Schwab'd," Chambers cautioned.

It's all the more important in the case of Internet deployment that the application of the technology is in close association with its users. The Internet is uniquely about context. According to a Cisco manager in Europe, "Our customers are directing the applications development. You have to be careful as you need to anticipate your customers' needs; they don't know what they don't know and in some instances you're leading your customers because you know them so well you are able to bring something to them and you can get their reaction to it and I think that's an important component as well. It's not just about reacting, particularly in the Internet space because if we're talking about doing things, I mean I don't know how in late 1994 a customer could have said to us, 'you know, I want to sit at my desk top and I want to be able to configure products, get order status and place the order and then order service parts and do all that from my desk top' – they wouldn't even have conceived of it. But yet what we knew was that they had a problem in they were dissatisfied in a number of ways around those processes and so therefore we developed a solution – the Internet."[27]

Interestingly, it is not so much cost reduction that drives what Cisco does. One of the key success factors in what it has done with the Internet is that it solved the customers' problem first and then looked for a technical solution. Electronic commerce started at Cisco because its products did not work well in the traditional EDI environment. Cisco makes highly configurable products with different chassis, different types of memory chips, modules, etc. and they are not interchangeable. As a result, before the e-commerce effort began, about one-third of all orders that came to Cisco were incorrect – wrong price, wrong part number, and invalid configuration. Typically what this would mean is a lot of call back to the customer and an increase in the product lead-times. Today, the system is updated regularly and wrong orders cannot be entered. Since Cisco has implemented e-commerce it and its partners have saved millions of dollars. However, the cost savings were not the goal of Cisco's foray into electronic commerce.

Action points

1. Is your organization a real-time organization? Is it capable of acting in real time? How long did it take you the last time to sense and respond to a major customer complaint?

2. Can some of the ideas of Oticon apply to (perhaps parts of) your organization? Is your organization caught in the trap of satisfactory underperformance? Are you realizing the creative potential of your employees?
3. What is your organization doing to attract and retain the best talent? Do people associate with your company because their employability is maximized?
4. Are there hidden assets in your network of partners that are not being leveraged? Can you create new value by combining your strengths with those of your partners?
5. Is information technology being used to connect all players (including customers) in your network of partners? Is technology enabling a seamless customer experience across your online and offline channels? And beyond to connect your customers to your firm's operational infrastructure (backend)?

Mantra

Oticon converted itself into the "ultimate flexible organization" because it aimed to be one. Oticon demonstrates how the design and implementation of operational infrastructure and practices becomes a great enabler and source of innovation, how leadership influences innovation, and how culture stimulates radical if not revolutionary innovation.

Three elements of the infrastructure – organization, partners, and information technology – provide a highly fertile substrate for growth through innovation. We call this potent combination the e-nfrastructure.

Organizations have to gear up to take the level of cross-functional integration an order of magnitude higher than was necessary in the past. A similar imperative holds true for integration with partners into a network and the quality of the integration will be critical for success. But such integration will not only be horizontal but many levels deep vertically too.

The dichotomy between man and machine is becoming meaningless. Technology, especially information technology, is getting interleaved with all operational processes – both online and offline. Technology adoption is no longer a simple technology issue. The (organizational) context of technology application plays the critical role in determining the innovative use of technology.

The innovation-ready e-nfrastructure cannot be achieved overnight, or even in months or years. From now on it'll always be an unfinished agenda. It must be in the (organizational) genes and the genes have to be mutated – organizational character is at the top of the change agenda. Middle-of-the-road organizational attributes can not support the demands of the emerging opportunities.

Notes

1. Labarre, Polly, (1994) "The dis-organization of oticon," *Industry Week*, July 18, pp. 23–8.
2. Labarre, Polly, (1994) "The dis-organization of oticon," *Industry Week*, July 18, pp. 23–8.
3. Victor, Bart and Boynton, Andrew C. *Invented Here*, HBS Press, pp. 193–5.
4. http//www.cisco.com/warp/public/749/ar2000/low/discover/supply_chain.html
5. www.oticon.com
6. Based on inputs from the company website www.ups.com
7. Based on the report by David P. Hamilton (2000) "At Hewlett-Packard, new boss remakes the gray lady," *The Asian Wall Street Journal*, August 23.
8. Based on the report by David P. Hamilton (2000) "At Hewlett-Packard, new boss remakes the gray lady," *The Asian Wall Street Journal*, August 23.
9. www.ge.com. Speech by J.F. Welch presented at the General Electric Company 2000 Anual Meeting, Richmond, Virginia, April 26, 2000.
10. Based on the article "Should you fear disruptive technology?" *Fortune*, April 3, 2000, pp. 89–90.
11. www.ge.com. Speech by J.F. Welch "Changing GE: Lessons learned from along the way."
12. James Collins (2000) "Don't rewrite the rules of the road," *Business Week*, August 28.
13. Byren, John A. (2000) "Visionary vs. Visionary," *Business Week*, August 28.
14. www.cisco.com
15. Smith, Randall and Gasparino, Charles (2000) "Late to the party: what took Merrill Lynch so long to respond to the Web?," *Wall Street Journal*, July 17.
16. www.cisco.com
17. www.ge.com. Speech by J. F. Welch, "A learning company and its quest for six sigma."
18. www.ge.com

19. De Meyer, A (1992) *Competing for Customer Value*, Pitman Publishing.
20. Elias, Paul (2000) "Is Jeff Bezos Father Christmas?", Redherring.com, August 11.
21. www.commerceone.com/news/us
22. Done, Kevin and Odell, Mike (2000) "European airlines may fly Internet travel agency," *Financial Times*, February 19.
23. eCompany (2000) "Napster is clouding Grove's crystal ball," *Fortune*, May 29, pp 77–8
24. Moran, Nuala (2000) "Intergrating systems," *Financial Times*, September 1.
25. "Business poses new challenge for IT architecture," *Information Week*, February 7, 2000.
26. Corcoran, Elizabeth (2000) "The Egang", *Forbes Global*, August 7.
27. Insead interviews.

Perpetual metamorphosis   10

Bookmark

The cove of economics is "scarcity." The economics of production is driven by scarcity. Indeed, the theory of constraints is most real to life. There is no life without constraints! But could you dare to imagine a life without most of the constraints around you? Difficult as it may be to imagine, it's getting to be a real thing. However, that also means organizations will secure changes in months which earlier took place over decades or years. The increasing pace of change is also leading to rapid-fire innovations. New innovation processes are emerging.

It's about the need for continuous change. Perpetual metamorphosis is the term we chose for this: the act of undergoing a slow death for rebirth – achieving a break from the past body and soul in order to build a new one, but having the humility to recognize failures and then metamorphose into yet another stage of experimental evolution. It is all part of the process of perpetual metamorphosis.

Read this chapter to see how companies are applying perpetual metamorphosis to live with the "unconstrained" context for innovation.

Changed forever

The previous chapters focused on how innovation will be enabled by restructuring existing resources like assets, processes, people, and connections with customers. There is another important driver for innovation – discontinuities in the external environment. A good example of this has been the remarkable spurt of innovation unleashed by the (commercial) arrival of the Internet. Thus, opportunities for innovation lie within and without. Organizations must reevaluate their businesses in the context of the changing business environment to maximize their opportunities – immediate and future.

The business environment is changing fundamentally because the Internet has given birth to a unique communication and delivery infrastructure. Trying to explain the phenomenon, Philip B. Evans and Thomas S. Wurster[1] pronounce that the trade-off between reach and richness of information is now being blown up. Reach represents the number of recipients of information. Richness represents the bandwidth (amount of information exchanged in a given time from sender to receiver), customization (degree of tailoring for the receiver), and interactivity. This pervasive trade-off has shaped how companies communicate, collaborate, and conduct transactions internally and with customers, suppliers, and distributors. This trade-off not only governs the old economics of information but is also fundamental to a whole set of premises about how the business world works.

According to them, what is truly revolutionary is the possibility that the Internet offers to unbundle information from its physical carrier. When information is carried by physical objects – by a salesperson or by a piece of direct mail, for example – it goes where things go and goes no further. It is constrained to follow the linear flow of the physical value chain. But once everyone is connected through the Internet, information can travel by itself. The reach versus richness trade-off would not be necessary anymore – both reach and richness could be achieved at the same time. For example, having an effective intranet within an organization will help unbundle knowledge about competitors and salespeople (the carriers of the knowledge). The unique knowledge content and experiences of all salespeople can be stored on the intranet. Any particular information easily could be accessed without the need to communicate with the concerned salesperson that provided that particular piece of knowledge. Consequently, the reach and richness of information within an organization increases manifold. A whole new way of operation is now possible!

> **eBay has changed auctions,
> E-steel has changed steel.
> Priceline is changing pricing.**

We've already seen in the cases at the start of the book how Amazon, E*TRADE, and Auto-By-Tel have each radically transformed their respective industries. And that is now happening in every industry. eBay has changed auctions, E-steel has changed steel, Priceline has changed pricing, MP3 and Napster have changed music. The list is endless. The consequence of these is that incumbents will have to reevaluate their businesses to compete in the changed business environment. That's not going to be easy at all. But at the same time, it's a great opportunity. An opportunity to rejuvenate your business opportunity-set. Some leading incumbents have been reinventing themselves off and on to redefine their businesses to make the most out of the emergent business environment.

IBM is a good example of a company reinventing itself every few decades. It was incorporated in 1911 to manufacture and sell commercial scales and industrial time recorders, meat and cheese slicers, and of course, tabulators and punch cards. It remained so for about three decades until the 1930s. Over the next two decades in the 1940s and 1950s it evolved into an office automation company (largely tabulating). In 1944 it launched Mark I, an electromechanical calculator. Over 50 feet long, 8 feet high, and weighing almost 5 tons, the Mark I took about six seconds for multiplication and twice as long for division! In 1952, it introduced the IBM 701, its first large computer based on the vacuum tube, and in 1957 added the IBM 305, the first disk storage system, and started billing, payroll, and inventory applications development.

The next two decades, the 1960s until the early 1980s marked IBM's evolution as a computer company – beyond hardware – into software and services. In 1964, IBM introduced System/360, a bold departure from the monolithic, one-size-fits-all mainframe; it allowed interchangeable software and peripherals. In fact, *Fortune* had indeed dubbed it "IBM's $5 billion gamble." Under Tom Watson Jr., in 1969, it changed the way it sold technology – "unbundled" the computer into hardware, software, and services components and offered them for sale individually – giving birth to the multibillion-dollar software and services industries.

During the 1980s and early 1990s, it tried to be a PC company and failed. IBM was thrown into turmoil – by its own creation, the IBM Personal Computer, or PC! By the late 1980s IBM had also laid a foundation for network computing and numerous other applications. But the PC and the client/server (network) revolution fundamentally rocked IBM. Result: by 1993, IBM's annual net losses reached a record $8 billion.

Louis V. Gerstner Jr. arrived as IBM's chairman and CEO on April 1, 1993. For the first time in the company's history IBM had chosen a leader from outside its ranks. Despite mounting pressure to split IBM into separate, independent companies (into PCs, services, and software divisions, for example), Gerstner decided to keep the company together. He asserted IBM's strength: combined expertise in solutions, services, products, and technologies. And yes, once again, customers were focused on integrated business solutions. And the stock value moved from under $20 in 1995 to around $110 in February 2000, including two 2:1 splits during this period.

IBM may just be one of its kind – it significantly influenced the evolution of the IT industry. Others did not have that fortune but some of them have at some points in their history significantly impinged upon their industry and at other times simply responded to their changing environment. Xerox, for example, gave birth to the "photocopy" industry but underwent two major business "reinventions" in the 1990s dictated by changes in its business environment. The first one started in 1994 and the other in 1999. In 1994, it unveiled itself as "The Document Company." That was the culmination of efforts between 1989 and 1994 to move away from a manufacturer of machines to a provider of solutions and from a specialist in copies to an expert in document management.[2]

In 1999, it reorganized itself to better capitalize on new growth opportunities and initiated the "Sharing knowledge through documents" initiative. "In the digital age, knowledge is our life blood. And documents are the DNA of knowledge," said Rick Thoman, the then president and CEO. Thoman bet that managing for knowledge will rejuvenate Xerox in the decade to come, just as managing for quality reinvigorated the company in the 1980s. According to Xerox, at least 46 percent of a company's knowledge is tied up in paper and digital documents. Do you know how to find it? Can you get to it when you need it? Can you put it to use? Xerox has a portfolio of products, services, software, and solutions for the same! It hopes that these might finally change it from a predominantly hardware company to a solutions company (see the next chapter for more on Xerox's efforts in knowledge management).

It take guts to reinvent yourself; you:

1 have to be prepared to change the rules of the game;
2 need top managers who can make bold long-term decisions;
3 have to be fearless about undergoing drastic strategic restructuring and organizational change; and
4 have to be ready to accept failure, learn from it and move on.

It's talking about helping companies to let their people do a better job of creating, finding, sharing, using, and reusing organizational knowledge. Assisting its clients to leverage new and existing technology investments, enhance productivity, reduce costs, and increase revenue and profitability. It has a suite of knowledge management products for:

- Sharing and distributing knowledge: the tools include Docushare, Flowport, Eureka, DataGlyphs and Chrystal.
- Finding, viewing, and navigating knowledge: the tools include Askonce, Inxight and electronic paper.
- Protecting digital intellectual property: the tool is Content Guard. It is an end-to-end solution for the management of digital content such as the granting of rights, the enforcement of rights during use and ongoing rights tracking. It also facilitates the acquisition and granting of rights and royalty accounting.

Evidently, organizations have been "reinventing" themselves time and again. Companies like IBM, Xerox, and others who have had the guts to reinvent themselves seem to have some common characteristics. First, they're prepared to change the rules of the game in their industry. Secondly, they have no fear of going through drastic strategic restructuring and reorganization of their competence base. Thirdly, top managers like Gerstner are willing to adhere to bold long-term decisions. Fourthly, customers and users play an important role in guiding the company's transition process.

The Internet is a new discontinuity requiring adaptation. A discontinuity in the way we communicate, manage information and act on it. Incumbents have to adopt and leverage this discontinuity, and at a rapidly increasing pace. Perhaps they find themselves in a continuous state of flux. But the one who thrives in the ensuing chaos becomes the winner.

Survival of the adept

It's finally survival of the adept. That biological truth is descending upon economic life (and death). Only the fittest among them all, the competing set of firms in a given "product category," at every moment, will thrive. To survive and grow, companies

To survive and grow, companies will have to do more than simply better competitors and predators.

will have to continuously do better than competitors and predators. One of the important manifestations of this will be that those who adapt fastest will thrive. The smallest of the start-ups could force an industry to move in a particular direction and then the option for the incumbent is binary –

change gears or lose the race. The past will be no passport for the future and in most cases it will be a mixed blessing.

Naturally, changes are happening across the board and not in the technology sector alone. Boaters.com (a portal on yachting, sailing, fishing, etc.) is "a blueprint for the reinvention of the company," vowed Eric Singleton, director of e-commerce at Raytheon.[3] "This is not a one-hit wonder." The backer for the site is none other than Raytheon Co., the $20 billion US defense giant, and maker of the famous Tomahawk cruise missiles among others. The only, remote, linkage between Raytheon and boats: $180 million of annual sales comes from the sale of radar for boats and other marine supplies. The company is hoping to boost its boat-radar sales. But it's also banking on commissions for every other item sold through the site, planned to be the site for yachting, sailing, racing, fishing and accessories, electronics, radars, safety, etc., through a network of participating retailers as well as sponsorship and advertising income.

For years, defense companies like Raytheon have viewed consumer markets as the Promised Land. But their past efforts to apply defense technology in commercial markets – attempting to hawk everything from electrically powered bicycles to windmills – have almost inevitably failed. As Norman Augustine, former chairman of Lockheed Martin Corp., has observed, the defense industry's record for such initiatives is "unblemished by success." And it is very committed; it even brought in a few bright high-school students to offer fresh perspectives. The result: Raytheon isn't locked into a "stodgy, risk-averse kind of business," noted James Infinger, CIO.

But Raytheon is no isolated instance and it's in the company of many incumbents already. In the cases (Chapters 3 through 5) we've already seen how Wal-mart, GM, and Merrill Lynch are all examples of the same.

According to Amazon CEO Bezos, "We'll be redecorating the store for every customer".[4] That quite epitomizes the vision today for continuous innovation! Bezos reaffirms, "we're not a book company. We're not a music company. We're not a video company. We're not an auctions company. We're a customer company."[5] And it started with books, then music, then video, then auctions but it finally did a major restructuring: "Clearly, Jeff has an 'I'm going to own the world' mentality," said venture capitalist Timothy M. Haley of Institutional Venture Partners. Today, Amazon.com is the place to find and discover many of the things you want to buy online. Similarly, Wal-Mart has been reinventing itself on the Internet. Its site offered more items online than it did in its giant stores. And in fact, the site's best-selling products in 1998 were Rolex watches and Nike T-shirts[6] – items not even found in Wal-mart stores.[7] Wal-Mart.com's music section is also very much expanded.

And what is Merrill Lynch doing? It survived and retained its preeminent position all these years but finally in December 1999 it did reinvent itself. And when it did, it did so dramatically. With features such as real-time account positions, tax-management information, the Global Investor Network for research, banking services, and online shopping with an exceptional Visa Signature Rewards program, self-directed investors will be able to use this site to help manage all aspects of their financial lives. Is it doing too much too fast? Maybe.

Merrill Lynch's eCommerce portal offers individuals and small businesses access to more than 450 vendors, from Toys"R"Us to Barnes & Noble Inc., and more than eight million products. Clients earn triple Visa Signature points for purchases made with the Visa Signature card and also may receive special discounts from participating merchants. Merrill account-holders purchased about $7 billion in goods and services with their Merrill Visa cards in 2000, John L. Steffens, vice chairman, said, and he believes that online sales could help raise that total to $100 billion annually within six years. Is Merrill trying to become an e-commerce company with its principal focus on brokerage? Not likely, but it's definitely more than a financial services company.

Perpetual metamorphosis – an innovator's innovation

Increasingly, for incumbents, perpetual metamorphosis is becoming a way of life: the act of undergoing a slow death for rebirth – achieving a break from the past body and soul in order to build a new one, but having the humility to recognize failures and then metamorphose into yet another stage of experimental evolution. It is all part of the process of perpetual metamorphosis.

Consider what has been happening at CompUSA, the biggest chain of personal computer stores in the United States. A retail group controlled by the Mexican billionaire Carlos Slim Helu announced on January 24, 2000, that it was buying the rest of CompUSA Inc. CompUSA, the Dallas-based network of computer stores, had been struggling with losses and declining sales. Net sales for the fiscal second quarter 2000 had decreased approximately 21 percent to $1.38 billion from $1.75 billion for the comparable period ending December 26, 1998 and the share price had fallen from around $35 two years ago to $6 just before the announcement of the deal. Mr. Helu cited the advantage of having 217 giant stores in 84 cities across the United States for filling orders quickly and aiding customers who feel overwhelmed by technology.

Like many retailers, CompUSA saw the Internet as another opportunity to rebuild the company. It had already created CompUSA Net.com in March 1999 to offer a comprehensive array of computer products, including certain other consumer electronics and technology products, on the Internet. CompUSA Net.com and CompUSA were managed as distinct entities. CompUSA Net.com and the company had entered into various arm's-length agreements and CompUSA Net.com utilized its own targeted marketing initiatives and advertising programs to reach a focused audience and position itself as a service-oriented provider of technology products via the Net. It also entered into separate agreements with various other distributors such as Ingram Micro.

As part of its metamorphosis on the Net, CompUSA Net.com re-created itself as a separate subsidiary called Cozone.com in October 1999 and severed the "umbilical" cord – the name CompUSA – with a redesigned website and an extensive marketing campaign. An entirely new entity was created. Cozone.com was something of an anomaly, though; it may have been the exceptional wholly owned subsidiary which bore no reference to its promoter. It had its own warehousing, distribution centers, and help desks. In fact, the name CompUSA wasn't even mentioned anywhere on Cozone.com's homepage. "CompUSA's board became our venture capital firm, really," explained Stephen Polley, CEO of Cozone.com. "We're kept completely at arm's length from CompUSA."[8]

The demise of CompUSA was thus only physical and the spirit lived. Couldn't have been better planned. An example of metamorphosis for a new lease of life in the e-era. For example, its offices were located in Marlborough, Mass., far from its parent's Dallas headquarters. CompUSA employees had no natural advantage in getting employment in Cozone; there was not a single CompUSA employee in Cozone. CompUSA was just one of the fulfillment agents and thus had no special pricing or servicing relationships. The pricing could not have been more different at the two companies. And overnight a global technology superstore with MP3 players, Sony PlayStations etc. was erected in place of a US computer superstore.

The basic ideas were quite sound. While many PC or electronic goods sites offer little more than an online catalog, Cozone.com was chock-full of information. One example: alongside pictures of its printers was a box of text explaining the difference between inkjet and dot matrix printers – in English, no jargon. The best feature on Cozone.com was its adviser, "Jill," a computer-generated brunette. She guided consumers through a series of questions, and then came back with a number of choices that customers could compare side by side. Executives planned to expand this feature to other products, including digital cameras and printers.[9]

However, life was not to proceed as planned. Cozone.com faced a whole mall of online competitors. Circuit City and Best Buy have websites, and retailers like Buy.com sell electronic equipment at cut-rate prices. Despite an aggressive advertising campaign, it proved hard to establish the new brand Cozone.com in an already crowded dotcom marketspace. Breaking the umbilical cord from the parent, a daring experiment, also caused problems. It deprived the new subsidiary of valuable experience and caused operational problems. Sales totaled $7.5 million in the fiscal second quarter ending December 25, 2000, with a pre-tax loss of $16.8 million. What to do given that an experiment had not proceeded as planned? CompUSA bit the bullet, shut down the new subsidiary and folded Cozone.com's operations into its home site, CompUSA.com. A failure? Perhaps. But it also gave CompUSA valuable learning to leverage as it continues its transformation as a leading retailer of the emerging bricks-and-clicks markets. The metamorphosis continues. Incumbents are re-creating themselves to create their e-incarnations.

And CompUSA is in good company. Recently 66 people left comfortable jobs at Autodesk[10] in San Rafael, California, to work for a start-up called Buzzsaw.com (a portal on the construction industry). The catch? Everyone departed with millions of dollars in funding from Autodesk and the unequivocal blessing of CEO Carol Bartz, Autodesk's CEO for seven years. And why did Bartz let so many valuable employees surrender? Because she had to. Bartz could have held on to Buzzsaw and run the new business herself. But she realized that wasn't going to work. Launching a new e-commerce company would eat up at least $60 million – a near impossibility. "I get killed if I'm down a penny," referring to what Wall Street does to a 17-year-old company whose earnings dip for the quarter. She was also resigned to losing staff. And even as Buzzsaw.com enters a crowded field (it will compete with Bidcom, Blue Line Online, BricNet, and Framework Technologies), Bartz expects it to be a worthwhile experiment! Buzzsaw will launch with the tag line an "autodesk venture." It's a bit of a misnomer – in a world of cannibalization, Buzzsaw could become the juggernaut behind Autodesk's future growth.

Retail: an example of an industry under reconstruction

At another level, we can see an entire industry, the retail industry, go through perpetual metamorphosis. The Internet-driven current revolution is only the latest in a series of radical transformations. Each of the transformations corresponds to a new business model for retail created by reinventing the elements of the principal value proposition of retailing. Clayton Christensen and Richard Tedlow mention in their writing[11] that "the essential mission of retailing has always had four elements: getting the right product in the right place at the right price at the right time."

We believe that only now, thanks to online retailing, is this mission getting realized. Retailing in the nineteenth century was driven by the right place, which is convenience. It was personalized and provided conveniences like credit, delivery at home, etc. The other three elements were incidental; prices were generally "high," product substitution was difficult, and volumes low.

All that changed with the advent of department stores in the early twentieth century. These stores brought the right product at the right place; they offered much bigger selections and were centrally located. It improved the model by adding the right products. They started with known products that required less personalized service and over time moved towards better prices as volume surged. Later they also added newer products at the higher end and supported that with their brand equity as a stamp of quality.

Then came the shopping malls – they improved the product and place criteria, by offering a deeper selection. In fact, the two competed and slowly the competition translated into, first, lower prices at department stores and second, better branded products at the department stores. The catalog businesses further deepened the price competition and brought in one more change: they helped the development of specialty products accessible to a much larger audience (much like the Internet).

The right price was still elusive and you still could not buy anything at anytime. The discount stores, the last wave of "retail invention," brought best prices. But just what the catalogs did for the department stores, new specialty stores, category killers like Toys"R"Us, did to the discount stores. The category killers got into discount selling in a given product category. And there has been a continuous evolution in how all of these players have behaved. Department stores, for example, moved from the lower-end products to mid-range products. They then shifted their merchandise mix towards higher-margin, more complex products to maintain their profits in the face of intense competition at the low end of their businesses.

The Internet is promising to serve all segments. Right product, price, and place certainly, but we can debate right time delivery. But the rising instant gratification "industry" only proves that even that is happening. It's happening because of richness and reach being possible simultaneously. A mix of catalog and department stores! It's about very high volumes and lowest prices.

How do e-tailers such as Amazon succeed? Clayton M. Christensen and Richard S. Tedlow explain, "In retailing, profitability is largely determined by two factors: the margins stores can earn and the frequency with which they can turn their inventory over. The average successful department store, for example, earned gross margins of approximately 40% and turned its inventory over about three times per year. In other words, it made 40% three times, for a 120% annual return on the capital invested in inventory. Compare that with the business model of the average successful discount department store, which earned 23% gross margins and turned its inventory over five times annually. … But if businesses such as Amazon.com continue to turn inventory at present rates of 25 times annually, they could achieve traditional returns with margins of 5%."[12]

What is evident from the above (and from Chapter 4) is that the perpetual metamorphosis is alive and well in the retail industry. What will the future face of retailing look like? How will the economics of "brick" and "click" retail differ from that of traditional departmental store retail? Retailing leaders such as Wal-Mart, Carrefour, and Amazon.com are exploring the answers.

Uphill task

Reinventing the business via perpetual metamorphosis is emerging as a dominant innovation model. And it is not easy even for the nimblest in Silicon Valley. Gary Hamel explains how Sun nearly torched its future several years ago.[13] In the early 1980s, its four founders created the high-end workstation business. Sun's early workstations sold for as much as $40,000. When one of the company's founders, Andy Bechtolsheim, suggested building a $10,000 workstation using a radical new chip technology, he ran headfirst into a wall of internal skepticism. The reason was simple: Sun's process for allocating product development resources heavily favored incremental improvements to existing products. Frustrated, Bechtolsheim left the company and used his own money to build a prototype. When they finally saw the elegant new computer, Sun's top managers quickly invited Bechtolsheim back into the fold. Within three months the new workstation, named the SPARCstation, was outselling every other product in the Sun line.

> **Given the imperative to grow, why can't organizations come up with breakthroughs more regularly?**

Consistently successful companies in the most innovation-intensive industries – those where the product life cycles are short and the need for breakout products is high – have pioneered a radically different approach to innovation. Given the imperative to grow, why can't product developers come up with breakthroughs more regularly? Eric von Hippel et al. noted that:[14] "they fail primarily for two reasons. First, companies face strong incentives to focus on short term. Put simply, although new products and services may be essential for future growth and profit, companies must first survive today to be around tomorrow. That necessity tends to focus companies strongly on making incremental improvements to keep sales up and current customers – as well as Wall Street analysts – happy. Second, developers simply don't know *how* to achieve breakthroughs, because there is usually no effective system in place to guide them and support their efforts." The latter is a problem for a company like 3M too, long known for its successful innovation. We discuss the latter issue in the next section.

PART FOUR DEFINING THE IMPERATIVES

How to change the strong focus from the short term to the long term to see reinvention opportunities? There is no short-cut solution. It requires a clever combination of strategic insight from top management and radical improvements in operational processes, competencies, and supply chain relationships.

We have seen that Schwab represents an excellent case study on these attributes. The specific circumstances that led to the development of online trading at Schwab should not be misconstrued as an accidental research discovery. It's important to recognize that Schwab's Internet success came about because the co-CEOs Schwab and Pottruck were willing to bet their company's future on the Web technology. They couldn't know for sure how their actions would turn out; all that their research told them was that lowering prices to compete on the Web would cost them as much as $125 million in forgone revenues. They created a separate unit to create the online application away from the usual business.

At IBM, Thomas J. Watson and his favorite slogan, "THINK," became a mantra for employees. Watson also stressed the importance of the customer, a lasting IBM tenet. He understood that the success of the client translated into the success of his company, a belief that, years later, manifested itself in the popular adage, "Nobody was ever fired for buying from IBM." Just as his father saw the company's future in tabulators rather than scales and meat slicers, Tom Watson Jr. foresaw the role computers would play in business, and he pushed IBM to meet the challenge. Under Tom Watson Jr., there also were innovations in marketing. In 1969, IBM changed the way it sold technology. Rather than offer hardware, services, and software exclusively in packages, marketers "unbundled" the components and offered them for sale individually. Unbundling gave birth to the multi-billion-dollar software and services industries. Today, IBM is the world leader in both industries.

At the operational level, the commitment to breakthrough improvements is unmistakable. For example, there has been a clear spiral in product development processes at IBM, all through its history – a very remarkable feat. It kept on improving its products to cannibalize its previous versions. It replaced its tabulating machines with the calculator in the 1940s. In the 1950s and early 1960s it replaced the calculator with monolithic computers. Starting April 1964 to well into the early 1980s it produced the System/360 where users could simply upgrade parts of their hardware; a bold departure from the earlier computers and which *Fortune* had dubbed as "IBM's $5 billion gamble." In 1969, it also unbundled the machine into hardware, software and services so that users could use competing solutions to their advantage. And of course it made the PC in the early 1980s that threatened to kill its product market and sales model.

Inventing capabilities through lead users

Coming back to the issue of developing an effective system to guide and support breakthroughs – a well-established method for increasing innovation within organizational boundaries, especially for inducing breakthrough innovations, is the Lead User Process. It is different from the usual research and development process where the engine of development is typically in-house creative power. The usual process is more of an inward-looking model where the innovations are somehow related to the existing core competencies or at best, users give their needs and the in-house development team gives it the shape of a product. P&G's entry into food, for example, evolved from its soap and candle businesses: with technical competencies in fats and oils, the company created Crisco, the first all-vegetable shortening. More recently, P&G used one of its laundry competencies – controlling calcium in hard water – to create calcium delivery technologies for food and beverage products and in leading-edge drugs like Didronel.

The lead user process starts outside the organization and the engine is the customer who tests the product (or the service) to the limits.

The lead user process starts outside the organization and the engine is the community of lead users. Lead users are those product users who exploit the product features at the limits or in novel conditions. Often they tend to improvise the products to suit their specific requirements and thus provide ready-made prototypes. The advantage of the lead user process is that it gives a structure and direction to what is mostly a very pliant subject. And no less important is the fact that the lead users' "community" (if they could be called a community), for any product category, is far more resourceful than any organization on this planet – in terms of numbers, intellectual capital (given the diversity among lead users), and monetary resources. But what's the catch in the use of the process? Who, where, when, what, how? Where are the lead users, for example? Because they're hardly a community and thus they're not identifiable and they do not know each other.

Eric von Hippel et al.[15] have written how 3M used the lead user process to "find a better type of disposable surgical draping" (the initial brief for the breakthrough innovation). They had technologically advanced disposable surgical gowns; surgeons loved the fabric, but insurers wouldn't pay for it (as managed health care was taking hold in the US), and sales were disappointing. The (research) group spent the first six weeks learning more about the cause and prevention of infections by researching the literature and interviewing experts, and then held a workshop with the management. The six weeks were spent on getting the important trends in infection control, including trends in developing countries. And they concluded that a crisis was germinating in the surgical wards of developing countries. And hence, even a drastic cut in the cost of drapes could not address that market. The team redefined its goal: find a much cheaper and more effective way to prevent infections from starting or spreading that does not depend on antibiotics (the usual solution in developing countries but not a long-term solution) – or even on surgical drapes. The team started networking again.

As is usually the case,[16] some of the most valuable lead users turned up in surprising places, e.g. leading veterinary hospitals, makeup artists in Hollywood, etc. For example, some leading veterinary hospitals were able to keep infection rates very low despite facing difficult conditions and cost constraints. As one of the country's foremost veterinary surgeons explained, "Our patients are covered with hair, they don't bathe, and they don't have insurance, so the infection controls that we use can't cost much." Another surprising source of ideas was Hollywood. One of the group members learned that makeup artists are experts in applying, to the skin, materials that don't irritate and that are easy to remove when no longer needed. As a final step, several lead users were invited to a two-and-a-half-day workshop. And in the end, the workshop generated concepts for six new product lines and a radical new general approach to infection control. The appropriate products are under development.

The Internet promises to make the lead user process much easier and to increase the rate of innovation manifold. The Internet not only makes it easier to create communities of lead users but also makes communication with them so much more intense and practical. And it gives it a real global scale. Perhaps, it will improve the quality of the community in another way – it will attract more of the leading lead users (the active lead users) who wish to know more about how they could do better.

Amazon's recent Toy Quest contest, for example, received thousands of dream toy ideas. CEO Bezos noted, "We want to see what … the world's coolest toy … will look like and what it will do…". Two youngsters were awarded the grand prize for their creations. Nadia Smith of Voorhees, New Jersey, won in the 9-to-12-year-old division for her character called Mr. Itchy Pants, and Nicky Englisis of Morganville, New Jersey, won in the 8 and under category for his My Favorite Friend doll. My Favorite Friend doll, for example, was described by Nicky Englisis as, "This doll has a picture frame for a face that lets you change the face of the doll to pictures of your friend's face. It could be soft, like a stuffed animal, or it could be like a doll. It should be small enough to hold in your hand, but big enough to see the photo face. It has a Velcro strip across the top that allows you to change the hair color and style. It comes as a boy or a girl…" How could Amazon ever know that kids would want such a toy!

The concept of lead users works very well for products or customer-oriented services. But how do you translate this for in-house processes, or for products for which the most sophisticated user is your next-door colleague? An interesting approach is the one proposed by Michael Schrage in what he calls "serious play." Successful innovation, asserts Michael Schrage,[17] demands more than a good strategic plan; it requires creative improvisation. Much of the "serious play" that leads to breakthrough innovations is increasingly linked to experiments with models, prototypes, and simulations. As digital technology makes prototyping more cost-effective, serious play will soon lie at the heart of all innovation strategies, influencing how businesses define themselves and their markets. Schrage studied the relationship between technology and work as a research associate at the MIT Media Lab, a Merrill Lynch Forum Innovation Fellow, and a columnist for *Fortune* magazine. In Serious Play, he argues that the real value in building models comes from the insights they reveal about the organization itself. Technological models, he insists, can actually change us – improving the way we communicate, collaborate, learn, and innovate.

Schrage shows how companies such as Boeing, DaimlerChrysler, Disney, IDEO, and Microsoft use serious play with modeling technologies to facilitate the collaborative interactions that lead to innovation. For example: Boeing's 777 engineers deliberately built conflicts into their Catia design program in order to flag and identify counterparts in other areas of the design team. They did so to see whom in the massive Boeing organization they didn't know but should get to know better, for teaming up in the future. Through the flag feature in the design system, Catia enabled a communication network for Boeing engineers who desperately wanted one.

The new project management challenge

We have discussed four challenges for incumbents in order to be able to react to the start-ups that threaten to disrupt their markets: the survival of the adepts, perpetual metamorphosis, a long-term vision to dare to climb uphill, and the need to listen to lead users. We would like to add a fifth challenge, which is less obvious from the lessons from IBM, Xerox, or others. We are convinced that incumbents will also have to reengineer their innovation project management methods.

PART FOUR DEFINING THE IMPERATIVES

> Consistently successful companies are more than consistently lucky. They have acquired special capabilities to stimulate continuous innovation.
>
> **1** They excel in generating and capturing new ideas – often in cooperation with lead users.
>
> **2** They have an effective capability to manage the innovation process – be it a classical stage/gate process or a more dynamic spiral approach.
>
> **3** They are able to focus on learning at every step – while sensing new opportunities, testing possible ideas, prioritizing value creation avenues, and acting to seize the opportunities.

As discussed in the previous chapters, we believe that the very focus of innovation is shifting to continuous value addition for customers. In a way this is a new approach to conceive and actualize innovative products.

Twenty years of research on innovation and the development of new processes and products have resulted in many questions, but also a few strong results. One of the latter is that a good development and innovation process requires a stage/gate approach. The essence of this is that the innovation process has to be structured in a number of sequential stages (specification definition, product planning, product development, process development, product launch), which are implemented in a cross-disciplinary way. These stages alternate with gates, or decision moments where a go/no go decision has to be taken, based on the results of the previous phase. This is not a plea for a sequential functional approach, because every phase requires cross-disciplinary implementation. This stage/gate model has been preached with almost missionary zeal at business schools in courses on innovation management, and its implementation has been the bread and butter of many consultants. Needless to say that we are careful to doubt it!

But a few years of successful innovation in the Internet world have created some doubt about its universal application. The stage/gate approach may still apply for normal product development. But as was already suggested with the description of Microsoft's development processes in *Microsoft Secrets*,[18] and their daily build approach, the development process in the Internet world is much closer to the spiral model that was described for software development. This model assumes that one will go rapidly through a repeated series of the different phases of the development process (specification definition, build, test, and launch), each cycle resulting in an increased performance and a rejuvenated product for the customer. This is perhaps to be expected, because Internet products are about software development. But we see in our cases that this approach is in many cases extended far beyond the software development, into the product definition and into the design of the complementary assets that are needed to deliver the final service.

Doing product development this way has a few uneasy consequences. Are we prepared to launch an incomplete product in order to capture the customer's attention? Surely not for a pharmaceutical product, for which the product liabilities associated with an incomplete product are too high. Surely not for a car where we will not disclose a model for which we have only designed the engine, but for which no innovative styling is available. But we do it often for Internet products, which we further develop in collaboration with the customers. And can we live with a product that changes every other week or every other month? What about customer service? How do we update the existing customer base, etc.? Yet these are the challenges we will have to come to grips with.

Action points

Perpetual metamorphosis is a way of life. It is no longer the exception. How can your organization succeed in its journey of perpetual metamorphosis?

1. Is your management ready to ask the tough questions? Is it ready to take the bold steps to reinvent your company?

2. Does your management have the right level of ambition to be a leader? Or are they satisfied to be a risk-averse follower? When was the last time your organization tried to redefine a fundamental precept of your industry?

3. How different is your organization today as compared to 10 years ago? Twenty years ago? Or more? Has your organization's business model remained stagnant over the last decades? Or has it evolved actively in a virtuous cycle of perpetual metamorphosis?

4. Does your organization really listen to customers? Can you identify success stories from your organization where listening to customers created significant innovations?

5. How good are you at managing the innovation process? Being successful at innovation requires more than the desire to do so. You need to be able to attract the best assets – people – and to provide them with the right context. Are you doing so?

Mantra

The past will be no passport for the future and in most cases it will be a mixed blessing. In fact, for many incumbents, the bag may have a disproportionate share of liabilities over assets. And incremental approaches will only pull the eventuality nearer – end of competitiveness. Organizations need to reinvent themselves continuously – perpetual metamorphosis is becoming a critical strategic tool. At times radically and at others times measured.

Interestingly, customers and users play an important role in guiding your transition process. The Internet has greatly strengthened the lead user approach to innovation because you can reach communities of lead users. And because lead users can create far more connected communities, their inputs are far more valuable.

A new model for innovation project management will also be necessary. The good old stage/gate approach will need changes. The common model will be spiral in nature in which customers will provide first-hand experience with the products. Products will be under perpetual development.

Notes

1. Evans, P.B. and Wurster, T.S. (1997) "Strategy and the new economics of information", *HBR,* September–October, p. 70.
2. Barth, Steve "Knowledge as a function of X," *Knowledge Management* (www.kmmag.com/kmmagn2/km200002/featal.html).
3. Squeo, Anne Marie (2000), "Raytheon to widen base via e-commerce sales," *The Wall Street Journal Europe,* February 22, p. 32.
4. Littman, Jonathan (1997) "The book on Amazon.com," *Los Angeles Times* magazine, July 20.
5. "Q&A with Amazon's Jeff Bezos," *Business Week,* May 13, 1999.
6. "Seashore to your door within 24 hours," Press release, July 30, 1997.
7. Steinhaufer, Jennifer (1998) "Old-line retailers resist online life," *The New York Times,* April 20.
8. Creswell, Julie, (1999) "CompUSA is killing itself-on purpose," *Fortune,* December 20.
9. Creswell, Julie (1999) "CompUSA is killing itself-on purpose," *Fortune,* December 20.
10. "In desperation, autodesk takes cannibalization to the extreme," Melanie Walker talk, *Fortune,* December 6, 1999, pp. 133–4.

11. Christensen, Clayton M. and Tedlow, Richard S. (2000) "Patterns of disruption in retailing," *HBR*, January–February, pp. 42–5.
12. Christensen, Clayton M. and Tedlow, Richard S. (2000) "Patterns of disruption in retailing," *HBR*, January–February, pp. 42–5.
13. Hammel, Gary (1999) "Bring Silicon Valley Inside," *HBR*, September–October, p. 76.
14. von Hippel, Eric, Thomke, Stefan and Sonnack, Mary (1999) "Creating breakthroughs at 3M," *HBR*, September–October, pp. 47–57.
15. von Hippel, Eric, Thomke, Stefan and Sonnack, Mary, (1999) "Creating breakthroughs at 3M," *HBR*, September–October, pp. 47–57.
16. von Hippel, Eric, Thomke, Stefan, and Sonnack, Mary, (1999) "Creating breakthroughs at 3M," *HBR*, September–October, pp. 47–57.
17. Schrage, Michael and Peters, Tom (1999) "Serious play: How the world's best companies simulate innovation," *Research Technology Management* Nov/Dec, Harvard Business School Press.
18. Selby, R. and Cusumano, M (1994) *Microsoft Secrets*, The Free Press.

Institutionalizing knowledge   11

Bookmark

All is fine with co-creation, e-nfrastructure and perpetual metamorphosis but how do you make them central to your growth strategy. In other words, how do you sustain them?

A new economy is emerging built on knowledge and innovation. Knowledge lies at the root of innovation and innovation creates new knowledge. In fact, there is a strong synergistic relationship between knowledge and innovation. The Internet provides a unique infrastructure that enables successful scope and scale for knowledge institutionalization within organizations and thereby makes it possible for firms to initiate and sustain the knowledge–innovation cycle. Knowledge management is becoming an integral part of the process of managing innovation.

A close look at the way Xerox and Arthur Andersen have attempted to institutionalize knowledge offers valuable insights into the new anchor for an innovative organization. There are some opportunities and imperatives in organization design.

Welcome aboard the bandwagon for the new knowledge-based organization. Read this chapter to detail the script for change in your organization.

A new battlefield

"Knowledge is the new battlefield for countries, corporations and individuals. We all increasingly face conditions that demand more knowledge for us to function and, in the long run, for us to survive," state Jonas Ridderstrale and Kjell Nordstrom, authors of the book *Funky Business* published by Financial Times Management in early 2000. Others are echoing this view. Nonakas writes in the book *The Knowledge Advantage*:[1] "In an economy where the only certainty is uncertainty, the one sure source of lasting competitive advantage is knowledge. When markets shift technology, competitors multiply, and the products become obsolete almost overnight, successful companies are those that consistently create new knowledge, disseminate it widely throughout the organization, and quickly embody it in new technologies and products. These activities define the knowledge creating company, whose sole business is continuous innovation."

> **Knowledge will be the asset to be managed and other assets will be the means for the competitive management of knowledge.**

A new economy is emerging built on knowledge and innovation. New economy? Yes, but not the B2B, B2C, or the C2C types, but one that's fundamentally different from the economic assets and processes we've thrived on all these years. In the emerging new economy, knowledge is not just another asset to be managed besides people, property, and capital. Knowledge will be the asset to be managed and other assets will be the means for the competitive management of knowledge. And how will knowledge be managed? Innovation. Continuous innovation is how knowledge will be managed. Knowledge is the fountainhead of innovation and the two form a closed-loop circuit. Knowledge fuels innovative initiatives and innovation creates new experiences to enrich knowledge. In fact, knowledge and innovation are only two sides of the same coin. We've already seen how co-creation and e-nfrastructure are enabling an intra-organizational market for creating and applying knowledge. As the new millennium unfolds, managers will have to transform their organizations into knowledge-based corporations. Organizations will have to learn to master the knowledge–innovation cycle, they will have to master knowledge institutionalization.

Knowledge institutionalization is not easily mastered. For evidence look around at corporations. Most organizations today have implemented intranets or a similar groupware system. However, a fraction of them can claim to have successfully leveraged their technology platforms to support an effective knowledge–innovation cycle. While it is true that the Internet provides a unique infrastructure to enable successful scope and scale for knowledge institutionalization, organizations have to combine people and technology in the right mix to start transforming themselves into knowledge-based corporations. But how is this mix of technology and people created? What's the knowledge we are talking about? How do organizations harness it to initiate and sustain the knowledge–innovation cycle? In other words, what will knowledge-based corporations look like? Let's begin with an initiative at Xerox to start exploring the answer.

Xerox: a knowledgeable company

Xerox presents a very interesting example of how a knowledge-based corporations can start to evolve. What started as a self-help tool invented by the service engineers at Xerox to become more effective and efficient has grown into a significant experience in knowledge institutionalization. By capturing and sharing the knowledge they amassed in their field experiences, Xerox service engineers created a community-based knowledge-sharing solution called Eureka. Eureka is a shared knowledge system in which customer service engineers can author, validate, and access repair solutions. It enables them to share "war stories" about problems, causes, and solutions in their own language.

In 1996, Eureka developed organically as an intranet communication system linked with a corporate database that helped customer-service engineers share repair tips. Respected peers who were subject-matter experts for the product family concerned validated these tips. Once validated, they were put into a searchable database that was available to all customer-service technicians through a Web-based browser. Authoring a tip or solution can be done either from the home screen under "Create a new technical tip" or while inside a tip. Database maintenance is everyone's responsibility through votes and feedback. Engineers are asked to vote whether the tips or solutions are useful and to provide feedback to improve them.

Xerox customer-service engineers worldwide make more than a million visits to customer sites every month to service printers, copiers, networks, and other aspects of customer operations. During these calls they are constantly discovering new and innovative solutions to unique problems that are not contained in standard service manuals. A good part of this knowledge is usually difficult, complex, or rare problems that are often passed along informally through the "war stories" within the community of customer-service engineers. Eureka was designed to capture as much of these war stories as possible into a "warehouse" of service tips to power high-quality and low-cost customer service. Eureka was co-designed by Xerox's service engineers and researchers at the eminent Palo Alto Research Center! And interestingly, Eureka initially started in France where it was fully deployed by 1996 on the Minitel system.[2]

While the overall objective was to improve customer service, Eureka's strategy was designed around four principles:

1. Never solve the same problem twice; no reinvention of existing solutions.
2. Make Xerox knowledge easily accessible to employees, customers, and partners at the point of need.
3. Create an environment where people develop and apply knowledge to prepare for the future.
4. Recognize and reward people for the creation, use, and transfer of knowledge.

But the success that Eureka is today has only been possible due to top management awareness and commitment to the institutionalization of knowledge. Paul Allaire, then Chairman of Xerox, noted this in November 1997: "Managing for knowledge is creating a thriving work and learning environment that fosters continuous creation, aggregation, use and re-use of both personal and organizational knowledge in the pursuit of new business value." A recent article in the *Harvard Business Review*, "Discovering New Value in Intellectual Property,"[3] adds: "most Fortune 500 CEOs, when asked how they intend to increase shareholder value, will talk about increasing sales, creating new leading-edge product lines, or pursuing mergers and acquisitions. But Xerox's [past] CEO Thoman isn't content with such conventional strategies. He believes one of the strategic keys to Xerox's future is something so intangible, so invisible to traditional bottom line thinking and corporate practice, that it doesn't even show up on the balance sheet: knowledge. Companies that are good at managing knowledge will win. The ones that aren't will lose."

The power of knowledge sharing via Eureka has become visible to all. Chris Wise, European Program Manager of Eureka, gave the following example: "In Holland, two engineers worked overnight to fix a problem. They had spent 16 hours on the customer site and tried everything that was in the service manual and from their own experience. Not being able to fix the machine, they called the national specialist who was 2½ hours' drive away. He jumped in his car, drove about 100 yards out of the garage. Then he thought that it might be worth checking in Eureka whether there was a repair tip. He found something, phoned up the two engineers and they fixed the machine! These engineers will never miss another opportunity to use Eureka."

Tom Ruddy, the previous Worldwide Customer Services Manager at Xerox, noted another example: "In Brazil, an intermittent failure kept bringing down a new DocuColor machine. The customer demanded an identical replacement ($40,000 cost to Xerox). Meanwhile, the technician tried a newly found Eureka solution from Montreal pointing out a potentially loose connector (90 cent part). The technician resolved the problem and the customer kept the original machine."

In 2000, the system held more than 36,000 solutions representing 12 countries and the database was growing at more than 400 tips per month. Sixteen thousand Eureka users each averaged over 18 solves per year, which meant that the user went to Eureka, applied the solution he or she found, and it fixed the problem. In 1999, over 260,000 problems were solved with the help of the Eureka system. Among the immediate direct benefits of Eureka are an average of 5 percent savings in parts cost and engineers' time and a 5 percent reduction in the length of repair time. Among the indirect advantages is that now Xerox trains employees primarily on the important generic problems that occur. Engineers spend much more time in the field dealing with real-life problems, rather than working on dummied-up simulations created by a trainer. Pierre Danon, president, Xerox Europe, has the last word: "Eureka represents the new face of Xerox as a solutions provider, as the world's sixth largest IT company, and as the company at the forefront of helping companies leverage knowledge for competitive advantage."

People: make or brake

"Eureka was a success because the system evolved out of the natural behavior of engineers, which was sharing stories. The other thing was high quality content. Engineers have to find a solution the first time they use Eureka. Otherwise they won't go back. Being engineers they also love smart tools," noted Tom Ruddy. "In the good old times we would meet in pubs for lunch and exchange stories. Whenever you put a bunch of engineers together they talk about technical things," explains one customer-service engineer who had been with the company for more than 20 years. Tom Ruddy explained what motivated the customer-service engineers to contribute to Eureka: "The customer-service engineers have a pecking order, based upon who has the most technical knowledge. Being recognized as the subject-matter expert is what gives you credit and status in this community."

Early on Xerox tried to give financial incentives but realized that it was not the best incentive to motivate this particular community. Engineers were motivated to contribute to Eureka primarily by recognition: the names of both tip-originators and validators are prominently displayed with each tip. The importance of peer recognition in this community was something the anthropologists at the Xerox Palo Alto Research Center (PARC) in California identified during their research, and it is what has been given much of the credit for Eureka's success. The ownership of tips improved the quality of the database. The ongoing dialog to send thank-you's and questions to the author kept improving the records and encouraged people to keep feeding tips into the system. "The behavior that we really want to reward is how much a tip is being used, has helped the customer, the technician and Xerox. The tips that are high usage and high benefit to all interested parties," noted Tom Ruddy.

Xerox set up the Eureka hall of fame for authors and validators. It is based on the thumbs up and thumbs down vote. Peers vote on tips when they apply them, to register whether they fixed the identified problems. Thumbs up vote – they applied the tip and it fixed the problem; thumbs down vote – they applied the tip and it did not fix the problem. The thumbs up are monitored. The authors then get identified into the hall of fame.

However, the average technician worked for Xerox for 20 and more years, and their dominant perception was that there was nothing about service they did not already know. The hurdle was to get them to use Eureka the first time. The first time an engineer used Eureka and it saved him time he was sold. Through peer testimonials and publishing newsletters Xerox tried to spread success stories. Active users started saying to their peers, "you have got to use Eureka because I found this." They started sharing success stories. Non-users started to get peer pressure. "Go look it up in Eureka. Why take up my time if you are not using the available tools!"

> Eureka has been successful because Xerox paid careful attention to the following fundamental building blocks of the knowledge–innovation cycle:
>
> **1** Communities: informal groups of people – often across organizational boundaries – sharing common interests or a common practice. Customer-service professionals within Xerox were the target community.
>
> **2** Knowledge repositories: a smart combination of technology and organizational culture helped Xerox to build and sustain a credible repository of the knowledge of its customer-services professionals.
>
> **3** Knowledge flow: Xerox successfully aligned resources and nurtured the Eureka community to accelerate knowledge creation, use, reuse, and transfer.

Initiation

Eureka is an illustrative example of how knowledge institutionalization occurs. Hopefully it must be evident from the Xerox study that knowledge is a direct outcome of personal experiences and reflections. Individuals are the fountainhead of knowledge origination and therefore, knowledge originates as tacit knowledge – tacit because it is not well structured and mostly resides as a cluster of ideas within individuals (similar to the war stories of the engineers). Tacit knowledge is primarily intuitive, non-verbalizable and related to individual experiences; individuals are the primary tacit knowledge agents.

Over time, out of repeated application and exchanges with others, certain clusters of ideas get articulated into a more coherent body of knowledge to become explicit knowledge at individual and group levels. Interestingly, however, a good part of that "explicit" knowledge again rests as tacit knowledge at the group level because until now it wasn't possible to secure appropriate dissemination (with respect to time and place) of a good part of that "explicit" knowledge. Attested Tom Ruddy, "Inside Xerox there is probably a known solution for 80% of all the technical problems that we get customer calls for. The problem is how to get to that knowledge when you need it." The problem has been one of connecting people seamlessly into a network because individuals in an organization are the source of its knowledge. Eureka is a living testimony of this fact.

> **Knowledge conversion is a "social" process *between* individuals and not confined to *within* individuals**

Ikujiro Nonaka and Hirotaka Takeuchi, in their book *The Knowledge-Creating Company*,[4] have discussed the dynamics of tacit knowledge and explicit knowledge. They assert that organizational knowledge creation is a continuous and dynamic interaction between tacit and explicit knowledge. They state that tacit knowledge and explicit knowledge are not totally separate; instead they are mutually complementary entities. They interact with and interchange into each other in the creative activities of human beings, a process they call knowledge conversion. They also state that their model is anchored on a critical assumption that human knowledge is created and expanded through social interaction between tacit knowledge and explicit knowledge. Thus knowledge conversion is a "social" process *between* individuals and not confined to *within* individuals.

Communities

The social process of knowledge conversion across individuals is embodied in communities. A community may be defined as a group of people who share some common identity. However, there is nothing unique about what communities do or exist for; the common purpose or need could be anything. And that's where communities display varying efficiency in knowledge conversion. If too formalized, communities become bureaucratic structures where social processes are so weak that interpersonal exchanges fail to sustain the demands of knowledge conversion (implicit to explicit conversion becomes the weak link). If too informal, social processes lack cohesiveness and thus, knowledge conversion again breaks down (explicit to tacit exchange becomes the weak link). If we understand that an organization is actually a community of communities, a community of departments/functions/regions, among many other communities, it becomes obvious that knowledge institutionalization in an organization is best originated from communities.

Knowledge-efficient communities need to be consciously nurtured because communities are unequal in their knowledge conversion efficiency. The key to nurturing communities is to tap their natural energy to share knowledge, build on processes and systems that they already use, and enhance the role of their natural leaders. This is amply evident in the success of Eureka where the natural energy and informal networks within the entire Xerox customer services organization has been leveraged. Communities can also transcend organizational boundaries and include customers, suppliers, professionals from other organizations, etc. Expectedly, nurturing such communities takes considerable effort.

The Internet is perhaps the best thing to have happened to the cause of knowledge institutionalization. The Internet has put communities at the center-stage of the new knowledge economy! The Internet has made it easier to create and sustain multiple communities based on shared interests and thus it has dramatically increased the capability of organizations to create knowledge-efficient communities. The Internet enables the creation of communities where the commitment to association is high because it's based on a far higher free will as compared to non-Internet-based communities. In the latter, the subjective reasons for associations like kinship, language affinity, geographic proximity, etc. tend to exert higher influence on the intra-community dynamics.

In the organizational context, another element becomes important in communities. Unlike other social communities, communities at the workplace are far more specialized because organizations are created to maximize the benefits from specialization (the so-called "division of labor"). Thus, at a broader level, there are two types of communities in organizations – reference communities (contributors) and user communities (learners). The reference communities determine the depth and the user communities determine the breadth of knowledge. The quality of the knowledge pool in an organization is a dynamic interplay of these two communities (though user communities are typically more difficult to create and sustain). In the Eureka example, "respected peers" is an example of a reference community and "engineers" is an example of a learning community.

It may be interesting to note that the critical role of communities in knowledge institutionalization is not new. Human evolution is perhaps the best example of such knowledge management. The cornerstone of our evolution is our ability to accumulate knowledge and pass it on to the next generation through various cultural institutions and processes. The ability to transfer the tacit knowledge of one generation to the next generation probably best explains why we're the most successful species on earth!

But how do you turn your organization into a collection of knowledge-efficient communities? How do you instill knowledge institutionalization across an organization? While Eureka represents a unique example of a successful knowledge community within a specific functional group, organizations face the larger challenge of managing the knowledge–innovation cycle across all functions and across geographies. Xerox has not yet been able to transfer the success of Eureka to the rest of the organization and the financial troubles of the corporation in the years 2000–2001 have certainly dampened many of its plans for such an institutionalization of knowledge. The corporate-wide transformation of Xerox into a knowledge-based firm is yet to happen, but we can learn from other organizations that have taken major steps toward transforming themselves into successful knowledge-based organizations. One such example is Arthur Andersen.

Arthur Andersen: combining people and technology

"$K = (P + I)^S$. This simple equation is the basis of our efforts to manage knowledge effectively and be competitive in the information age," noted Jesper Jarlbaek, the Managing Partner of the Business Consulting Practice at Arthur Andersen Denmark. He continues: "We see knowledge (K) as being captured by people's (P) ability to exchange information (I) by utilizing technology (+), exponentially enhanced by the power of sharing (S). The power of this simple equation is tremendous. It is clear and it has universal appeal. When you explain it to someone, everything makes sense, everything falls in place!"

$K = (P + I)^S$. The power of this simple equation is tremendous.

Arthur Andersen (AA) is one of the world's largest professional services organizations. An ability to organize and communicate knowledge seamlessly on a worldwide basis is viewed as the critical competitive factor in the auditing and consultancy tasks performed by AA. Compounding the challenge is the realization that the global volume of knowledge is doubling every fifth year and is predicted to double every 72nd day by the year 2020. AA, more than many other organizations, has long realized the importance of managing organizational knowledge effectively to be competitive in an ever-changing, intensely competitive information age. An internal document described the issues thus: "Our objective is to develop and maintain our knowledge capital so that, as a company, we will command the greatest, best structured and most valuable knowledge capital in the knowledge society.... Our unique strength lies in the fact that we have always worked with intensive knowledge sharing. Since Arthur Andersen's origins in 1913, we have had centralized knowledge databases, to which employees all over the world have contributed Best Practices examples ... Arthur Andersen was applying the science of the knowledge society long before the notions of information and knowledge societies were invented."

We studied in depth the Danish office of Arthur Andersen which has developed a distinct competence in knowledge management that has been widely quoted and has been copied as an example of best practice in knowledge management within the larger AA organization. However, despite extended experience in knowledge sharing, the intricacies of managing knowledge in the information age are only starting to be understood. Jesper Jarlbaek continued: "We thought we understood the equation, $K = (P+I)^S$, but as we go forward we continually discover new issues, interpretations and problems inside the equation. We are finding that knowledge management is not simply a task of building technological systems or collecting information. Questions are raised about our entire organization and about how people relate to each other. Our journey has only begun!"

Architect your knowledge

Each service line within the worldwide AA organization has a knowledge manager who is responsible for the collation and dissemination of knowledge related to that service line on a worldwide basis. Each AA office also has a manager responsible for knowledge management. Carsten Dalsgaard, the partner previously responsible for KM within AA Denmark, elaborated on his role: "I have to ensure that our Danish offices are plugged into the AA global knowledge network. This means two things. First, we should be making effective use of the global AA knowledge base. Second, we should be making our contributions to the development of the knowledge capital within AA. This latter aspect is particularly important – if you see value in and use knowledge created by someone else, but you do not add to it, it is unfair."

After the completion of each project, project team members are required to fill in a report summarizing their key learning from the assignment experience and also mentioning any best practices which they may have observed within the client's organization. These observations are summarized and shared locally, and also transmitted to the global AA knowledge managers. Global knowledge managers filter through the "incoming knowledge," distill key messages and incorporate them within appropriate firm-wide knowledge bases.

The degree of knowledge shared also influences the evaluation of personnel at all levels of the organization. Carsten Dalsgaard elaborated: "Project team members are required to search for all possible sources of relevant knowledge within the global AA organization. They are rated by project leaders on the degree to which they have used firm-wide resources. The effective leverage of global AA resources is one of the components in the annual ratings of staff. Even partners are subject to a peer evaluation of the degree to which they have been helpful and cooperative."

Advanced decision support

Global knowledge sharing via online knowledge bases often provides a unique competitive advantage. Jesper Jarlbaek provided an example: "We have an online knowledge-base called the Proposal Toolbox which contains details of all proposals submitted by Arthur Andersen worldwide. In one instance we were required to submit an urgent bid in a industry sector which was completely new for the Danish office. Using the Proposal Toolbox, we found all other proposals made by AA worldwide in this industry sector, reutilized parts of proposals prepared by other offices, located and called upon other AA employees who had actually worked on the proposals, and submitted a professional, complete bid within three days!"

The constant need to render client-oriented processes at AA more effective and efficient has led to the development of a number of advanced decision support and expert systems for decision support. These systems have had a major impact on improving the quality of the auditing process and improving client satisfaction.

For example, prior to embarking on any auditing or consultancy services, a risk analysis of potential client arrangements is performed to sketch out and delimit the auditing process. Winsmart is a user-friendly expert system that optimizes and rationalizes a qualitative decision-making process. Winsmart is engineered as a workflow, guiding the user first through questions ranging from the general to the specific. When all questions have been answered, the risk profile for the commitment is computed, resulting in completed forms ready for signing by the management of Arthur Andersen and a graded risk profile in the range of low to maximum risk. Depending on the risk computed, consultative comments are generated on the forms. Winsmart is used more than 100,000 times a year worldwide. The results of all these analyses are centrally consolidated and used to update the weightings of the risk drivers. This knowledge is incorporated and distributed in new versions of Winsmart and forms the basis for the computation of the updated risks for assignments.

Win PROCESS is another complex and sophisticated expert system. As its database, Win PROCESS takes the completed Winsmart and a wide range of benchmark analyses classified by industry in a workflow-controlled application with the following objectives: (a) to comprehend, communicate, and evaluate the client's expectations of the auditing process; (b) to provide the client with relevant suggestions for possible added value initiatives; (c) to match detailed, client-specific accounting data with relevant historical and benchmark industrial data to identify risk and variance and to form a basis for creative proposals for improvements; and (d) to generate cost-effective planning on major auditing assignments.

> Arthur Andersen has been successful in building a K-Corp because it has worked on the following five dimensions:
>
> 1 Strategy: a fundamental belief in the criticality of knowledge as a key driver of competitive advantage lies at the heart of the corporation's strategy.
>
> 2 Infrastructure: it has created a leading-edge physical and technological environment to support knowledge sharing.
>
> 3 Processes: all critical business processes have been reengineered to integrate knowledge sharing.
>
> 4 Organization: it has consciously designed the organization to support the knowledge–innovation cycle such as by having designated knowledge officers across offices with an explicit mandate to identify and collate new knowledge and to feed them back into the larger organization for sharing.
>
> 5 Products and services: the corporation emphasizes knowledge-based relationships with customers and enhances its products and services by embedding knowledge at appropriate customer interactions.

Issues and concerns

Despite a long and successful history in implementing knowledge management, several challenges remain for AA. A particular concern relates to the fact that different practice streams exhibit different attitudes to knowledge sharing. This is particularly evident in the differential rates of adoption of groupware for knowledge sharing within the practice streams. Jesper Jarlbaek elaborated: "The business systems consulting practice stream has been very successful over the years in sharing knowledge with groupware on a global scale. They have a natural inclination to share. In contrast, the audit practice streams, while being good users, have been poor adopters of groupware for knowledge sharing. I think that the difference is mainly due to differences in the nature of the skills used. Knowledge within the business systems area is specialized, technical in nature and fluid. Auditing, on the other hand, relies on well-documented rules and models, much of which were developed several decades ago."

While AA has developed a special competence in the use of technology for top-down sharing of knowledge through an impressive array of online knowledge bases, the overall "write/read ratio" is not very high, i.e., the amount of new knowledge contributed by employees is low as compared to the use of existing knowledge by employees. A partner speculated that the reasons for this were probably rooted in the culture of the company: "Most employees of Arthur Andersen, specially at the senior levels, are focused on chargeability – as this is a key figure of their performance evaluation. This may lead to a natural inclination to not share information with each other, to read more and to write less! However, everyone has to be writer and not only be a reader for the network to succeed."

Another manager noted that the organizational structure is perhaps not the most conducive for sharing: "Today we have profit centers per office and per practice stream within each office. While this sharpens our focus and increases accountability, it does not always create the right incentives for sharing. I do not believe that we really understand how to measure knowledge management and create the right incentives for effective knowledge sharing."

In addition, there are challenges along the international dimension. Jesper Jarlbaek added: "You need an environment of trust and openness for effective knowledge sharing. But the reality is that there are large differences in management styles and trust levels across European countries. For example, there was significant resistance to giving junior staff access to Lotus Notes within the international tax practice stream in a neighboring country. It was feared that the staff might send the wrong information to other AA offices and increase legal liability. The answer is not to shut off the use of the enabling technology; rather there should be organizational mechanisms to ensure that people have adequate skills, talk to each other and trust each other."

While employees universally praise the global knowledge management infrastructure of AA as unique, many are critical of information overload in the existing system. A manager commented: "There is too much information today. I spend a lot of time reading and listening, not enough doing. At our billing rates, this can be deadly! While technology makes it easier for me to accomplish certain things, it does not help in differentiating us from our competitors."

Another junior staff member added: "There is information overload. There is a need to structure knowledge better to make it more useful. There needs to be a higher degree of quality control into what goes into our knowledge bases. For example, the reporting of key learnings required after the completion of each project occurs in a relatively ad-hoc manner. Thus the quality of knowledge input varies widely from project to project."

Technological progress and trends in knowledge sharing are also threatening to change the very nature of AA's business. Jesper Jarlbaek elaborated: "The trend is to share our knowledge directly with the client. For example, for the first time we have packaged our knowledge about accounting principles and started selling it to clients as a CD-ROM/Internet-based knowledge product. If you start sharing everything, what do you have left to generate revenue with? Market trends are forcing us – and everyone else too – to start moving further up the value ladder!"

The agenda

Obvious as it may be from the AA case, knowledge institutionalization is now an explicit task at individual, group, and organizational levels. In the past, like the implicit role of knowledge institutionalization in the evolution of societies, the role of knowledge in organizational settings was implicit. But why has it today become explicit? The answer – $K = (P + I)^S$. The Internet has dramatically increased "S" – sharing. And given the exponential effect of "S" in the equation for knowledge creation, we're witnessing a phenomenal boom in the knowledge created within organizations.

Internal knowledge and customer knowledge must fuse to be strategically meaningful to organizations.

To us, there is another important dimension – the increasing amounts of knowledge being created at the customer interfaces. A similar equation holds true for the knowledge created by "customers" (P) ability to exchange information (I) by utilizing technology (+), exponentially enhanced by the power of sharing (S). We've already seen in the co-creation chapter how customer interfaces are getting increasingly more critical in sharing information with customers. A major knowledge pool is being created at the customer interfaces.

Knowledge institutionalization has to be worked upon at two levels – one with internal knowledge (organizational and operational) and the other with external knowledge (customer related). While the two must fuse to be strategically meaningful to organizations, the imperatives for managing the two are different. The imperative for the first is the speed and spread of knowledge institutionalization because internal knowledge institutionalization always happened. Employees within an organization always shared; the Internet is making it many times faster and wider in scope. The imperative for the second is the digital infrastructure to capture and store customer knowledge and appropriately deploy it for institutionalizing customer knowledge. The issue here is that the Internet makes it manifold easier for organizations to integrate their customers into their critical processes. This is a new imperative.

Internal knowledge

Nonaka and Takeuchi put the issue of the institutionalization of internal knowledge in perspective. They define four modes of knowledge conversion:

- Socialization – tacit to tacit
- Externalization – tacit to explicit
- Combination – explicit to explicit
- Internalization – explicit to tacit.

Learning starts usually with an individual experiencing a success or failure – a tacit knowledge. Over time the individual, given the right incentives, externalizes or conceptualizes the knowledge to apply to different instances, and thus makes it explicit. The explicit knowledge combines and diffuses throughout the organization. Slowly, the new explicit organizational knowledge gets internalized and transformed into the unquestioned routines of the organization. It becomes tacit knowledge again – at group level. The tacit organizational knowledge is shared with newcomers through socialization practices, e.g. on-the-job training or mentoring. The individual who has absorbed this organizational knowledge is then ripe for new experiences, and the cycle starts all over again. In a knowledge-based economy, competitive advantage will come from being able to go faster through this cycle, from the ability to learn faster and then to build up the knowledge to innovate faster while involving the entire organization – across function, division, and geography.

To be faster, the present focus needs to change – from managing knowledge workers to managing knowledge work. Managers have long treated the way knowledge workers performed their activities as an impenetrable "black box." Organizations can do better than the current black box approach by applying a process approach. A process approach to knowledge work attempts to capture knowledge – at least to some degree – from particular knowledge workers into the work itself. This is what is often referred to as embedding more intelligence in the processes. And this becomes feasible only when the processes rest on an intelligent infrastructure and not on a paper-driven system. Intranets provide just that very infrastructure.

Intranets have helped solve one major problem in knowledge application: enabling a collective and randomly accessible "memory." This is particularly important because organizations are distributed knowledge systems (distributed in departments/functions/divisions, etc.). Intranets facilitate knowledge integration by "routinizing" the capture, storage, and retrieval of information. Emerging intranet applications are enabling "electronic" processes wherein the entire contextual knowledge is automatically captured, organized, and communicated. IT enhances knowledge application too, the ultimate value of knowledge institutionalization, by making greatly improved collaboration possible.

Ford, as another example of knowledge institutionalization, manages its business on the intranet; the internal web is the backbone of Ford's business today. "It's even more important than our mainframe infrastructure. We have become much more disciplined about managing our intranet because we can't afford anything less than top performance," said Ford Motor's previous CIO Bud Mathaisel.[5] CEO Jacques Nasser hosted a series of online chats focused on the launch of the Mercury Sable 2000. Top execs have pushed for web-only publication of divisional business plans, engineering best practices, and product-development specs. Every car and truck model has its own website to track design, production, quality control, and delivery processes. Will a new dashboard design slow assembly? How many blue fenders are coming in tomorrow's shipment? To seek answers for such questions, employees do not have to sift through stacks of paper; they know that the online version is up to date and that co-workers and suppliers around the world are looking at the same data. The knowledge pool residing in the corporate intranet thus drives organizational processes.

However, cautions Xerox Chief Scientist John Seely Brown,[6] "The social processes underlying knowledge creation and sharing are as important as the technological processes. We don't think of knowledge as being in the document as much as being around the document, because of the conversation the document fosters... The document (is) an evocative object around which knowledge gets shared." It is not surprising, in the above context, that documenting procedures, creating databases, discussions groups, etc. have not been enough to get people to think together, share insights they didn't know they had or generate new knowledge.[7] Xerox says that Eureka is successful because it was designed to be 90 percent about sociology and 10 percent about technology.

Incidentally, one of the important dimensions of the 90 percent sociology is the need to dramatically reduce the gulf between the two worlds – the formal and informal worlds of an organization. For example, if the answer to "Is there one way of doing things here?" is "Yes," and you wish to promote a creative and knowledge culture, there is a wide gulf. Anyway, strengthen the informal organization to build stronger peer cooperation and coordination. Also create simple but coveted "rituals" around the use of the knowledge system to reinforce the role of knowledge in the growth of the organization.

Knowledge switchboard

The interface of organizations with customers is fast becoming a hotbed of activity in knowledge management. This is natural as it provides a couple of advantages. First, it increases the potential to learn more about customers. Cisco, for example, mines into detailed knowledge of customer interactions to get a better profile of each customer in order to proactively prepare its infrastructure for a delayed fulfillment. Second, it helps customers and the organization to enter into an interactive dialog as to what is possible and under what terms. The organization becomes a "café" where consumers can walk up and configure their product/service and the organization translates the same into deliverables.

Palma, Lazar and Ulsh is a simple example of how knowledge institutionalization can transform an organization into a "serve-yourself" entity. Not long ago, Palma, Lazar and Ulsh[8] (PLU) the oldest flood certification company in the industry, found itself submerged in a very different kind of a flood. With 13,000 pages of flood certification requests arriving daily – and customer service agents searching for a specific fax at any one of 50 fax machines, countless in-baskets or even among two million pages of filed documents – the company struggled to keep its corporate head above water.

Top management at PLU started to realize that it needed to reexamine its internal procedures. "Many of our problems arose because we had simply expanded our existing processes, rather than redesigning them, as our business grew," explained Kruszczynski, PLU's director of management information systems. The new system (appropriately dubbed "Noah") allows users to send and receive flood hazard information over a modem.

The flood-related data is maintained locally and flood certifications are printed at the customer's local facility, allowing for fast and reliable data transmission – a key consideration, since PLU is legally liable for the accuracy of these documents. Incoming faxes are now automatically imported into the system, identified, split into individual requests and then dispersed to different departments, drastically reducing the time required to complete certification.

The paper chase at PLU has ended as well. Customer-service agents can now call up information in real time and answer questions on the spot, and everyone in the organization has access to the current, accurate information they need, when they need it. Not only has PLU entirely eliminated paper from the process, but by using intuitive forms that fill in information like the date automatically, PLU has eliminated two million wasted keystrokes in three months, reducing data entry efforts by 25 percent. For Krusczcynski, however, the system's chief value lies in the ability "to finally be in control of our business; to understand statistically what we're doing right and wrong; to better meet the needs of our clients." A digital interface has come in between PLU and its customers that acts more like a large switchboard to connect customers to the right information needed.

Knowledge-based corporations

Knowledge communities, internal knowledge and the knowledge switchboard together form the foundations knowledge-based corporations. An organization where the knowledge–innovation cycle is a routine part of the processes. Beware that the resulting organization will actually be a fundamentally different organization. In a way, the very *raison d'être* of organization will shift.

Traditionally, it has been argued that organizations exist to minimize "transaction costs." Minimizing transaction costs is portrayed as the glue that holds an organization together and justifies the economic rationale of organizations. More simply, by bringing different specializations or functions within the boundaries of a single entity, a lot of cost is saved. A significant part of transaction costs are due to search costs and inefficiencies in communication.

A knowledge-based corporation is "part technology, part work practice, part sociology."

But some see knowledge creation and nurturing as taking over the very rationale of organizational existence.[9] They argue that organizational knowledge provides a synergistic advantage not replaceable in the marketplace. Pharmaceutical companies, for example, are discovering that knowledge about how to administer drugs, avoid complications, and manage side effects is as desirable to customers as the drugs themselves. Thus, it's knowledge, not just transaction costs, that holds an organization together. As the Internet becomes more and more pervasive, and as knowledge management becomes increasingly embedded within corporations, such a view will only gain momentum. Companies have no alternative but to turn themselves into knowledge-based corporations.

Japanese flat-panel displays[10] producers provide another example of successful knowledge-based corporations. The Japanese flat-panel displays producers, who dominate the industry with over 90 percent of the world market, are extensively using various knowledge management options to ensure that their market lead is sustained. For example, they use knowledge management to achieve economics of scale by reusing and recombining knowledge in multiple ways, cost reduction through process innovation and knowledge internalization, and insuring against technological discontinuities by having multiple options for pursuing new flat panel options.

Specifically, Fujitsu, for example, has maintained its leadership in PDP[11] technology over the last 25 years. It deploys the following knowledge evolution and knowledge leveraging strategies extending the cognitive boundaries of knowledge (with low appropriatability by competitors):

- Knowledge envisioning: It has identified a generic technology which has long-term growth opportunities.
- Knowledge evolution: It has rapidly evolved knowledge ahead of others to gain competitive advantage.
- Knowledge internalization: It has internalized knowledge to become the first firm in the world to mass-produce plasma display panels.
- Knowledge externalization: It has evolved a variety of products using the same knowledge to derive scope economics.
- Knowledge protection: It has obtained 300 patents on plasma display panels to make its proprietary technology the de facto standard.
- Knowledge complementing: It has joined with Ashahi glass to produce large glass panels so that 100,000 large panels can be produced a month.

Similarly, internal knowledge is used for creating entry barriers for new players. Some of the strategies used for this are:[12]

- rapidly evolving new knowledge through knowledge search and creation;
- rapidly combining internal knowledge for leveraging existing knowledge as a platform for creating a variety of new products;

- introducing new products rapidly through knowledge leveraging so that competitors can not catch up in terms of speed and variety of offerings; and
- continuously offering new features along with an existing technology so that competitors can not match the cost effectiveness.

But there is more behind this example – the excellent management of tacit knowledge. We must remember that critically important tacit knowledge can get de-emphasized if the dissemination of information is mostly "impersonal" (e.g. online databases/discussions forums/document exchanges). Most knowledge systems take a very technical view of the required IT infrastructure. They end up laying high-end technological solutions over cumbersome and inefficient processes. Some hints for improving the use of IT in knowledge systems are:

- Reengineer processes before applying IT solutions.
- Do not create islands; link customers, suppliers, investors, etc. to your knowledge system.
- Be prepared to invest much more on maintenance than design and implementation.

Obviously, building up a knowledge-based corporation is "part technology, part work practice, part sociology." Therefore, reengineering the existing knowledge system is a very comprehensive organizational intervention. While Internet-enabled IT solutions create a highly facilitative infrastructure, other organizational dimensions such as leadership, group dynamics, reward and recognition system, and work processes provide the superstructure for effective knowledge institutionalization. And it's here that you can unleash your innovative genius.

Action points

1. Does the term "knowledge" appear in your corporation's mission statement? Does your CEO understand the strategic importance of knowledge to innovation?
2. What are the best practices of knowledge sharing that you can identify within your corporation today? Do you have any "Eureka-like" examples? What are the principles underlying these success stories? How can you leverage these best practices across your entire organization?
3. Are your technology systems capable of providing a seamless environment for communication and collaboration across the enterprise? Is the technology integrated with your work processes (such as in Arthur Andersen)?

4. How is your knowledge switchboard at your customer interfaces? Is all relevant knowledge being applied at customer interactions? What knowledge remains to be integrated into your knowledge switchboard?
5. How do your organization's culture and incentive practices support the knowledge–innovation cycle?

Mantra

Knowledge fuels innovative initiatives and innovation creates new experiences to create knowledge. Organizations will have to learn to master the knowledge–innovation (K-I) cycle; master knowledge institutionalization. Fortunately, the Internet provides a unique infrastructure for knowledge institutionalization within organizations and thereby makes it possible for organizations to initiate and sustain the K-I cycle. Knowledge institutionalization has to be worked upon at two levels – one with internal knowledge (organizational and operational) and the other with external knowledge (customer related). The two need to fuse to create an effective knowledge-based corporation.

But organizations are social entities too. People dynamics must not be ignored. Individuals are the original knowledge creators and their tacit knowledge is the source of group and organizational knowledge. And indeed, this "knowledge conversion is a 'social' process between individuals and not confined within individuals." This social process is embodied in what we call communities – contributing and learning communities. Turning your "social organization" into knowledge-efficient communities requires innovative inputs because communities are all unequal in their knowledge conversion efficiency.

Notes

1. Ruggles, Rudy and Holtshouse, Dan (1999) *The Knowledge Advantage*, Capstone US Business Books Network.
2. Minitel: a passive terminal provided by France Telecom to businesses and consumers since mid-1984. Users can access private or public services through the national Transpac France Telecom network, such as doing online reservations, search telephone directories, etc. It is, however, fairly rudimentary as it provides information in text form with very simple graphics. Today Minitel can be integrated in a laptop environment.

3. Rivette, Kevin G. and Kline, David (2000) "Discovering new value in intellectual property", *Harvard Business Review*, January–February.
4. Nonaka, Ikujiro and Hirotaka, Takeuchi (1995) *The Knowledge-Creating Company*, Oxford University Press, p. 61.
5. Brown, Eryn (1999) "9 ways to win on the web," *Fortune*, May 24, p. 51.
6. www.xerox.com
7. McDermott, Richard (1999) "Knowledge management," *Californian Management Review*, 41 (4), Summer, pp. 110–16.
8. http://knowledge managementmag.com/knowledge managementmagn2/microsoftsup/home.htm
9. Brown, John Seely and Duguid, Paul (1998) "Organising Knowledge," *Californian Management Review*, Spring.
10. Bowonder, B. and Miyake, T. (1999) "Japanese LCD industry: Competing through knowledge management," *Creativity and Innovation Management*, 8 (2), June.
11. One of the leading technologies in flat-panel displays.
12. Bowonder, B. and Miyake, T. (1999) "Japanese LCD industry: Competing through knowledge management," *Creativity and Innovation Management*, 8 (2), June.

Preparing for action   V

The backpack 12

Bookmark

Innovation was always a guest item on the agenda of boardroom occupants. It was strategic but exceptional. It was planned but not effectively monitored. It was too technical for most directors and located within an island within the organization. And external stakeholders had little to do with the innovation processes.

We hope you appreciate that all this has changed for good.

What's your agenda for change? Let's open the backpack.

Reality plus!

You were right – enough of virtuality – get real. Get focused on value delivery and build competencies for the same. Business remains business-as-usual! Products have to be produced, delivered, and serviced as always. But the foundation of the real is increasingly being enhanced by the virtual. It is not about virtual reality but about reality plus!

For some years, many believed that the Internet would create a virtual world where organizations and individuals would cohabit and interact in virtual ways. In fact, this has been the fundamental goal of virtual reality – how to create a virtual world which provides a "real-life-like" representation for individuals and firms. However, our experiences over recent years have shown us that people still like to lead real lives. Technology cannot replace the real world but can certainly provide a more enhanced version of the real world that compensates for many of its limitations.

Consider a simple example. When you visit a convention or a fair, you typically gain the most from meaningful conversations that you conduct with other interesting individuals whom you also meet at the fair. How many such conversations can you conduct over a day at a typical convention? Do not count the dozens of quick acquaintances that you make in such a setting. If you had extended conversations with about half-a-dozen interesting individuals, you have probably gained a lot from your day at the convention. How many other such conversations were possible? Assuming that there were 500 individuals at the convention, there were at least 493 other one-to-one conversations that you potentially could have engaged in (and many more in groups of different individuals). Granted, you would probably not have wanted to have one-on-one conversations with all 493 other attendees, but there were probably certainly several other attendees that you missed connecting with. This happened because you were limited by time and due to the simple fact that it was probably not easy to determine who among all 500 attendees were interesting individuals for you.

Imagine a scenario where your personal digital assistant had some knowledge of your interests and could communicate with the digital assistants of other conference attendees. Each digital assistant, with knowledge of the interests of its "owner," could determine the degree of interest in initiating a conversation between its owner and other individuals. Your digital assistant could propose a set of relevant individuals to you and you could select and request your digital assistant to schedule appropriate meeting slots. Suddenly technology is enabling you to get more out of your time at the convention. Technology is not replacing the physical convention, but is creating new possibilities for you and helping you to get more out of the real world. As we noted before, it is not about virtual reality but about reality plus – reality enhanced by the power of technology.

The new organizational frontier is the "**Real Virtual Corporation**" – corporations which are able to leverage the power of the Internet and associated technologies to enhance customer relationships to create value, manage integrated supply chains to improve the efficiency of all players, and empower their employees to be more productive and innovative. It is about using the power of the virtual to enhance the real! The Internet is pushing a growing amount of intelligence onto the communication infrastructure and that will significantly impact how we produce, deliver, and service. It also implies that, for once, business practices and opportunities for companies anywhere in the world will be driven by a truly ubiquitous resource – the Internet. They all have a chance to compete on an even keel irrespective of their origins. Companies are set to witness a defining moment: there would be one organizational form – globally – the real virtual corporation.

There is going to be no digital divide in business! The Internet is not a tool/window channel. It's the channel of channels. It's an infrastructure. It's the new backbone. And the message in this book is simple:

- Reconstruct your business on to the new infrastructure, and
- make innovation your corporate, tactical and operational mainstay.

From now on, innovation is going to be an imperative for survival, not just growth. Innovation is going to be routine. The quantity of innovation will count no less than the quality. And there will be no simple short cuts or organizational islands for innovation – you're an innovator or you aren't. You'll innovate both how you do business and what your business is all about.

> **There is going to be no digital divide in business!**

And innovation will not be a "cost center." The Internet is creating a unique infrastructure – customizable, intelligent, and scalable; it's the new Edison's laboratory. Take as much of your assets and processes online as possible.

The underlying tone of the book is that we are convinced that incumbents can be as nimble footed on innovation as start-ups. We appreciate that this may be a tall order for many incumbents. But Barnes & Noble, GM, Charles Schwab, Merrill Lynch, and others prove that it can be done. We're therefore revisiting the innovation agenda to offer you the essential conclusions that are especially drawn for the incumbents. Here is the exploratory backpack – get set – good luck!

> **The quantity of innovation will count no less than the quality.**

Packers' mantras

It would be foolish to argue that the new economy has nothing to learn from the old economy. The basic mantras of innovation management apply in both worlds. Expect more innovations if you have an entrepreneurial organization, if you listen to your customers, if you create a flexible fulfillment infrastructure, and if you have visionary leadership. These and other powerful ideas that you can find in any good book do also apply in the Internet world. But there are more specific and actionable lessons from the past. In particular, our earlier experiences with service innovation and innovation under technological discontinuity have a special significance. Let's just revisit them once again.

In service innovation, one of the major design parameters is the degree of overlap between you as a supplier of the service and the customer. Many organizations have poured the design of that overlap in concrete. Committing your organization to the Internet is a unique opportunity to deeply question the design of that overlap. And to redesign it, either by increasing or decreasing the overlap.

In doing so, you also need to understand that the Internet is a new technological infrastructure. We do know that incumbents have a tendency just to transpose the current business model onto the new infrastructure. Once they do that, they may think about improving the quality of their service and then, only then, will they think of new applications. It is perhaps not intrinsically bad to follow that sequence, but we need to develop speed. No cross-country skiing, but a ski jump is what we need!

Lessons from the past give you a good head start, but they cannot keep you ahead.

To do so we need to carefully manage the hurdles for the adoption of an innovation. We have described six types of hurdles in Chapter 6, and you may want to turn back to them and analyze which of those are the most important in your company and with your targeted customer base.

The Internet has several characteristics in common with other occasions of technological discontinuity. Learning from these other historic moments in business, we'd like to re-emphasize two points.

The first is that your organization needs to develop flexibility and an ability to learn. This is particularly important in the initial fluid phase of experimentation following a technological discontinuity. What you think is right may not be right. What you think your customers want may not be what they need. And your customers may not be able to articulate their needs precisely. A difficult scenario, indeed! But also a scenario full of opportunities, if only you are able to be flexible and are able to learn.

The second is that leadership in developing a new dominant design following the emergence of a discontinuous technology is critical. Such a dominant design is something you will have to develop with allies and you will probably need to shape the sectoral boundaries anew. Are you prepared to give such leadership? Do you have the imagination to see your industry disappearing and new ones arising out of its ashes? If you are not an active leader in shaping the dominant design, you risk being left with only crumbs from the new pie being created.

If this order is not tall enough for you yet, we have a few more pieces of advice ready. They have to do with the really new stuff. But for this we will offer you a roadmap. Your backpack is almost ready!

The roadmap

The lessons from the past give you a good head start. But the lessons from the past cannot keep you ahead. You need a roadmap of the new contours being paved by the Internet. The previous four chapters detailed the roadmap that we must follow. Each of the chapters sounds very demanding, and they are. And they may sound more so for incumbents because they literally have to deconstruct a legacy and then reconstruct it all over again with a different architecture but with the same people. It's with this imperative in mind that we've attempted to revisit the chapters once more to identify the milestones to help you measure your progress in converting your organization in "simpler" actionable steps.

Co-creation

Customization is becoming real and simple – just ask for it. Customization will be the standard – you'll not usually pay a premium for customization "efforts." Welcome to the age of individuality. Interestingly, whenever a customization is sought, it will be a win-win situation for both – customers and producers. The current push technology of production is sub-optimal for all. But there hasn't been an alternative. The Internet has changed all that.

We're entering an era where perhaps the greatest value-creating virtue is to enable customers to give wings to their imaginations. And how is that good news for incumbents? It's simple. As incumbents, you already have customers! They may not necessarily all be very happy customers but they aren't probably a community either!

The greatest value-creating virtue is to enable customers to give wings to their imaginations.

Thus, you still have a chance to build it up into a great competitive resource for yourself. New as it is, co-creation is a major innovation window. How do you get to co-create?

The first step: Reach out to your customers and bring them home. Invite them into your organization. Work together with them to better understand their needs. Provide relevant information to help them to decide upon their own needs. Do not forget that customers need your help to define and satisfy their needs. Are you ready to provide that help? Do all you can to enhance knowledge within your employees about your customers.

The second step: Sensitize all your customer interfaces for an informed dialogue with your customers. Give them a facelift. Interconnect them seamlessly. Deploy the Internet to connect disparate and distributed databases about customers. Focus on making the process of purchasing through your interfaces "real" – attempt to give them a personalized and trustworthy experience.

The third step: A strong customization ability without a robust pricing strategy could be dangerous. Develop comprehensive cost data for the production and delivery of customized solutions. Make relevant data relating to possible customizations, costs, and deliveries, etc. available to your employees and your customers. Do your homework rigorously – keep your own notes on each customer. Use those notes in real time while interacting with your customers.

The fourth step: Reach out to all of your customers and convert them into a community. Facilitate lateral communication among them – online and otherwise. But why should they talk to each other? Plan some tangible incentives for them if they do – financial or otherwise. At the top of the incentives list should be an opportunity to undo the past – promise to bring customer delight in all future purchases. And let your community facilitation be the biggest proof of your intent! Assert that you're now clear about your destination – customers.

E-nfrastructure

Middle-of-the-road organizational infrastructure cannot support the demands of the opportunities that co-creation will generate. Organizational infrastructure is becoming ever more important in the quest for excellence and innovation. The three elements of the infrastructure that we observed – organization, partners, and information technology – provide a highly fertile substrate for growth through innovation. You need to be state-of-the-art in each one of them. How do you achieve that?

The first step: Think people. Think leaders. Think about how you can create an organizational environment that brings out the best in each employee. Do you recall the story of Oticon (from Chapter 9)? Can you take the leadership to create an environment that attracts the best talent? Are you inspired enough to set an ambitious agenda to develop talented employees? Doing all of this is non-trivial. Because change begins with you. You have to change in order to help others. The creation of the right organization may create psychological and emotional traumas for you and for your employees. You have to be sure that you can deal with it first. This is critical.

The second step: Think partners. Think virtual factories. A strong partnership with customers was the focus of the first imperative, "co-creation." If you have understood your customers' needs well, you have realized that you are unable to fulfill those needs alone. There are others who are critical for your success – suppliers, resellers, and R&D partners. You need the help of your partners. Are your organization's processes woven with those of your partners to create the right virtual factory for you? Take a close look at all your critical processes. Are you exploiting the unique strengths of each partner to make your virtual factory a significant source of innovation? Or are your processes hidebound by inter- and intra-organizational boundaries? Do you have what it takes to build your virtual factory?

The third step: Think technology. Information technology. Most likely you currently consider information technology to be a limitation as opposed to a great enabler. You are probably hostage to a fragmented information architecture and suffer from the harmful effects of having multiple systems that cannot talk to each other. If these statements do not apply to you, consider yourself very lucky. But if they do, it is time for you to start investing in a business redesign of your technology infrastructure. You probably do not have either the necessary resources or the luxury of time to do a complete overhaul of your IT systems. This may also be futile as technology systems are constantly evolving. What you should do is to carefully identify the needs of your critical business processes – such as those to build your virtual factory – and then apply the power of the Internet and new technology to support those processes appropriately. Build a strong supply chain that is electronically linked to your customers – consider yourself as a gatekeeper of the supply chain to your customers. The key to success is the ability to discern the business value of processes and to lead the organization in the adoption of the new technology-enabled process. Remember, this is what leaders like Schwab and Cisco have done.

> **Organizational infrastructure is becoming ever more important in the quest for excellence and innovation.**

The fourth step: Integrate the above – great people, good partners, and effective processes and systems – to create a real-time organization. Gone are the days when you could wait weeks before sensing that something was not right for your customers. Gone are the times when you could wait days before informing your supply chain partners about business changes. Today you need to be able to quickly sense the pulse of your customers, feed that information down your network of partners, and mobilize your people across functions to provide the right response – all in "real-time." It is not simply a question of sensing problems. Probably much more important is the fact that you have to continuously evaluate the opportunities that emerge out of exploiting online digital assets – about customers and about operations. Innovative business modeling is the most potent innovative opportunity.

Perpetual metamorphosis

One aspect that has become painfully evident to managers over recent years is that continuous change is here to stay. No longer can a firm assume that it has earned and guaranteed its success for a decade – an eternity in today's business environment where in many sectors product life cycles are measured in weeks and days. A best-selling product or service that seemed to work so well just a few weeks or months ago can be rapidly challenged by a new entrant or supplanted by a new business proposition.

Leading firms continuously re-evaluate their businesses in order to maximize their opportunities – both immediate and future. Recall the changes at IBM over the past decade from Chapter 10. Though no dotcom start-up, Big Blue has retained the mantle of leadership by continuously reinventing itself over the past century. The Internet has changed the pace and scope of innovations and thus increased the pressure on companies for perpetual metamorphosis – the act of breaking away from past body and soul to build a new one. What should you do to succeed in your quest for perpetual metamorphosis? We have some suggestions.

The first step: Lose your fear. Lose your fear of failure. Lose your fear of rocking the boat. It is said that entrepreneurship is a story of mainly failures and a few scattered successes. The same applies to intrapreneurship – entrepreneurship within your own firm. Yes, you are very successful today. Yes, it seems like that your products and services are going to remain successful for a few more years. But your success today is no guarantee of success in the future. There is no reason to be complacent. If you are not ready to rock the boat – you cannot start the journey of perpetual metamorphosis. The first step is therefore having the courage and the willingness to start on the journey: a journey of innovation, a journey of considerable uncertainty.

The second step: Design your organization for learning. It is true that our organizations are today designed largely for execution and not for learning. If perpetual metamorphosis is inherently an uncertain process – how can we succeed without a strategy for experimentation and a model for learning? Note that there is a good reason why schools and universities exist. Despite all their limitations, they impose a certain process and structure to learning. What is your process for managing learning? You may choose a classical stage/gate approach or a more recent spiral approach or a hybrid approach. Regardless, you have to carefully reexamine your processes for managing innovation. Never forget that learning is central to innovation and learning cannot happen in a vacuum, just based upon random serendipity.

The third step: Assimilate the drivers to build a portfolio of learning projects. The drivers for your metamorphosis could be your customers – recall the importance of lead users from Chapter 10. Or the drivers could be partners from your alliance network. Or more likely, some high-performing groups and individuals within your firm can provide the right stimuli for metamorphosis. Regardless of the drivers for your journey of perpetual metamorphosis, it is important to anchor your journey on these drivers. Build a portfolio of experiments with them. Some experiments will have a short-term focus. Others should have a long-term focus. Some ideas will be quick wins – achievable with low risk. Others may be breakthrough concepts with significant risks. You have to leverage the ideas into a balanced portfolio of learning projects. Few firms manage continuous change as the managed impact of a portfolio of learning projects. Make perpetual metamorphosis a managed journey and not a random experiment.

The real opportunity offered by the Internet is to undertake rebirth.

Institutionalizing knowledge

A new economy is emerging built on knowledge and innovation. As discussed in Chapter 11, knowledge will not be just another asset to be managed besides people, property, and capital. Knowledge will be the asset to be managed for competitive advantage. Knowledge fuels innovative initiatives and innovation creates new experiences to create knowledge. Thus knowledge will be at the root of innovation. And innovation will be better managed if knowledge management is institutionalized in the firm.

In Chapter 11, we observed how Xerox and Arthur Andersen have each focused on institutionalizing knowledge. How do you start? We have the following recommendations.

The first step: Make sure that your top management truly understands the meaning and implications of institutionalizing knowledge. This is important. All too often, managers equate knowledge management with the installation of intranets or similar groupware systems. The task of institutionalizing knowledge is far more comprehensive and far more complex than simply installing the technology platform. The evidence is clear. While most firms today have installed intranets, few can claim to have institutionalized knowledge with any degree of success. Once top management understands the strategic importance of institutionalizing knowledge, this needs to be reflected in your business mission and value statements. Also, make sure that your top management clearly articulates and communicates this vision.

The second step: You need to act. If you are new to knowledge institutionalization, you need to start somewhere. You probably need to begin small with a clear focused application – much like the Xerox's Eureka system. A good place to begin your first project(s) is the customer interface. Think about what knowledge is required to bear upon each point of contact with your customers and how you can better manage the knowledge transfer associated with each point of contact. Also, do not forget the lessons from perpetual metamorphosis. The institutionalization of knowledge has to be managed like any other learning experiment. If done right, it can create a virtuous cycle of innovation.

The third step: Adopt a holistic approach to knowledge institutionalization. Recall the lessons from the story of Arthur Andersen in Chapter 11. You will need to act along multiple dimensions – strategy, process, technology, incentives, and communities – to ensure that knowledge gets successfully institutionalized across the organization. Do not forget that knowledge institutionalization is as much a social process as a technology-enabled phenomenon. Pay particular attention to social processes within and across different knowledge communities in your organization (and its network of customers, suppliers, and partners). You need to tap into the natural energies of people to share knowledge and feed the innovation process. Reduce the gulf between the two worlds – formal and informal organization – and strengthen the informal organization to build stronger peer cooperation and coordination. And create simple but coveted "rituals" around the use of the knowledge system to reinforce the role of knowledge in the growth of the organization.

The sum of parts

INNOVATION is NOT a big word anymore; it's no more the privilege of the mighty like GE, GM, Cisco, Wal-Mart. You may also add eBay.com and Amazon.com if you wish. It is your privilege now. It's your time to make your mark!

Index

AA (Arthur Andersen) 39, 136, 219–24, 230, 244
Abernathy, W. and Utterback, J., technological life cycle model 107–10
ABT *see* Auto-by-Tel (ABT)
adoption hurdles for innovators 121
advertising online 15–16
airline industry 7–8, 14, 19, 20, 26
   collective enterprises 181–2
   destination-bound capabilities 149
   and efficient interfaces 155
   reverse product life cycle 119–20
   and value pricing 158, 159–60
Allaire, Paul 214
Allyn & Bacon 15
Alsop, Stewart 78
Amadeus Global Travel Distribution 153
Amazon.com 12, 19, 20, 27, 32, 33, 37, 38, 65, 66, 69–71, 105, 244
   and Barnes & Noble 73–4, 75
   books-return policy 70
   collective enterprises 180
   and comprehensiveness 161
   continuous innovation 77–9
   customers 69–70, 77, 134
   Gift-Click 154
   innovation strategy 128–9, 131, 134, 135
   and the knowledge–innovation cycle 136
   and perpetual metamorphosis 77, 135, 193, 196, 200, 201, 204
   and service innovation 116, 118
   and the technological life cycle 111, 113
   Toy Quest 70–1, 134, 204
   and Wal-Mart 72, 80
   zShops 160
AOL 12, 27, 97, 160, 162
   LiveProducts 153
Apple Computer 112
Arthur Andersen (AA) 39, 136, 219–24, 230, 244
Asia Pacific firms, and the Marketspace model 20, 21
Asian managers, and Internet-based transactions 122
AT&T 27
Augustine, Norman 196

Auto-by-Tel (ABT) 19, 38, 83, 84, 86–94, 100, 123
   after-market program 92–3
   Certified Car Cyber-Store 91, 129
   Dealer Real Time system 88, 94, 135
   dealer referral network 89–90, 91, 93, 135
   factors in the success of 94
   and GM 5, 95, 96, 97
   iManager 88–9
   innovation strategy 130, 135
   and the knowledge–innovation cycle 136
   locate-to-order model 100–1
   online auction services 87
   and perpetual metamorphosis 193
   and service innovation 114, 115
   vehicle financing and insurance 92
Autodesk 199
automobile industry 38, 83–7
   changing dealerships 85–7
   innovation strategy 132
   learning from the past 106
   retail prices 84
   used car sales 84–5, 86
   see also Auto-by-Tel (ABT); GM (General Motors)
AutoNation 86
Avnet Inc. 186
Axon 183

backend systems
   and customers 6, 31, 32, 33–4
   and dotcom failures 6, 35
   and the frontend 32–3
   recreating on an Internet backbone 7, 17
Barnes & Noble 33, 37, 38, 60, 65, 73–5, 80, 105, 237
   and Amazon 73–4, 75
   and Fatbrain.com 75
   innovation strategy 129
   and Internet Service Counters 74
   and Merrill Lynch 197
   origins 73
   strategic investments 75
   "superstore" concept 73
   and the technological life cycle 111, 113
   University 75

Barras, R. 119
Bartz, Carol 199
Bechtolsheim, Andy 201
Bertelsmann 5
Best Buy 198
Bezos, Jeff 69, 70, 71, 128, 135, 196, 204
boaters.com 196
Boeing 3, 205
Bond, Sir John 31
Boo.com 6
Border Books 156, 180
Borders.com 77–8
Boston Consulting Group 35–6
Boynton, Andrew C. 170
brokerage industry 38, 46–63
  bulletin boards for secondary trading 62
  changes 46
  Direct Public Offerings (DPOs) 62, 63
  discount brokers 47, 48
  "full-service" brokerage firms 47
  innovation strategy 131
  and Internet-based stock trading 47–8
  long-term impact of the Internet 62–3
  and Mayday 1975 47
  regional brokerage firms 47
  see also E*TRADE; Merrill Lynch; Schwab, Charles
Brown, John Seely 226–7
business models
  innovating 133
  new 11, 12, 25, 26
buy.com 35, 159, 160, 198
BuyEnlarge 75
Buzzsaw.com 199

Camdens 154
CarMax 86
Carrefour 201
Case, Steve 160
CDNow 5
Celebrity Sightings 118
Chambers, John 176
Chase Manhattan Bank 58
chemical companies, product information 15
Christensen, Clayton 199, 200
  The Innovators' Dilemma 175
Chrysler 100
Circuit City 198
Cisco 4, 19, 26, 27, 30, 32, 170–1, 175, 241, 244
  call centres 34, 187
  Cisco Connection Online (CCO) 171
  as a collective enterprise 179

and custom manufacturing 34–5
Internet customer-care solutions 171–2
Manufacturing Connection Online (MCO) 170–1
and technology adoption 186–7
Citigroup 3
Clauden, Ron Jr 98
co-configuration 170
co-creation 38–9, 134, 141–64, 239
  and comprehensiveness 148, 160–3
  and destination-bound capabilities 148–52, 164
  and efficient interfaces 148, 152–6
  and value pricing 39, 148, 157–60
collective enterprises 179–83, 241
communities, and institutionalizing knowledge 216, 217–19, 231
comprehensiveness 148, 160–3
CompUSA 197–9
Compuserve 119
connectivity, and the Marketspace model 9, 30
Cotsakos, Christos 49, 51–2, 57–8, 175
Covisint 99, 111
Cozone.com 198–9
custom manufacturing 34–5
customer relationship management (CRM)
  and ABT 88
  and E*TRADE 58
customer relationships
  and the Marketspace model 9, 11, 13, 18
  use of the Internet for 13–14, 32, 33
customers
  and backend systems 6, 31, 32, 33–4
  central role of 27, 28–30
  changing behaviour of 123
  and co-creation 15, 38–9, 134, 141–64, 239–40
  and cyber-communities 3, 13, 14, 150–2
  E*TRADE 51
  and efficient interfaces 148, 152–6
  gatekeepers 62
  and innovation strategy 132–3
  interfaces 28, 38
  and knowledge institutionalization 227–8
  and the lead user process 203–5, 208
  restructuring of customer interfaces 36
  as a source of competence 147
  user friendliness of Internet sites 121
  Wal-Mart 67–8
customized products 15, 142–5, 147, 150, 156, 239–40

DaimlerChrysler 205
Dalsgaard, Carsten 220, 221
Dammerman, Dennis D. 175
Danon, Pierre 215
Dell 19, 30, 143, 184
DeLuca, Tony 186
destination-bound capabilities 148–52, 164
DiMaggio, Dan 172
Direct Public Offerings (DPOs) 62, 63
discontinuity
    the Internet as a 25, 26, 27, 107, 238–9
    management of 107–10
discounts on Internet orders 15
Disney 15, 205
dominant design, and the technological life cycle 109–10, 124
dotcom companies
    failures xi, 4, 5, 6, 35
        and the brokerage industry 62–3
    and pricing 159
DPOs (Direct Public Offerings) 62, 63
Dykema, Evie Black 161

E*TRADE 19, 37, 38, 45, 46, 47, 55–8
    Access 57
    Business Solutions Group (BSG) 55
    Center 57–8
    customers 51, 56–8
    and cyber-gatekeepers 62
    E*TRADE BANK 55
    and e-infrastructure 175
    growth and innovation 49, 51–2
    impact of the Internet on 62
    innovation strategy 129, 130, 131, 134
    key strengths of 56
    and the knowledge-innovation cycle 136
    market share 48
    and Merrill Lynch 60, 61
    and perpetual metamorphosis 193
    revenue 49
    and success by empowerment 55–6
    and the technological life cycle 112
    "Virtual Credit Union" 56
    Zones 57
e-nfrastructure 134, 167–88, 240–2
    and co-configuration 170
    and collective enterprises 179–83, 241
    and employees 241
    and the innovative use of IT 171–3, 241
    and naturally innovative organizations 173–8
    and technological savviness 183–7, 188
E-steel 193
eBay 111, 121, 158, 193, 244

Edmund's 88, 90
electronics firms
    and the Marketspace model 18, 19
    online ordering of products 16
Ellis, Peter 87, 88, 92, 93, 94
Ellison, Larry 27, 28, 180
Ellspermann, Randy 92
employee stock option plans (ESOPs) 175–6
enews.com 75
Ericsson 21
ESOPs (employee stock option plans) 175–6
European firms, and the Marketspace model 20, 21
Evans, Philip B. 192
Expedia 7–8, 14, 182

Fatbrain.com 75
Fidelity 49
financial services sector 12, 36–7
    and the Marketspace model 18, 19
    see also brokerage industry
Fine, Charles 145
Finland 21
Fiorina, Carly 174, 180
1stUP 160
Flextronics 183–4
fluid phase, of the technological life cycle 108–9, 111–12, 124
Ford 26, 27, 33, 84, 85, 86, 90, 129
    and co-creation 146, 147
    and GM 98–9
    and knowledge institutionalization 226
    and the UPS Logistics Group 172
Forrester Research 161
4Ps (Product, Price, Promotion and Place), and the Marketspace model 9–11, 12–19
France Telecom 11
Frazier, Michael D. 130
Fujitsu 229

Galloway, Joe 182
gay and lesbian websites 162
Gazoo.com 99–100, 161
GE xii, 3, 7, 26, 27, 175, 244
    culture of learning 177–8
    destination-bound capabilities 148–9
    innovation strategy 130
    secrets of success with e-business 6
    and Six Stigma Quality 6
    and value pricing 157, 159
General Motors *see* GM (General Motors)

Gerstner, Louis V. 193–4, 195
global business transformation, research on 8–12
GM (General Motors) xii, 15, 19, 26, 27, 38, 83, 84, 89, 90, 94–101, 237, 244
    and co-creation 146
    and Covisint 99
    e-GM 96, 97–8
    and Ford 98–9
    GM BuyPower 95–6
    GM International Operations (GMIO) 94
    GM Robotics Corp 95
    GM-North American Operations (GM-NAO) 94
    innovation strategy 129
    locate-to-order model 100–1
    OnStar 98
    and service innovation 114
    and Toyota 99–100, 161
Goldstein, Michelle V. 90
Google, PageRank technology 185–6
Grove, Andy 182
Guenthard, A. 155

Habern, Glenn 76
Haley, Timothy M. 70
Hamel, Gary 201
Hamilton, Stuart 183
Helu, Carlos Slim 197
Hewlett-Packard (HP) 26, 174, 176, 180
Hippel, Erich von 201, 203
Hogan, Mark 96, 97
Home Depot 20
HP (Hewlett-Packard) 26, 174, 176, 180
HSBC Holdings plc 31, 60–1
Huber, Chet 98

IBM xii, 16, 27, 112
    and perpetual metamorphosis 135–6, 193–4, 195, 202, 205, 242
IDEO 205
ImageX.com 181
Infinger, James 196
information technology (IT)
    and e-infrastructure 183–7, 241
    innovative use of 171–3
    stocks 3
ING Group 16
innovation
    as an imperative for survival 237
    quantity of 39–40
    service innovation on the Internet 114–18, 124
        hurdles for innovators 120–3

stage/gate model of 206–7
as strategy xi–xii, 38, 127–38
    the four imperatives 133–6
through a new infrastructure 118–20
see also perpetual metamorphosis
innovative organizations, and e-nfrastructure 173–8
institutionalizing knowledge 39, 134, 211–31, 243–4
    advanced decision support 221–2
    architecting your knowledge 220–1
    and communities 216, 217–19, 231
    and customers 227–8
    holistic approach to 244
    initiation 217
    internal knowledge 225–7
    and knowledge-based corporations 228–30
    and the knowledge–innovation (K–I) cycle 39, 136, 212, 216, 228, 231
    and peer recognition 215–16
    and "write/read ratio" of employees 223
insurance companies 15
Intel 4, 175, 182
IntelliChoice 88, 90
interactivity, and the Marketspace model 9, 30
Internet
    as a broadband infrastructure 22, 28
    as a discontinuity 25, 26, 27, 107, 195, 238–9
    dotcom failures xi, 4, 5, 6, 35
    and innovation 5–6, 118–20, 237
        service innovation 114–18, 120–3, 124, 238
    lack of exploitation by large firms 3, 5, 11–12
    merging old and new 7, 21, 30–2, 238
    and new business models 11, 12, 25, 26
    new strategic architecture 7–8, 31
    as a publishing medium xi, 11
    and the technological life cycle 110–14
    uniqueness of the technology infrastructure 4–5, 135, 192
Intranets 226, 244

Jackson, Jeanne 37, 66, 76
Japanese companies
    7-Eleven retail chain 153
    flat-panel displays 229
    and the Marketspace model 20
Jarlbaek, Jesper 219, 220, 221, 223, 224
Jeppensen, Christian 171

Kelley Blue Book 88, 90
Kenney, Jerome P. 59
knowledge-based corporations 228–30
knowledge-based economies 225
knowledge-innovation (K-I) cycle 39, 136, 212, 216, 228, 231
Kolind, Lars 168–9
Komansky, David H. 59, 60, 177
Kozmo.com 6
Kutner, Harold 98–9
Kwik-Fit 84

Landsend.com 149–50
large firms, lack of exploitation of the Internet 3, 5, 11–12
lead user process 203–5, 208
leadership, and the emergence of discontinuous technology 239
learning culture, and e-infrastructure 177–8
Lepore, Dawn 50, 53, 54, 176–7
Listwin, Donald J. 35
Lorimer, Mark 93
Lucent 4

m-commerce (mobile commerce services) 79
McKinley, John 59
Maddox, Matt 32
managers
  Asian 122
  and Internet-based IT systems 28
manufacturing sector, and the Marketspace model 18, 19
Marketspace model 3, 8–21, 22
  and customer relations 9, 11, 13, 18
  place dimension 10–11, 13, 16–17, 18
  price dimension 10, 13, 17–19
  product dimension 10, 13, 14–15, 18
  promotion dimension 10, 13, 15–16, 18
  regional variations 20
  sectoral variations 18–20
  and technology 8, 9, 10, 13, 18
Mathaisel, Bud 226
media firms
  exploiting the Internet 12
  and the Marketspace model 18, 19
Merck 13
Merrill Lynch xii, 19, 37, 45, 46, 47, 48, 58–61, 177, 237
  and cyber-gatekeepers 62
  and fee-based accounts 60
  HOLDRS website 61
  innovation strategy 130, 131
  lessons from the experiences of 59
  Merrill Lynch Direct (ML Direct) 59–60

organizational culture 60
partnership with HSBC Holdings plc 60–1
and perpetual metamorphosis 196–7
and Schwab 58, 60, 61
and the technological life cycle 112
Unlimited Advantage 59
Microsoft 112–13, 171, 205, 206
Mightywords 75
Minitel 11, 213
Motorola 171
MP3.dom 5, 193
music industry 29–30

Napster 29, 35, 182, 193
Nasdaq 3, 4, 132
Nasser, Jacques A. 33, 84, 98, 226
new business models 11, 12, 25, 26
new technology, deployment of 4–5, 7, 21–2
Nextel Communications Inc. 79
Nokia 21
Nomura Securities 160–1
Nonaka, Ikujiro 212, 217, 225
Nordstrom, Kjell 212
North American firms, and the Marketspace model 20–1
notHarvard.com 75

Oracle 26, 27, 78, 180
Orbitz 8, 20, 182
Oticon 167, 168–70, 179, 188, 241

P&G 203
Palma, Lazar and Ulsh (PLU) 227–8
Pappas, Krista 8
parcel delivery companies 20
PayPal.com 154
perpetual metamorphosis 39, 134, 135–6, 191–208, 242–3
  and Amazon 77, 135, 193, 196, 200, 201, 204
  inventing capabilities through lead users 203–5, 208
  and learning 243
  and the new project management challenge 205–7
  reach versus richness trade-off 192
  reinventing the business via 201–2
  and the retail industry 199–201
  and the survival of the adept 195–7
pharmaceutical companies 13, 228–9
Pisz, Jim 100
place dimension, in the Marketspace model 10–11, 13, 16–17

PlanetOut 162
PLU (Palma, Lazar and Ulsh) 227–8
Polley, Stephen 198
Polymerland 150
Porter, Bill 49
Pottruck, David 31, 32, 50, 52, 53, 54, 135, 156, 175, 202
Prahalad, C.K. 147
Priceline 159, 193
   WebHouse Club 28–9, 30–1
prices
   Auto-by-Tel 94
   co-creation and pricing strategies 39, 148, 157–60, 164, 240
   and customer savings 28–9
   price dimension in the Marketspace model 10, 13, 17–19
   price/performance hurdles for innovators 121, 122
   Wal-Mart 68–9
process approach to knowledge 226
process innovation, and the technological life cycle 110
product dimension, in the Marketspace model 10, 13, 14–15
products
   catalogs 14
   customers and online product design 15, 146
   customization 15, 142–5, 147, 150, 156, 239–40
   information on 13
   and online retail 32
   ordering 16, 17
   payments 17
   reverse product life cycle 119–23, 124
   stage/gate approach to product development 206–7
   value pricing 148, 157–60
project management 205–7
promotion dimension, in the Marketspace model 10, 13, 15–16

Quick & Reilly 49

Ramaswamy, Venkatram 147
Raytheon Co. 196
Real Virtual Corporations xii, 237
reality plus 236–7
realization hurdles for innovators 121–2
Redfield, Carl 35
Reel.com 6
Reiner, Gary 157
Research and Development (R&D), and innovation strategy 128

research on global business transformation 8–12
retail industry
   changes 130–1
   and the Marketspace model 18, 19–20
   and perpetual metamorphosis 199–201
   see also Amazon.com; Wal-Mart
reverse product life cycle 119–23, 124
Reynolds, Jerry 172
Ridderstrale, Jonas 212
Rose, M.J., *Lip Service* 77, 134
Rothnie, James 149
Ruddy, Tom 214–15, 216, 217
Ryan, Gerry 101

Sasson, Gideon 50, 53, 55
Scandinavian companies 21
Schmit, Tracey 149
Schrage, Michael 205
Schuman, Susan 162
Schwab, Charles xii, 19, 30, 31, 32, 36, 38, 45, 237
   and co-creation 156
   culture of innovation 53
   customer centricity 53, 54
   customer interfaces 152
   and cyber-gatekeepers 62
   and discount brokerage 47
   and e-infrastructure 173–4, 175, 241
   growth and innovation 48–9, 50
   impact of the Internet on 62
   innovation strategy 129–30, 131, 135
   and Internet-based stock trading 48, 52–4
   and the knowledge-innovation cycle 136
   Learning Center 55
   and Merrill Lynch 58, 60, 61
   and perpetual metamorphosis 136, 202
   revenue 49
   and service innovation 115
   technological curiosity cabinet 46
   and the technological life cycle 112
   visionary leadership 53
   Women Investing Program 54–5
Sears 35
Secure Electronic Transaction (SET) 72
service innovation on the Internet 114–18, 124, 238
   hurdles for innovators 120–3, 238
Seven Cycles 142–3
Siebel 185
Singleton, Eric 196
software firms 12
Sony 175

Southwest Airlines 76
Sprint Corp. 79
Standard & Poor (S&P) MidCap 400 Index 56
Steffens, John L. 59–60, 197
Sun 201

tacit knowledge 225, 230
Takeuchi, Hirotaka 217, 225
Taylor, Frank 172
technological life cycle
   Abernathy and Utterback's model 107–10, 124
   and the Internet 110–14
technological savviness 183–7, 188
technology capability dimension, and the Marketspace model 8, 9, 10, 13, 18
Tedlow, Richard 199, 200
Teloquent 184–5
Thorman, Rick 194
3–M 180, 201, 203–4
Tierney, Mike 142
Toyoda, Akio 100
Toyota 26, 84, 99–100, 161, 175
Toys"R"Us 20, 33, 60, 78, 180, 197, 200
transaction costs, minimizing 228
Travel & Transport sector, and the Marketspace model 20
travel industry
   and efficient interfaces 155–6
   and value pricing 159–60
Travelocity 7–8, 76, 182

Uniglobe Travel International 155–6
United Auto Group 86
UPS Logistics Group 172
US Postal Service 16
user friendliness of Internet sites 121

value pricing 39, 148, 157–60, 164, 240
Vandermark, Rob 142
Verizon Communications Inc. 79
Victor, Bart 170

virtual factories 179–81, 241
visionary leadership 37
Vivendi 5
Volkswagen 15, 16, 86

Wal-Mart 12, 20, 29, 32, 35, 37, 65, 66–9, 80, 105, 167, 175, 244
   and Amazon 72, 80
   closure of website 66
   customers 67–8, 71
   early forays into the Internet world 71–2
   innovation strategy 128, 130, 131, 134
   Internet travel service 153
   key strengths of 68
   and lower prices 68–9
   online products 72
   online strategy 67, 75–6
   ownership 66
   and perpetual metamorphosis 196, 201
   SAM'S CLUB 71, 72, 152
   and Secure Electronic Transaction (SET) 72
   and service innovation 115
   sundown rule 69, 128
   and the 10-foot attitude 68, 128
   and the technological life cycle 111, 113
Walton, Sam 68, 69
Watson, Tom Jr. 193, 202
Welch, John F. Jr. 6, 7, 11, 35, 130, 157, 174, 175, 177
Western Geophysical 150
White, Suzi 56–7
Wintel 179
Wise, Chris 214
Wurter, Thomas S. 192

Xerox 39, 136, 194, 195–6, 205, 213–15, 243
   alliance with 3M 180
   Eureka 213–16, 217, 218, 219, 226–7, 244

YadaPrice 162
Yahoo! xi, 4, 12, 27, 61, 62, 111, 160, 185